# The Psychic World

*By*

Hereward Carrington

*Director of the American Psychical Institute;*
*Member of the "Scientific American" Committee;*
*Permanent American Delegate to the*
*International Psychical Congresses.*

G·P·PUTNAM'S SONS
*NEW YORK*
1937

# By Hereward Carrington

*The Story of Psychic Science,*
*Modern Psychical Phenomena,*
*The Coming Science,*
*The Physical Phenomena of Spiritualism,*
*The Problems of Psychical Research,*
*etc.*

PRINTED IN THE UNITED STATES OF AMERICA
AT THE VAN REES PRESS

*Dedicated to*

MARIE

MY COLLABORATOR IN LIFE,

LOVE AND LETTERS;

*Without whose presence I could never have begun this book; without whose absence I could never have finished it.*

# Preface

THE RECENT marked revival of interest in psychic topics has prompted me to submit this book to the reading public. In it will be found, I believe, a considerable amount of new material, which has thus far not been covered by other books dealing with this subject—much of it representative of my own thought, after having devoted more than thirty-five years of my life to this interesting question.

The book falls naturally into two parts, the first being composed of discussions of particular problems connected with psychical research; the second dealing with psychic phenomena among primitive peoples. The latter subject is of interest for the reason that it has in the past rarely been touched upon from any point of view other than that of the anthropologist, who almost invariably regards such cases as *necessarily* fictitious, and as representative, merely, of the erroneous beliefs of primitive minds. If such phenomena have any actual bases in reality, however, and can be found paralleled in our own society, this throws an entirely different light upon the whole problem, since they are at once removed from the realm of folk-lore and placed into that of psychic science. The changes which this would necessitate in anthropological research are obvious.

In Part I, devoted to modern psychic phenomena in our own civilization, some of the more difficult problems are dealt with—in a semi-popular fashion, however, rendering them (I hope) of interest to the general reader. The solution of some of these riddles in turn throw light upon the primitive phenomena, so that the two parts of the book thus fit together like a jig-saw puzzle.

Some of these Chapters have already appeared in psychic Journals, and thanks are due their Editors for permission to reprint them here.

Also to The Macmillan Company, for permission to quote from Dr. William McDougall's *Body and Mind;* to Henry Holt and Company, for permission to quote from Bergson's *Mind Energy* and from Giles' *Civilization of China;* to G. P. Putnam's Sons, for permission to quote from Jevons' *Personality;* to Harcourt, Brace and Company, for permission to quote from Seabrook's *Magic Island;* to Houghton Mifflin Company, for permission to quote from Percival Lowell's *Occult Japan;* and to various publishers for the shorter quotations included.

H. C.

# Contents

x    Contents

# INTRODUCTION

# The Tyranny of Dogmatism

A HISTORY of popular opposition to new ideas or new truths would fill a volume of many hundred pages, and would constitute a melancholy human document. This opposition is doubtless almost as old as human thought itself. Plato, in his *Republic,* tells us that when Socrates stated his conviction that only philosophers should be appointed rulers of the people and of the state, his listener, Adeimantus, replied:

"Socrates, what do you mean? I would have you consider that the word which you have uttered is one at which numerous persons, and very respectable persons too, pulling off their coats all in a moment, and seizing any weapon that comes to hand, will run at you might and main, before you know where you are, intending to do heaven knows what; and if you don't prepare an answer, and put yourself in motion, you will be 'pared by their fine wits,' and no mistake."

It is hardly necessary to remind the reader of the bigotry and intolerance of the Middle Ages when men burned, tortured and killed one another because of the slightest difference in point-of-view, the interpretation of a word or the rendition of some Biblical text. Those days, we trust, have gone forever; but the spirit which inspired that opposition and those cruelties is still strong, and the basic resistance to any ideas running counter to those of the Herd is still a fundamental part of human nature. Nowadays this usually takes the form of ridicule or attempted disproof of the ideas offered, but the psychological mechanism involved is fundamentally the same. Let us take a few examples of this, drawn from our own times—or within the past century—and we shall see that scientific truths which today are accepted by us as a matter-of-course were at first received with the utmost incredulity and aroused the greatest opposition—largely from the scientific men of the time.

When railways were first constructed, engineers predicted that they could never become practicable; and that the wheels of the locomotives would simply whirl round and round without moving forward. In the French Chamber of Deputies, in 1838, Arago, hoping to throw cold water on the ardor of the partisans of the new invention, spoke of the inertia of matter, of the tenacity of metals, and of the resistance of the air. M. Prudhom said that "it is a ridiculous and vulgar notion, that railways will increase the circulation of ideas." In Bavaria, the Royal College of Doctors having been consulted, declared that railways, if they were constructed, would cause the greatest deterioration in the health of the public, because such rapid movement would cause brain trouble among travelers, and vertigo among those who looked at moving trains.

I myself remember that an expert mathematician once explained to me how heavier-than-air flying machines could never become practicable, because gravity would overcome any possible upward pull by the engines and wings of the machine.

It is a matter of history how the banks of the Hudson River were lined with jeering crowds, to see the utter failure of Fulton's steam boat, which nevertheless steamed majestically up the river.

When it was first proposed to lay a submarine cable between Europe and America, in 1855, one of the greatest authorities on physics, Babinet, a member of the Institute, wrote:

"I cannot regard this project as serious; the history of currents might easily afford irrefutable proof that such a thing is an impossibility, to say nothing of new currents that would be created all along the electric line, and which are very appreciable even in the short cable crossing from Calais to Dover...." (*Revue des Deux Mondes.*)

The first bathtub in the United States was installed by Adam Thompson, a wealthy grain and cotton dealer of Cincinnati, in 1842. He had lately returned from London where he had heard that the Prime Minister had such a device. On December 20, 1842, he had a party of gentlemen to dinner, all of whom tried out the new invention. The following day, the story was in the papers and Thompson was attacked both by doctors and politicians. We do not find that Thompson was required to pay a fine, but the discussion in connection with the bathtub resulted in various measures for the restriction of its use. The Common Council of Philadelphia considered an ordinance to prevent any such bathing between the months of November and March! Virginia had a tax of $30.00 a year on all bathtubs and extra heavy water rates. In Boston there was an ordinance forbidding their use except on medical advice!

Camille Flammarion tells us:

"I was present one day at a meeting of the Academy of Sciences. It was a day to be remembered, for its proceedings were absurd. Du Moncel introduced Edison's phonograph to the learned assembly. When the presentation had been made, the proper person began quietly to recite the usual formula as he registered it upon his roll. Then a middle-aged academician, whose mind was stored—nay, saturated—with traditions drawn from his culture in the classics, rose, and, nobly indignant at the audacity of the inventor, rushed towards the man who represented Edison, and seized him by the collar, crying, 'Wretch! We are not to be made dupes of by a ventriloquist!' This member of the Institute was Monsieur Bouillard. The day was the 11th of March, 1878. The most curious thing about it was that, six months later, on September 30th, before a similar assembly, the same man considered himself bound in honor to declare that, after a close examination, he could find nothing in the invention but ventriloquism, and that 'it was impossible to admit that mere vile metal could perform the work of human phonation.' The phonograph, according to his idea of it, was nothing but an *acoustic illusion.*"

Murdoch, who invented the gas light, was ridiculed by a Committee of the English Parliament, because he was so "crazy" as to claim that a lamp could burn without a wick. Galvani was called the "frog's dancing master," because of his experiments on frogs' legs, stimulated by weak electric currents. Harvey was ridiculed and professionally ostracized because of his advocacy of the circulation of the blood. It is a matter of history that no physician more than forty years of age at the time of his discovery ever accepted it. The inventor of the umbrella barely escaped from being killed by an angry crowd because he was interfering with "God's rain." Only by running through a shop was he enabled to escape his pursuers. In 1890 doubts were still expressed as to the reality of thunder-bolts, and the "Specter of the Brocken" was said not to exist, because it could not be explained.

Lavoisier, one of the most learned men of his day, wrote a report to the French Academy, asserting that stones could not fall from the skies—it was contrary to common sense to think so. Gassendi asserted the same thing. In Provence, in 1627, an aërolite weighing thirty kilograms had fallen. Gassendi saw it, touched it, examined it—and attributed it to an explosion of the earth in some unknown region.

The evidence afforded by fossils, evolution, and a thousand other things, had been opposed and ridiculed in the same manner. Indeed, it would be possible to fill many pages with illustrations of precisely the same character. Animal Magnetism was utterly condemned by the French Academy of Sciences and by the Faculty of Medicine. Men waited before they would believe in it (and even after!) to see the result of an operation by Jules Cloquet, for cancer of a woman's breast, which was performed without pain, after she had been previously "magnetized." The early advocates of mesmerism and hypnotism were ridiculed and attacked on all sides in a most shameful manner. It was said that the subjects of these painless operations were merely "hardened rogues" who submitted to the ordeal for pay. When Dr. Tanner fasted forty days, medical men said he was a humbug, and few believed him. Now, scores of like cases are on record, and have been studied by nutrition experts. For years psychologists opposed the theory of the subconscious mind, contending that everything was the result of "unconscious cerebration." And so it goes; the list could be continued almost indefinitely.

And this same opposition exists today, in a greater or lesser degree, to all forms of psychic phenomena! We still see them ridiculed, misrepresented, maligned by press and public. Very few psychologists today would accept the reality of telepathy—to say nothing of more startling manifestations! Even many psychical researchers will not accept the reality of "physical phenomena." Only very gradually are these phenomena gaining acceptance and becoming recognized by official science. It is our duty to continue piling-up well authenticated cases of the type until their reality can no longer be doubted. This, however, can only be brought about by well-controlled, scientifically-conducted researches in which no loop-hole for fraud or possible error can be found. This is a fundamental requisite, if our subject is to gain ultimate acceptance. The Societies for Psychical Research have made great headway in this direction; we should see to it that the work is carried on in such a manner that the scientific world, press and public will eventually be forced to acknowledge its reality and authenticity. When that turning-point has been reached, there can be no question that adequate funds for the work will be forthcoming, and that rapid progress will be made in all branches of this investigation. Implications and interpretations will follow. Our prime need, still, is well-observed, thoroughly authenticated *facts*.

# PART I

## Psychic Phenomena in Modern Civilization

# I

## The Confessions of a Psychical Researcher

EVERY one, I suppose, has some hobby or special interest. My own interest happens to be psychical research —and I believe that I am not generally considered a "crank." Why, then, should I be interested in Psychics, and such oddities as ghosts, astral bodies, ectoplasm, clairvoyance, and possible spirit-communications? And what's more, seriously interested? Well, I suppose it is for the same reason that one man is interested in politics, another in antiques and a third in astronomy. It is a sort of innate thing, dependent partly upon heredity and early environment, no doubt, but also upon some instinctive desire, which psychologists have not yet succeeded in fully analyzing. An incident which I vividly remember may help to illustrate this.

When I first came from England to America, I was about eight years of age. My mother, my sister and myself were crossing on the North German Lloyd boat, the *Elbe,* afterwards wrecked on the coast of Ireland, if I am not mistaken. On the boat were three enormously fat men, who said that they had traveled back and forth several times because they liked the food served on it better than that in hotels! From which the reader may gather that they were not excessively esthetic, and that they did not altogether despise the material pleasures of this life. Nevertheless these men had a keen interest in psychic phenomena. That famous book, *Phantasms of the Living,* had just been published, and I vividly remember them discussing it with my mother: the evidence for telepathy, the fact that a large number of apparitions had been found to coincide with the death of the person thus represented, and so on. I sat there, open-mouthed, drinking in this conversation, absorbing it. It left a vivid and never-to-be-forgotten impression upon me. Yet I was only eight! Which makes me feel that some innate mental predisposition must have been present, as I have said, in order to account for the curious interest thus aroused. For my interest had not been at all in the "ghostly horrors" discussed, but in the scientific marvel of it all.

When any fairly normal and intelligent man becomes in any way publicly identified with spiritualism or psychic investigation, the general public immediately endeavors to discover *why,* in order to "explain" his odd interest or belief. This man is getting old and doddering, perhaps in his second childhood. That man lost a son in the war, and of course was emotionally biased, because of his desire to "communicate" with him. Another was "always rather religious." And so it goes. Doubtless, many of these criticisms have an element of truth in them. But it is by no means true that the majority of scientific investigators are in any way influenced by such factors. They are interested in psychic investigation just as they would be in any other scientific problem, and do not let their feelings run away with them in the least. They do not desire to prove—or to disprove—anything! They desire only to ascertain the truth, to discover some new and hitherto unsuspected facts.

It is a great mistake to assume that, just because some man is interested in these investigations, therefore he is unduly credulous, or overly anxious to "communicate" with some loved one who has died. Such may be the case, but it is not necessarily so. Nor need one be in any sense "religious," in the orthodox sense of the word, in order to be interested in this field. One may be a "Rationalist," and yet a sincere student of psychic phenomena.

To take my own case, for example. Both my parents were (I am inclined to think) Agnostics; at all events I never heard any talk of religion at home, and received no training in any orthodox sense. They had lived in the Orient for many years, were strongly anti-missionary on that account, and were, I am inclined to think, more Buddhists than anything else; though of this I am not sure. At all events, they always took the stand that, just because I happened to be born in a Christian country (so-called) I need not necessarily be a "Christian" when I grew up; I might choose to become a Mohammedan or a Confucian, or anything else, for all they knew. The result was that I grew up with practically no religion at all, and no instinct for or belief in it. I had a perfectly open mind upon the subject; more or less interested in all religions from the purely historical or anthropological point-of-view, but by nature and feeling a rationalist and an agnostic.

Nevertheless, as the result of my researches, I have become quite convinced of the reality of some superphysical or psychic world of some sort, and of the actuality of supernormal (psychic) phenomena. But this belief has been based solely upon evidence—upon *facts*. What are these facts and how did I become interested? Let me answer the second of these questions first, since this has a rather curious history.

Early in life I became an amateur conjuror, interested

in the history and technique of magic. I gave my first "performance" when I was thirteen. The literature of the subject I read with avidity. When I was eighteen, I picked-up a few books dealing with what are technically known as "pseudo-spiritualistic tricks"—imitations, by conjuring, of certain alleged mediumistic marvels. This line of reading I followed up assiduously, and for many months thought that any one who believed any of these alleged marvels was simply ignorant of how they were done, and that I was particularly "clever" and knew! (Many conjurers today take the same attitude.) Then I happened to run across a book entitled *Essays in Psychical Research,* by Miss X— now out of print. The author wrote in an eminently fair, sane, judicial style, it seemed to me; she was not an out-and-out spiritualist; nevertheless, she had experienced many of these strange happenings herself, in her own person, and wrote of them impartially and intelligently.

"Well," I thought, "if an apparently sensible woman such as she asserts these things to be true, there may be something in it after all! I shall join the Society for Psychical Research, read their publications, experiment for myself, and see!" I accordingly did so. This was in 1900. I have been a member, and actively engaged in this research work ever since—for my reading soon convinced me that many of these phenomena were undoubtedly supernormal, and that the general character and tone of the Society's publications were eminently scientific and skeptical, as well as fair and open-minded. And I think that any impartial student of their Reports must agree with me.

This, then, was how I became interested in psychical

investigation: not through the death of some loved one; not through any desire to communicate; not because of any religious belief, nor the "will to believe." Nothing of the kind. I became interested through magic. I am just as skeptical now as ever, when it comes to any individual case. But my own personal investigations have convinced me that many of these things do occur. Therefore I consider their investigation important, and the subject unduly misrepresented and neglected. This, it seems to me, is a logical conclusion to reach, in view of the general attitude toward these questions.

But is not the public attitude perhaps justified? Is there not much fraud, illusion, hysteria and error in this field? Every other sphere of human activity has been subjected to a rigid process of "debunking" of late. Is not the public constantly being imposed upon by fraudulent mediums and self-styled Teachers of Truth?

Indeed it is! The credulity, superstition and nonsense which one encounters is simply amazing. Yet the fault lies largely in the public, and not in the subject itself. We encounter the same sort of credulity, stupidity and sheepish belief in religion, politics, business—in every walk of life. All this has nothing to do with the reputable psychical investigators and their methods. One must judge a subject by the best minds which it attracts, and not by the worst. Unfortunately, this particular subject attracts more silly people than any other, because of the element of wonder in it; and the crowd often follows because of mere curiosity. All of which is fully realized by the leading men in this field; but if the reader should care to spend a little time glancing through the publications of the Society, he would find nowhere any mention of the numerous fortune-tellers, clairvoyants and advertising mediums which are just the ones which the amateur investigator would be apt to encounter in his preliminary quest. We know as well as any one else that nothing of value is to be found here.

Good mediums are rare—probably much rarer than great singers or painters or etchers, who are rare enough. What our Society has always done has been to concentrate upon two or three promising cases, more or less to the exclusion of all others. Thus, Mrs. Piper, of Boston, has been under constant observation and subjected to test séances since 1885. In a lesser degree the same is true of other cases. But nowhere will the reader find mention of the hoi-polloi of mediums which the average investigator is liable to encounter.

Have I in any degree succeeded in convincing the reader that a psychical researcher may be a sane, sensible person, and yet vitally interested in this particular subject? If so, I shall feel that I have accomplished a great deal! One need not be a credulous dupe merely because he investigates certain odd facts, and analyzes and subjects them to every conceivable test—instrumental and otherwise—before accepting them. Furthermore, facts and the interpretations of those facts are two very different matters. Many psychic investigators admit the reality of certain phenomena, admit that they are supernormal, yet do not admit their spiritistic interpretation; or they hold their judgment in abeyance. Professor Richet belongs to this group. The same may be said of many others. On the other hand, there are psychic investigators who are spiritualists. It is largely a question of individual interpretation of certain facts. But the facts themselves are invariably granted.

Spiritualism and psychical research, then, are two very different things. The former is a religio-philosophical scheme, built upon certain alleged phenomena; the latter is merely a scientific attempt to investigate and interpret these phenomena—to expose them, if fraudulent; to record and file away all doubtful cases, to study at length all apparently genuine cases. And the methods employed in doing so have been as accurate and careful and scientific as the newness and difficulty of the investigation has rendered possible. Let me emphasize this point: the most critical acumen has been displayed in analyzing and sifting this material. Years ago, Professor William James wrote:

"Were I asked to point to a scientific journal where hardheadedness and never-sleeping suspicion of sources of error might be seen in their full bloom, I think I should have to fall back on the *Proceedings* of the Society for Psychical Research."

The first President, Professor Henry Sidgwick, was described as "the most incorrigibly and exasperatingly critical and skeptical mind in England."

More exposures of fraudulent mediums have been made by members of the Society than by all the conjurers combined. And when skeptics wish to quote authoritative exposés, they almost invariably have to fall back on our publications, or upon books published by psychical researchers themselves! It is a curious situation, and one very little realized by the public.

Nevertheless, we psychic investigators believe that certain supernormal facts exist—both physical and mental. . . .

Have I myself seen any such manifestations, which I consider genuine? I certainly have, and I am as sure that these things occur as I am that I write these pages. But—let me make this very plain—genuine phenomena are rare, and for every real case one encounters, one is liable to encounter a hundred worthless imitations. However, the mere fact that "old masters" can at times be so skillfully imitated that no one but an expert can detect the difference, does not prove that there are no old masters. On the contrary it proves, if it proves anything, that there are some genuine old masters to imitate. So, here. There are individuals in the world possessed of unusual and extraordinary powers, and, in our commercial age, they often decide to capitalize them. Seeing which, clever and shrewd knaves decide that they will do the same thing, by trickery, and set up an establishment of their own, in which they practice their arts, until exposed. This is the sort of thing we encounter all the time, and that is why investigation is so difficult and so annoying!

It is obvious that every Tom, Dick and Harry is not competent to pass judgment upon these phenomena, or the subject in general. An expert in psychic investigation is slowly and painfully evolved. We go to an expert chemist for an opinion upon some technical chemical problem; and the public should be educated to believe that expert opinion is just as necessary in this question as in any other. For, in our opinion, this is a new branch of science, and a most difficult and baffling one, at that!

# II

## Some Personal Psychic Experiences

It is, I believe, highly probable that practically every one—no matter how "normal" he may be—has had a certain number of odd psychic experiences in his life, which would make an interesting collection, if he were to take the time and trouble to record them. Heaven knows, no one is naturally more "unpsychic" than myself, and my friends are frequently upbraiding me for my critical attitude toward mediums and psychic phenomena generally! When first I became interested in this subject, I spent hours upon hours trying to develop automatic writing, crystal-gazing, a psychometric faculty, trance, or anything that might come along, but the results of these experiments were, generally speaking, *nil*. It is true that I worked quite hard at Yoga for some two years, during which time I lived entirely upon fruits and nuts (uncooked), spoke to no one, and lived completely alone. In this, I obtained some curious and interesting results, mostly of a physiological nature. While I did not actually attain the state known as Cosmic Consciousness I approached it sufficiently closely, on some occasions, to convince myself that there is some real state of the kind, which various writers have tried to express in words.* It was soon after this that I experimented considerably with "astral projection," in which I seemingly attained some degree

---

* See *Cosmic Consciousness,* by J. M. Bucke; *Cosmic Consciousness,* by Ali Nomad; *Higher Psychical Development,* by H. Carrington; also a number of Oriental works dealing with Tantra, Yoga, etc.

of success on at least one occasion. I have recorded this in the Preface to our book *The Projection of the Astral Body,* pp. 34-35, so that I shall not do more than refer to it here.

Soon after this, however, I decided that I would no longer try to develop psychic powers myself, and for two reasons: first, because such scant results had hitherto been forthcoming; but second (and mainly) because I deemed it a wise policy not to do so. I said to myself: "Here I am, a psychic investigator, carrying on inquiries in a scientific field. Suppose I *should* develop a certain psychic faculty in myself? Suppose I should then attend a séance, and bring in a report, stating that such-and-such phenomena occurred. I might lay myself open to a certain type of criticism, from various individuals. They might say: 'Oh, well, Carrington has hallucinations; his testimony is no good!' " So, in order to prevent this, I shut-off all further attempts at psychic development—this permitting me to say: "I am as normal as you are! If you had been there, you would have seen the same things I did, just as I saw them."

Under the circumstances, I think it wiser that I took this course—though it was only for the above reason, and not because of any "fear" connected with the subject. I have often thought that many people are terrible cowards, when it comes to this question of psychic experimentation—an attitude with which I have but little sympathy. On the other hand, I should be quite ready to admit that a sound, well-balanced physical and mental constitution is essential to any one taking up this line of inquiry, and that the neurotic, the psychotic and the weak-willed had best leave it severely alone.

All this, however, is by way of introduction, and merely to give the reader an idea of my mental background and ordinary lack of psychic ability. Notwithstanding this, I have had quite a number of striking spontaneous experiences—a few of which I propose to give here very briefly, together with an account of some "cases" which have come under my observation, or which I have from time to time investigated.

The first case is one which made a deep impression on me at the time, and which I have ever since remembered vividly. It was in connection with the death of a friend of mine, whom I shall call Ida P. She was at the time a woman in the prime of life, and so bubbling over with health and animal spirits that one could never associate her with death or illness. The last time we had met was on the street, nearly a year before.

I was seated at my desk, writing, when I suddenly had the impulse to call her up on the telephone. I did so, and a woman's voice responded. I asked for Ida P. The reply was, "Why, didn't you know? Mrs. P. passed away yesterday!" I was so thunderstruck that I do not remember what I said in reply, but hung up the receiver.

Soon after this, the feeling of a *presence* (not *her* presence particularly, but *a* presence) made itself very manifest in the apartment. I could "sense" it now here, now there, but most frequently in a particular spot, a dark alcove, just inside the front door. It was so "strong" here that I caught myself, on several occasions, momentarily hesitating before passing this spot! On the afternoon of the second day, a neighbor of mine stepped just inside my front door to say a few words (I had left it open, as the weather was extremely hot) when he suddenly turned sharply, exclaiming, "Oh, I thought some one was standing there!" (Naturally I had said nothing to him about the experience.) Yet the spot he turned to was that little dark alcove, where I had so frequently sensed my "presence."

This lasted for nearly three days. During those three days, I had "rappings" at irregular intervals all over the place—on the walls, the floor and the furniture. These were sometimes quite loud and utterly unlike anything heard before or since. On the afternoon of the third day, I was sitting at my desk, writing, when a note on the piano in the next room was distinctly struck. I immediately rushed into the next room, and picked out the note on the piano with my finger. I was quite alone at the time, and had no cat or other animal in the apartment. I was busily engaged when this occurred. From that moment nothing further was noticed—no more "presence," no more rappings, nothing! What *appeared* to be happening was that some invisible entity had endeavored to attract my attention, and, when it had finally succeeded in doing so, in an unmistakable manner, had been "satisfied" and taken its departure! At least, I gained the very strong impression at the time that this was the case, and I have come no nearer any other solution of the problem since then.

These "rappings" are very curious phenomena. They are quite unlike any other raps or sounds which may be noticed on other occasions, and totally unlike the "creaks" often noted when a draught of cold air strikes some door, for example, causing it to contract. I have occasionally noted these raps just as I was falling asleep; a sharp rap would then resound, waking me up suddenly. I observed a certain coincidental relationship here. Just as I would "let go," preparatory to falling asleep, a rap would occur. I found that I could in some measure *control* the rap by "hanging-on" to myself, as it were, and not relaxing completely for some little time. Then, as soon as I thoroughly relaxed, bang would go the rap! I was forced to the tentative conclusion that there was a certain relationship between the rap and the release of control over the bodily energies. This is, I think, a point well worth studying, and bears a distinct analogy to the famous Karin case,* concerning which it was said:

"... the various attempts made by Karin to influence the phenomena (rapping) by her will seem to show that such influence, when it took place, never could be exercised *directly*, but only by way of a subconscious mental state that lay beyond the control of her will."

Mr. Wijk, the author of the article, suggested that such influence might perhaps be exercised by means of *hypnotism*. (Dr. Osty's later observations in this direction are of great value here.)

One other instance of a very mysterious character should perhaps be included. At the time I was living in a studio apartment, on the fourth floor. A large brass knocker was on the door, a sort of Sphinx head. One morning I was awakened from a sound sleep by the knocker being rapped violently. I jumped out of bed, put on a dressing gown, and was standing by the front door, tying the rope about my waist, when it was knocked again, as insistently as before. *Immedi-*

* "Karin: A Study of Spontaneous Rappings," *Annals of Psychic Science,* Sept., 1905.

*ately* I opened the door. The hall was empty! Not two seconds had elapsed between the knock and the opening of the door. It is hardly necessary to say that I was wide awake when the second knock was heard, though the first one had awakened me from a sound sleep. I explored the hall and the stairway; no one was to be found. This happened only once, and I have never been able to find a satisfactory "explanation" for this extraordinary occurrence.*

Speaking of raps reminds me of another curious experience I once had—though this time the phenomenon was certainly subjective or interior, being inside my own head. It was a peculiar "snap," which I distinctly heard, just as I was awakening from sleep. In those days I was always fully awake the moment I opened my eyes. On this particular occasion, however, I felt dazed and confused for some considerable time, and it took me three or four minutes to regain normal consciousness. I could not help thinking of the "head-snapping" so frequently reported by Mrs. Piper, when emerging from trance, and I imagine the phenomenon was very similar in the two cases—whatever it was. I have however reported this case in full in the *Journal S.P.R.*, Jan., 1925, where similar experiences were also reported by Miss H. A. Dallas and Miss Eleanor B. Kelly.†

Before leaving this subject of quasi-physical phe-

---

* It should perhaps be added that this happened on the third morning of my Ida P. "haunting," and seemed somehow to be connected with it.

† The author of that remarkable book *The Maniac* dwells upon this phenomenon, and is inclined to believe that it is in some way closely connected with insanity, and with the severance of the "astral" from the physical body. The interest of several psychiatrists has lately been aroused in this question.

nomena, I might mention a curious case, which I was called upon to investigate, some twenty-five years ago, in which I succeeded in curing a poltergeist by means of hypnotic suggestion.

A most circumstantial account had been furnished by the mother, and, upon visiting the house, I found a most peculiar child there, about fifteen years old, who nevertheless appeared to be eleven or twelve—so under-sized and almost abnormal was she. The disturbances centered about her, taking the form of articles thrown around the house (even inkpots, with imaginable results!) and small "apports." It did not take long to discover that the girl was responsible for the mischief, and that she skillfully threw these objects at a moment when no one was looking. Nothing was said to her at the time, but that night, after the girl had gone to sleep, her mother and I quietly entered her room, and I took a chair beside her. I then "suggested" to her that she could no longer throw things about, that she would feel no desire to do so, that she would feel a restraining influence, preventing her from doing so, whenever she made the attempt, etc. This was continued for some twenty minutes. The next day the "phenomena" materially decreased, and the following day ceased altogether. They have never, I believe, recurred since. This is rather an interesting case, in view of its possible implications.

We now come to a few *dream* cases of an unusual nature. The first involves a sort of "cross-correspondence," inasmuch as three persons dreamed a very similar dream the same night, and by a fortunate coincidence met and compared notes the following day. To take my own dream first: I dreamed that I was walking along a country lane, a tall hedge on my right and a curious, barn-like structure on my left. From this barn projected a large, iron hook, and from the hook hung a *black baby,* the hook passing through its clothes. The baby was yelling and screaming—which was perhaps only natural! As I looked, the clothes of the baby gave way, and it fell to earth, being dashed to pieces and killed instantly. The thing which struck me particularly, in my dream, was the curious "plop" sound of the impact, which I likened (in my dream) to a paper bag filled with water, and dropped from some considerable height. Although there was much blood, this somehow did not seem to offend me—as it certainly would have in life, under similar circumstances.

That same night Miss Elizabeth Smythe, connected with the ... Hospital, dreamed of a *black baby* falling and being smashed to bits, and she awoke to hear her own lips reciting a curious little verse, in which this incident was described.

My friend Mr. Fred Keating also dreamed the same night of *two black bears,* one of which fell from the roof of the Woolworth Building—where they were playing—and was killed on the sidewalk below. Both Miss Smythe and Mr. Keating commented on the peculiar "plop" sound made by the impact of the bodies. We compared notes the following day at tea.

In connection with the next dream was associated a remarkable coincidence—if coincidence it was. During all the years that I had known Dr. Hyslop, I had never once dreamed of him, to the best of my recollection, except on this particular occasion. I then had a very vivid dream, apparently lasting for some time, during which we discussed the work of the S.P.R. I awoke, the dream still fresh in my memory. *Within three seconds* of my awakening, a clatter-clatter was heard in the next room, as though some picture had fallen from the wall. "Well," I thought to myself, "if that is Hyslop's photograph, it will certainly be a remarkable thing!" I jumped out of bed and ran into the next room. Sure enough, Dr. Hyslop's signed photograph was lying on the floor, the string having broken! Did he inspire the dream, and subsequently produce the "phenomenon"? Was it a mere coincidence? It must be conceded as remarkable that the only dream I ever had of him—and an exceptionally vivid one—should have been thus associated with the fall of his picture, which had been hanging on the wall for years. I made a written note of the occurrence at the time, which I still have.

The next case is a delightful example of the type of "wit" perpetrated by the subconscious mind. It took the form of an amazing series of puns. I dreamed that two white, phantom forms were standing, one on either side of me. They were talking to one another, quite regardless of my presence. One of them said:

"What nationality is Pola Negri?"

To which the other replied: "She is Pole and egg-ri."

The first held up his hand and said: "Enough!" (An oeuf.) *

Here is another curious case of dream-punning. I dreamed one night that I was playing Bridge, and that I played a card—a curious looking thing, covered with green swirls and dragons' heads, differing from anything I had ever seen before in any illustration, so far as I could remember. At the same moment that I

* Oeuf, of course, being the French for egg.

played the card to the center of the table, I also bid! I said: "I bid one George." That is all the dream that I remember.

The next day I puzzled my brains for a solution of this seeming mystery. A partial explanation was forthcoming when I recalled the famous "Grypholife" story, often told by my friend Sidney S. Lenz, in which he describes a card (the Grypholife) bearing these same curious green scrolls. [It had figured in a dream phantasy of his own.] So far, so good; the design on the card might thus be accounted for. But why "one George"? Looking through the New York *Times,* the next day, my eye happened to light upon a large advertisement by "George the Tailor," and in big type the words "New Suits and Overcoats." Looking back, I found that the previous day's issue had also carried this same advertisement. Here, then, we have the solution of the mystery. The card I played evidently belonged to some *new suit;* it was not one of the traditional four —Spades, Hearts, Diamonds and Clubs. And this "new suit" was sponsored by George the Tailor! When I played and bid, therefore, I said "one George," thereby combining the elements of the advertisement, which I had doubtless unconsciously noted, in looking through the paper, the day before.

In the *Journal* A.S.P.R., August, 1908, I reported an interesting case, in which abnormal and supernormal phenomena seemed to go hand in hand—as they so often do. It was that of a young lady who spontaneously developed clairvoyance, during a period of convalescence, but woke up one morning, feeling much better, only to find that her clairvoyant faculty had completely gone, never to return! This is in some ways analogous to the famous case of Molly Fancher. It has also been stated that the mediumship of Eusapia Palladino dated from an accident, in which she fell against a cart wheel and cut her head open.

In any event, this interesting connection between the abnormal and the supernormal must not be lost sight of. The mistake of the psychiatrist lies in attempting to *explain* the supernormal by reason of the abnormal —which of course he can never do. One might readily grant any amount of hysteria, dissociation, actual insanity, or whatever you like. The problem still remains: How account for the actual supernormal knowledge displayed? No purely physiological explanations can ever do that. The same objection applies to many of those curious "obsession" cases, where the abnormal mental state is very evident, and yet occasionally, coupled with it, undoubted supernormal elements are displayed. I have, during the past thirty years, observed a great many cases of this character—and I am happy to say I seem to have been instrumental in helping several of them to recover a normal equilibrium again— but such cases must be handled "just so," and the possibly supernormal elements of the case kept constantly in mind. I do not doubt that suggestion is an enormously important factor, even when the subject is cured by some "spiritualistic" means, but all this material dovetails in so complex a manner that it is often most difficult to disentangle it—just as it is difficult to designate the point where subconscious play-acting ends and possibly genuine "communications" begin.

Speaking of the extraordinary powers of suggestion reminds me of a most interesting case which I have had in my possession for many years, in written form, but have never yet published. I do so now, copying the original document as it lies before me. It runs as follows:

"On the afternoon of May 1, 1916, I was standing in my hall, preparing to go out, when I saw the knob on my front door slowly turn. I stood still, awaiting developments; gradually the door opened, and I saw a man standing there. As he saw me, he quickly closed the door, and ran down the stairs and out of the front door. (He was in fact a burglar, trying to enter my apartment.) The interesting thing about the experience is this: that, during the moment he was standing in the door, although he did not actually move, I had the distinct impression that he had run up the hall, and grasped me firmly by the arm, and I was for the moment petrified with fear. The next day my arm was black-and-blue, in the exact spot where I thought he had pinched me; and this mark continued for several days, until it finally wore off. I told Dr. Carrington about this two days later, when he called, and showed him the mark."

(Signed) LOUISE W. KOPS.

"I remember hearing the story as above narrated, and Miss Kops showing me the black-and-blue marks on her arm at the time."

(Signed) HEREWARD CARRINGTON.

The above is, doubtless, a sort of transition case between the normal physiological effects of suggestion and instances of real stigmata.

It would be impossible for me to begin to enumerate the scores of public and private mediums with whom I have obtained sittings. "The hours I spent with thee, dear heart" are nothing to the hours I have spent with amateur mediums claiming to produce extraordinary phenomena.

And such phenomena! Complete Levitations, which turned out to be mere tippings of the table; remarkable Spirit Messages, which turned out to be the veriest drivel; and so on. Well, I suppose that is part of the penalty one pays for being a psychical researcher! However, one is rewarded, from time to time, by stumbling upon some really remarkable case, and then all the fruitless labor of the past is forgotten, and one becomes absorbed in observing these baffling phenomena, and in endeavoring to discover the laws and causes underlying them, and instigating them. No study could then become more thrilling. No astronomer in his observatory, seemingly on the eve of some great discovery, could be more enthralled than the true psychic investigator witnessing a series of phenomenal happenings, of the supernormality of which he has become convinced. No biologist, performing some daring experiment, could seemingly touch life so intimately. No religious enthusiast could come more closely in touch with some spiritual world. It is that Great Possibility which always lures us on. For, in the words of Frederic Myers:

"That which lies at the root of each of us lies at the root of the Cosmos too. Our struggle is the struggle of the Universe itself; and the very Godhead finds fulfillment through our upward-striving souls."

# III

## What Constitutes a Psychical Researcher

THERE is probably only one thing more difficult than defining an ideal psychical researcher—and that is, *being* one! For whatever attitude one may assume, it is sure to be wrong in the estimation of a large number of persons interested in this subject. If he be somewhat hyper-critical, he is attacked by those convinced of the truth of spiritualism; if he be a virtual spiritualist, he is similarly attacked by those who desire to maintain the ultra-scientific attitude hitherto maintained by the S.P.R.—one which has, it is true, been instrumental in influencing various eminent men of science, and even forcing the newspapers and general public to pay some respect to this subject. If, finally, he be on the fence, holding his final judgment in suspense, and endeavoring to see both sides of any question with rigid impartiality, he is attacked from both sides—neither of which is satisfied with his non-committal attitude. One group regards him as too critical and negative; the other as too credulous and positive. Even William James, one of the sanest and most balanced minds who ever lived, was subjected to criticism of precisely this character.

Intellectual honesty is, I believe, one of the most difficult things in the world to maintain in this subject. There is, in the first place, always the tendency to be swayed by the opinions of the majority, instead of standing up for what one considers the truth, even in the minutest detail. This fear of opprobrium or unpopularity tends to sway the verdict or cloud the judgment. The fear of social ostracism is a most important factor in the lives of many. The Almighty Dollar proves itself to be powerful, here as elsewhere, and many are influenced by the fear of possible loss, which might result were their true convictions known. It is undoubtedly true that there are many men in the country today who are only prevented from publicly stating their views because of this practical consideration. This applies especially, perhaps, to men connected with our Universities.

A true psychical researcher must determine, first of all, to set all these considerations to one side. He must remain impervious to the opinions and criticisms of others; he must have the courage of his own convictions, no matter how unpopular these may be, and he must be unswayed by any pecuniary interests. Above all, he must be loyal to the truth, wherever that may lead him,—no matter if this result in the exposure of some fraudulent medium, or in the frank admission of some incredible supernormal occurrence.

There have been investigators in this field, as we know, who were undoubtedly hyper-critical in their attitude. I mean by this, unreasonably so. They stressed every negative argument and minimized every positive account. They ignored much of the most striking and evidential matter, in order to make out a case and write a Report which would sound plausible and redound to their own credit. There is perhaps a certain tendency to do this with nearly all of us, under certain conditions. Thus, suppose a certain medium is being investigated: ninety-eight per cent of the phenomena are unquestionably fraudulent. Two per cent remain inexplicable. There is always the tendency to throw-in the two per cent, and make the Report one hundred per cent negative! This, in my opinion, is not honest. A frank statement should be included in the Report regarding this two per cent, together with the writer's opinion as to why they were possibly valid. Any critical remarks concerning this material may rightly be included in this section of the Report.

Take, on the other hand, the convinced spiritualist. He is often indignant when any one dares to raise the question of fraud, in connection with the phenomena produced by his pet medium. He insists that the conditions imposed by the medium (no matter how preposterous these may be, obviously intended to facilitate fraud) are perfectly right and justifiable. He roundly accuses the investigator of unwarranted skepticism, of blatant materialism, of wishing to expose every medium who may come under his scrutiny. He is so intent upon proving the continuity of life, and the reality of his "spirits" that he has no patience with and no respect for any one who may venture to question the conclusiveness of his "messages" or the accuracy of his control. He closes his mind to anything which might tend to interfere with his set convictions. Worst of all, he even refuses to listen to certain definite, negative evidence, which may run counter to his preconceived opinions and beliefs.

Both of these attitudes are, in my opinion, equally fallacious, misleading, and intellectually dishonest. The true researcher should not endeavor to prove or to disprove anything; his sole aim should be to arrive at the truth, whatever that may be. His duty is to record *facts,* and draw logical deductions from those facts. If the observed facts seem to indicate a positive conclusion, this should be given fully and frankly. If they point in the opposite direction, this should be stated with the same impartiality. The will-to-believe or the will-to-disbelieve should never be allowed to influence the judgment in one way or the other.

Dr. Richard Hodgson expressed what I am endeavoring to say very clearly when he wrote (*Proceedings,* IX, p. 366):

"There is no royal road to sound opinions on such matters generally; there is nothing for it save to examine each narrative on its own merits, and with close individual care; the mind meanwhile prepared for either fate—whether to prick some bubble of pretension into empty falsity, or to discover beneath some unpromising envelope a germ of inexplicable truth."

That is the attitude of the psychical researcher who endeavors to occupy some middle ground and maintain a rigid impartiality with regard to these phenomena. In my estimation it is the only correct attitude —though it is undoubtedly the most difficult and uncomfortable one. There are two sides to this question, and every competent and experienced researcher knows there are genuine phenomena, and also that there are spurious imitations. It becomes a question of sifting the wheat from the chaff. This is often a most difficult thing to do, and that is why, as I have often said, psychical research is the most fascinating and the most annoying topic in the world. Just when one feels that a definite decision may be arrived at, some little incident crops up which entirely upsets the apple-cart. And this is true no less of positive than of negative conclusions.

Take, for example, the difficult question of spirit communication. There are many, as we know, who accept *all* communications of the kind as genuinely spiritistic—messages through mediums of all sorts and descriptions, automatically written books, etc. In the opinion of other spiritualists, this is far too inclusive and positively erroneous. They would contend that, while veridical messages are undoubtedly received at times, they are relatively rare, and that the vast majority of messages received are obviously subconscious in their origin. This is the attitude of the more intelligent spiritualists, and is doubtless correct, so far as it goes, inasmuch as many of these messages have been traced to their source or origin, and shown to be such.

There are those again who, while freely granting the supernormal character of much of this material, are inclined to doubt the spiritistic source of any of it. A number of prominent investigators were of this opinion —men like Schrenck-Notzing, Morselli, Richet, Sudre, Flournoy—and, though constantly quoted by spiritualists, yet wrote strongly against it! They doubtless realized the enormous psychological difficulties involved, and also the problems presented by such cases as that of Gordon Davis (*Proc.* 35, pp. 560-90) and that of Mme. Dupont (*Spiritism and Psychology*, pp. 72-82), where long and most circumstantial communications were received from the *soi-disant* communicators—who subsequently turned up alive and well!

In these instances, the source of the information was certainly *not* spiritistic; yet the general tenor and appearance of the communications were precisely similar to many of those which are said to be so. No definite conclusions can be drawn from such cases beyond the one which I desire to stress, viz., that they *enormously complicate the problem.* They justify a certain reserve of judgment with regard to this question, and permit the cautious researcher, who is in possession of these facts, to avoid any rash jumping to conclusions.

In all psychical investigation, we should, I think, be governed by two general propositions. These are:

1. All is possible.
2. The strength of the evidence should be proportioned to the strangeness of the facts.

The first of these indicates a certain open-mindedness: the willingness to grant the theoretical possibility of any fact, no matter how bizarre it may appear, and to accept it upon sufficient evidence.

The second deals with the sufficiency of that evidence. The more unusual and seemingly impossible the alleged phenomena, the stronger the evidence should be, before accepting it. This is perfectly logical, and as it should be. If a certain alleged fact departs only a little from the generally accepted facts of science, the mind can more readily assimilate it, and it appears to us *a priori* more credible. If, on the other hand, it totally violates (seemingly) some of the very fundamentals of modern science, the evidence for the actual occurrence should be proportionately strong, in order to overcome our natural mental resistance to it.

As an example of this latter type, I might cite lycanthropy, that is, the alleged ability of certain men to transform themselves into wolves, hyenas, or other animals. Any one who may care to look up the existing evidence for this will find an extraordinary mass of case-records in its support; yet no one, I imagine, seriously believes in it today. Why? Because of its seeming impossibility. The first-hand, circumstantial evidence is not *sufficiently* strong to warrant our belief. Similarly, many psychic phenomena appear relatively incredible to different minds: telekinesis and materialization to the physicist and the biologist; clairvoyance and spirit communication to the psychologist. The first set of alleged facts run counter to the experience of the former, and the second set of facts run counter to the philosophy and experience of the latter. Hence their mental resistance or opposition to them. This is quite intelligible, and is a constituent part of our human nature.

And why should the spiritistic theory prove so difficult of acceptance by the psychologist? The religiously or mystically-minded man finds little difficulty in accepting it. To him it appears quite reasonable and rational, and only what we should expect. To the ordinary physician or psychologist it is a fact "most strange." Why? Because he realizes that so much of our mental life is indubitably bound-up with the functionings of the brain. Not only are there certain definite areas wherein sensory impressions are received, and motor impulses given forth, but whole sections of our memory (so to say) seem to be stored in certain definite areas of the brain structure—the memory of names, of written words, of musical notes, of spoken words, etc. —so that an injury of that localized area will destroy the memories connected with it.

For example, a man can no longer read and understand musical notes, while he can still read the printed word perfectly. Now, inasmuch as our personality depends largely upon memory (there is an old saying: "no memory, no personality") and inasmuch as memory seems to be so intimately bound-up with the activities of the physical brain, it is almost unthinkable to the psychologist that the human personality can exist and remain intact in the absence of a physical brain altogether. It is considerations such as these which have caused men such as Richet, Sudre, Schrenck-Notzing, etc., to reject the spiritistic hypothesis, while accepting the supernormality of the facts.

It must be admitted, of course, that this argument is purely *a priori,* and if the facts *prove* survival, it must be accepted, and physiological theories adjusted accordingly. I merely state the case here in order to show why it is not possible for the psychologist to accept the idea of survival easily, and why he is so insistent upon absolute demonstration before conceding it to be a proved fact. His natural mental resistance to the idea is very great, and can only be overcome by an overwhelming mass of facts for which there seems to be no other reasonable explanation.

Every fair-minded student of this subject must admit that there is a great deal of very respectable evidence in favor of survival. *Evidence,* however, is not the same thing as *proof,* and the average scientific man wants proof before accepting it. This, as we know, is difficult to obtain, and the number of clean-cut cases is relatively rare. On the other hand, there is a great mass of seemingly spiritistic material which is certainly not due to that source (*spiritoid,* as Boirac calls it) which fact has been emphasized over and over again by Hyslop, James, Lodge, and every investigator of note. In view of these facts, it obviously behooves us to exercise due caution, when dealing with this material, and not to "swallow everything" offered us in the name of spiritualism.

I trust that the reader will understand that I am not attacking the validity of the spiritistic theory, in anything that I have said. There is much to be said in favor of it, and many eminent and fair-minded men have declared themselves spiritualists, after carefully weighing the pros and cons of the subject. I think there is a growing mass of evidence in its favor, and a gradual tendency to accept it as the correct explanation. I myself have written strongly in favor of the *theory* of spiritualism, in reply to certain critics of our evidence. It is a perfectly justifiable working hypothesis. I am only contending that the attitude of balanced, suspended judgment is perfectly logical, and is, in my estimation, the correct attitude for the average psychical researcher to take in the present state of our knowledge.

I am inclined to think that our general mental attitude toward this question is largely determined by our early religious training. If the mind has been imbued, from early childhood, with the reality of a spiritual world, a certain set predisposition toward that belief is almost inevitable. If, on the other hand, the child is brought up with little or no orthodox training, this attitude is frequently lacking. The "craving for immortality," which so many feel keenly, is not experienced in these cases. This "craving" is, I am convinced, often the deciding factor, in making our decisions in these matters. Given the same set of facts, they will prove conclusive to one mind and not to another. The psychological background or setting is responsible for the final choice. There is rarely any certitude in matters psychic. There is always a *balance of probability:* whether this interpretation or that one be the more reasonable, in view of the recorded testimony. As William James said:

"We all live on an inclined plane of credulity. The plane tips one way in one man, another way in another; and may he whose plane tips in *no* way be the first to cast a stone!"

It may be next to impossible to find any one possessed of this perfectly balanced mind: but the point I wish to emphasize is that this was held up as an ideal to be attained by no less an authority than William James, and certainly no man can be censured for trying to attain it. On the contrary it is, I believe, the very essence of a psychical researcher to achieve this end—allowing himself to be swayed by no emotions, and holding his mind perfectly open to the reception of new truths.

In my *Story of Psychic Science* I endeavored to summarize what I considered were the chief essentials of a competent psychical researcher. I then said:

"...A specialized training is necessary for this work; our ideal investigator must have a thorough knowledge of the literature of the subject; he must have a good grounding in normal and abnormal psychology; in physics, chemistry, biology, photography, and some laboratory experience; he must be a keen observer, a good judge of human nature and its motives; he must be well trained in magic and sleight-of-hand; he must be shrewd, quick of thought and action, ever on the alert, patient, resourceful, open-minded, tolerant, rapid in his observations and deductions, sympathetic, and have a sense of humor! He must be free from superstition, and at the same time unswayed by bigotry, theological or scientific. In short, our ideal investigator is hard to find, and it is probable that such a man is born rather than made...."

I can see no reason to change the views therein expressed. This attitude of open-mindedness, of suspended judgment, seems to me to be the soundest and the best—not only because of the fact that one's own decisions are probably more accurate on that account, but also because the general public has, as a rule, more confidence in such a man and his leadership. It must always be remembered that each individual case stands on its own merits, and that because a certain set of phenomena, occurring through the instrumentality of one medium, may be accepted as genuine, that by no means proves that the same phenomena produced through the instrumentality of another are genuine also. That is far from being the case! It is also true, on the other hand, that negative results may be obtained time after time, and that positive results may ultimately be forthcoming, in the presence of another medium. This has been my own experience, and has doubtless been the experience of many other researchers also.

Thus, before attending my first séance with Eusapia Palladino, I had sat with dozens of "physical mediums," every one of whom had turned out to be fraudulent. Yet I became thoroughly convinced of the genuineness of her phenomena, and so stated. The result was that my "conversion" carried due weight— Professor Flournoy being kind enough to say, when reviewing my book *Eusapia Palladino: and her Phenomena:*

"... It is hardly necessary to add that this difference of theoretical interpretation between Mr. Carrington and myself does not in the least diminish the value which I attach to his researches; and that, in particular, I hold his report on Eusapia to be the most valuable contribution to the subject in the whole history of the supernormal, and the one which pleads the most powerfully in favor of the authenticity of the Palladino phenomena. . . ."

I cite this for no personal reason, but merely to justify an *attitude*—the attitude, namely, of the man who decides to hold his final judgment in suspense, with regard to the ultimate interpretation of these baffling phenomena. The man who is always "on the fence" is, I am fully aware, a source of constant annoyance to his fellow workers—who are always urging him to get off the fence on one side or the other! [As a matter of fact "the other" (complete negation) does not enter into their calculations at all. What they really want him to do is to come out flat-footed in favor of spiritualism.] But—as I have tried to show —there are many reasons why certain individuals cannot bring themselves to do so. They may ultimately arrive at this conclusion, and a number of them have, but there are many who prefer still to hold their final verdict in suspense, while continuing their accumulation and study of facts. And this is, it seems to me, an attitude which cannot reasonably be criticized.

Much that I am saying here has been said in other and doubtless better words by F. W. H. Myers, in his paper on "Resolute Credulity" in the S.P.R. *Proceedings*. And, as Dr. Hyslop has reminded us: "Faith no longer charms with her Magic Wand, except among those who do not accept or appreciate scientific method, but whose flimsy standards afford no criteria for defense against illusion and deception." Dr. Hodgson maintained his critical attitude to the day of his death, when called upon to investigate any new medium. Emotional cravings should not be allowed to sway the judgment, nor should any particular philosophy of the Universe which one may care to hold. Psychical Research consists, or should consist, of much more than evidence for survival—though this is, naturally, the central and most absorbing topic to the majority of investigators.

The scoffer and the critic are, on the other hand, far more easily disposed of. They have on their side as a rule no evidence, no facts and usually no logic! They know nothing about the subject and are merely ignorant. Such critics often make themselves ridiculous, without in any way affecting the evidence or influencing those who happen to know what they are talking about. Serious criticism is always valuable, but this has rarely been attempted: the majority of such criticisms have merely served to display the bias and prejudice of the critics themselves. All of which reminds me of Dr. Hodgson's old saying that "if we could only get the scientific men to attack us, our case would be won!" What is needed above all else is helpful criticism, patient investigation, and the constant accumulation of new facts.

# IV

# The Psychology of Genius

## CONTENTS

## What is Genius?

GENIUS may roughly be defined as original, brilliant and creative work of some sort, and the man of genius as one who has the faculty or ability to produce results of this character. But it will be realized at once that this definition is superficial and tentative, and that it does not attempt in any way to define the nature of the product, far less the *modus operandi* of its production. Yet, from the psychological point-of-view, that is the interesting problem which confronts us! How account for such extraordinary powers? Whence do they originate? What happens inside a man when he is in the throes of some creative effort? Is the man of genius a normal individual? Is there any traceable connection between the inspirations of genius and other supernormal powers? These are a few of the questions which at once come to mind as soon as we begin to discuss this

37

question, and seek to discover its inner nature. In view of the scarcity of material available, and the scant references to it in the literature of borderland psychology, an analysis of this problem can hardly fail to be of interest.*

In the first place, then, what do we mean by genius? Is this word to be used as synonymous with talent? With intellectual brilliance? With original, creative work? With musical or artistic or scientific ability? With inventiveness? With originality? Are the various musical and arithmetical prodigies to be counted as geniuses? Are all geniuses necessarily erratic, defective or mad? Or are they superior individuals? Is genius merely hard work? Each of these questions must be considered in turn before we can hope to come to any clear understanding of the problems involved.

The first serious attack upon this vital problem was made by Sir Francis Galton, in his book *Hereditary Genius*. His inquiry was however largely statistical, and constituted an attempt to show that genius probably was hereditary, inasmuch as a brilliant man frequently had a brilliant father, or various members of a family showed marked ability, if one of them did. The number of families that had served as the basis of the work was about 300, and included nearly 1,000 men of note, of whom 415 were illustrious. Taking judges, statesmen, generals, men of letters, scientific men, poets, artists and divines, as the basis for his calculations, Galton concluded that "the probability that a man of mark would have remarkable kinsmen is, on the average, for

* For example, the word "genius" does not even appear in the Index of McDougall's *Outline of Abnormal Psychology;* only the most fleeting references are made to the subject in William James' *Principles of Psychology,* etc.

his father thirty-one per cent; brothers, forty-one per cent; sons, forty-eight per cent; grandfather, seventeen per cent; uncle, eighteen per cent; nephew, twenty-two per cent; grandson, fourteen per cent;" etc.

Galton's figures have been considered problematical for various reasons, though they *do* seem to indicate, in general, that genius of a sort may often be hereditary, just as other psychological factors are.* Galton apparently made genius more or less equivalent to intellectual brilliance, or outstanding artistic merit, but, as we shall presently see, this conception is far too limited in its scope, and not nearly comprehensive enough to include all types and varieties of genius. We shall return to this question, and also that of the possibility of hereditary genius, however, later on.

Let us now, first of all, examine a few of the various tentative definitions of genius which have been given in the past, in order to discover, if possible, in what genius consists, and what it is and is not. We shall reserve our general discussion of the question until later. These definitions, and a brief discussion of them, each in turn, will at least serve to clear the air and perhaps enable us to arrive at some sort of understanding of the nature, functions and peculiarities of genius.

### Is Genius Originality?

Undoubtedly a genius, in order to be such, must be original. Royse says: "We can not conceive of genius except as something extraordinary, and of this quality originality is the very essence." Doctor Johnson, in his essay on Milton, says that "the highest praise of genius is original invention." Emerson says: "Every great

* Cf. Ribot, *Heredity, A Psychological Study,* etc.

man is unique.... The highest merit we ascribe to Moses, Plato and Milton is that they set at naught books and traditions, and spoke not what men, but what *they* thought." George Eliot declares: "Genius itself is not *en règle;* it comes into the world to make new rules." Hazlitt, in his *Table Talk,* says: "Genius, or originality, is for the most part some strong originality of the mind, answering to and bringing out some new and striking quality in Nature.... Originality consists in seeing Nature differently from others, and yet as it is in itself." Lowell asserts that "to make the common marvelous, as it were a revelation, is the test of genius." Bain contends that "the principle of like recalling like, through the disguises of diversity, *this* I count the leading fact of genius." William James, in his *Principles of Psychology* states that "the most elementary single difference between the human mind and that of brutes lies in this deficiency on the brute's part to associate ideas by similarity.... Genius is identical with the possession of similar associations to an extreme degree" (11, p. 360). Such opinions and quotations could be multiplied almost indefinitely.

It is undoubtedly true that where there is no originality there is no genius; hence originality is an essential, constituent factor. But does this serve in any way to *explain* the genius? Or does it not rather define its quality—*one* of its qualities? We are assuredly no nearer a solution of the main problem: what constitutes genius—*why* and *how* the original ideas come into the man's head, where they come from, and why he should see similarities and associations which another man does not see. Certainly this does not consist in mere intellectual clarity or in profound learning. Many men have exceptionally clear and logical minds who are not in the least original, and there are many men of great erudition who do not show the slightest indications of true genius. Nor does the sparkling, versatile mind, as a rule, make any real mark in the world; it is usually a pseudo-genius rather than a true one. Invention shows originality; but this is often only on one line, and the man is otherwise anything but a genius; he is more likely to be a mere crank. Franklin was a real discoverer when he drew lightning from the clouds; so was Edison when he invented the electric light bulb; yet the great scientifico-philosophical geniuses (Darwin, Laplace, Kant) must surely rank as the greater. Artistic, musical and literary geniuses each shine in their own sphere. Finally, such definitions of genius as those given above do not in the least explain or help us to understand *why* such men as those already mentioned possess the originality they do, or *why* they are enabled to perceive differences and make associations other men do not. In short, all they do is to point out and emphasize one essential element of genius, without in the least making plain to us the underlying psychological factors involved, or what happens in the mind of the genius when his original ideas are created or brought into being.

### Is Genius Concentration?

Goethe, Johnson, and others, defined genius as concentration, but it is very evident that thousands of individuals concentrate, none of whom are geniuses! It is probably true that genius of a certain type (as we shall see) *is* brought into action by means of concentration, but there are geniuses of another type who do not have to concentrate in the least, and their best work is produced when their minds are more or less blank and seemingly inactive. Some artistic and musical geniuses are of this type, and the same is true of arithmetical prodigies, etc. It cannot be said, therefore, that concentration is essential to genius, though may geniuses have possessed unusual powers of concentration.

### Is Genius Patience?

Buffon gives us this definition, but in many ways it is precisely the opposite of the truth. The slow plodder is, as a rule, just what he appears to be, and is such because of his lack of the true spark. Hard work may prepare the soil of the mind, so to say, and cultivate it, so that genius may sprout in it, if the germs are really there. But it is a palpable truth that there are tens of thousands of hard workers for every true genius, and, as we shall presently see, genius is not the result of work but rather the cause of it. This definition, therefore, places the cart before the horse, to a certain extent, and is in no sense a true definition of genius.

### Is Genius Common Sense?

To ask this question is to answer it. Genius consists essentially in *un*common sense, in originality, in the ability to think differently from other people. This is precisely what genius is *not*.

### Is Genius Constructiveness?

Emerson says: "Genius is intellect constructive"; and Matthew Arnold and Taine seem to agree with him. But, in order for the mind to construct anything, it must first of all have a vision of the thing to be constructed. Every engineer must possess this faculty to some degree: but every engineer is not a genius! It represents, rather, a special talent which has been trained; and as we shall see more fully later on talent is not at all the same thing as genius. Also, there are many types of genius which are not at all constructive, in the ordinary acceptation of that word, and are even altogether unconscious of how their results are obtained. It cannot be said, therefore, that this is in any sense a true definition of the essential constituent of genius.

### Is Genius Anticipation?

Longfellow, in his "Hyperion," says: "It has become a common saying that men of genius are always in advance of their age; which is true. There is something equally true, yet not so common; namely, that, of these men of genius, the best and bravest are in advance not only of their own age, but of every age. . . ." Macaulay says much the same thing, and so do Richter and Alison.

What has been said above, with regard to originality, applies here also to a great extent. In order for the possible future to be in any way envisioned, there must be originality and fertility of imagination. Every man possesses this to some degree. But the vast majority of our prophets fall hopelessly by the wayside, and the degree of originality they possess is soon found to be far from surprising. The true genius anticipates because he is a genius, but anticipation does not make him such. In short, the cart has again been placed before the horse, here as elsewhere.

## Is Genius Breadth?

Grant Allen, in one of his *Essays,* has this to say:

"The peculiarity of a genius is that he possesses in some one department a few more elements of mind than most other people, his contemporaries; that he combines in himself a certain large number of mind-factors, all, or nearly all, of which are to be severally found in other people, but which are not to be found in any other one person in the same combination."

Much this same thought may be found expressed in the writings of Carlyle, Emerson, Lowell, DeQuincey, and others.

This vast, almost cosmic, sweep of the mind is to be found in many geniuses, such as philosophers, great generals, etc. If it is not "shallow breadth," it undoubtedly constitutes a variety of genius. Such minds cannot be bothered with details, with minutiæ. But just because of that fact the majority of men of this stamp fail to become geniuses: they cannot gather and patiently assemble vast quantities of facts, as Darwin did. Many of them are, therefore, their own worst enemies, and the peculiar constitution of their minds prevents them from becoming geniuses. True, the majority of geniuses probably possess great breadth of mind, but breadth of mind does not in itself constitute genius. The "divine spark" is not present, and it is that which constitutes the very essence of the state we are considering.

## Is Genius Merely Hard Work?

There are many, as we know, who hold this view, but we have very largely answered it in what has been said before. Hard work *per se* will rarely develop the genius, though it may prepare the soil in which genius may sprout—especially genius of a scientific character. But there are many other varieties of genius of which this is not at all true, and any definition of genius which we may be tempted to give must be more or less inclusive of all types. The spark of genius may cause a man to work hard, but hard work is more likely to develop a (more or less) latent talent, rather than develop true genius. The God-given fire is lacking, and it is that which constitutes the true essence of the genius, as we are attempting to define it.

### Is Genius Character?

John Burroughs was of the opinion that the former depended to a large extent upon the latter, but this is directly contradicted by Lowell who, in his essay on Rousseau, stated that "genius is *not* a question of character." And it may be said that the whole experience of mankind is against this view; for many men of irreproachable character have been anything but geniuses, while, on the other hand, some of the greatest geniuses the world has ever known have been men whose character was deplorable. It cannot seriously be contended that there is any essential connection between the two.

.    .    .    .    .    .    .

Having now cleared the ground of much of the rubbish and under-brush growing about this subject, and having shown that the various definitions of genius which have been attempted in the past do not really define genius in any true sense, we may now pass on to a more general theoretical discussion of our problem, considering various aspects of it in turn, and see what light, if any, may be thrown upon it, before advancing any explanatory hypotheses or attempting to draw any conclusions or similes. Let us begin with a brief discussion of that moot question—the possible connection or inter-relationship between

*Genius and Insanity.*

This aspect of the problem was brought prominently to the fore by Max Nordau (*Genius and Degeneration*), Lombroso (*The Man of Genius*), F. Nisbet (*Insanity and Genius*), and many others. Nordau and Nisbet attempted to show that the "eccentricities of genius" were often so glaring that they bordered upon true insanity, while Lombroso endeavored to prove that certain definite "stigmata" were invariably present, just as they were claimed to be present in the cases of criminals—a theory now almost entirely abandoned. The idea that there is some connection between the two dates back from the veriest antiquity. Both Plato and Aristotle drew attention to the fact, as did Pascal, Diderot and Lamartine. Perhaps the oft-quoted lines of Dryden sum-up this point-of-view with precision:

"Great wits are sure to madness near allied,
    And thin partitions do their bounds divide."

One of the best summaries of this theory is doubtless that of Dr. James Sully, who endeavored to prove the point by a collection and analysis of numerous incidents in the lives of well-known men. Thus: we find instances of extreme abstraction, amounting almost to absence of mind—Archimedes; so absorbed in a problem as not to be aware of the approach of his Roman slayer; Newton, judging from the plate that a prankish friend had emptied that he had really eaten his dinner; Beethoven standing in his night-clothes before an open window, etc. The persistence of vivid ideas has also been noted in men of genius: Peter the Great afraid to cross a bridge; Johnson's repugnance to certain alleys in London; Pascal's fear of a gulf yawning in front of him; Marshal Saxe terrified at the sight of a cat; Schiller keeping a row of rotten apples in his study as a necessity of living and working, etc. Hallucinations were experienced by Luther, Malebranche, Descartes, Goethe, Pope, Byron, Napoleon, Shelley and many others. Extraordinary violence of temper was common, while melancholy and hypochondria were frequently noted in men of this type. In a number of cases, this terminated in clearly developed mental disease. Whimsical and erratic ideas were frequently noted, while inconsistencies and contradictions were observed in many instances. Dr. Sully thus sums-up his argument:

"Our conclusion is that the possession of genius carries with it special liabilities to the disintegrating forces which environ us all. It involves a state of delicate equipoise, of unstable equilibrium, in the psycho-physical organization. Paradoxical as it may seem, one may venture to affirm that great original power of mind is incompatible with nice adjustment to surroundings, and so with perfect well-being.* The genius is a scout who rides out well in advance of the intellectual army, and who by this very advance and isolation from the main

---

* Psycho-analysis has, of course, thrown considerable light upon this question, of late years.

body is exposed to special perils. Thus genius ... is a mode of variation of human nature which, though unfavorable to the conservation of the individual, aids in the evolution of the species. ..."

It is doubtful, however, if most of these charges against men of genius can seriously be maintained. How many tens of thousands of cases of violence of temper, irrationality, hallucinations, temptation to commit suicide, hypochondria, irritability, etc., might not be cited in cases of men who were not at all geniuses? These are semi-morbid traits which occur in all walks of life, and the mere fact that a few men of genius similarly displayed these traits does not in the least prove that they were the *cause* of the genius, or even necessary concomitants of it. Rather, the man was a genius in spite of these handicaps of temperament! The mere fact that the man was a genius made him a marked character—one subject to public criticism and analysis. And the mere fact that one or more of these peculiarities was found in him by no means proves that they were, of necessity, connected with his original, creative powers. Many geniuses appeared to be eminently sane; while many, possessing not a spark of genius, exhibited them in a striking degree. The only charge which might perhaps "hold water" would be that of occasional fits of abstraction; but these were surely due to extraordinary concentration upon the problem in mind, and represent a supernormal, rather than a sub-normal, mental functioning.

It is obvious, therefore, that no logical connection exists between genius and insanity, as commonly understood; however, we shall return to this question again in due course, after having made a more systematic psychological analysis of the whole problem. This we shall now accordingly attempt; and I shall begin by calling attention to a very illuminating distinction between the various types or kinds of genius—first advocated, if I am not mistaken, by Prof. Ostwald, the famous physicist, of Germany, noted for his theory of "energetics."

### Classical vs. Romantic Geniuses

There are those, as we know, who contend that genius consists mostly in hard work, while there are others who contend that work has little to do with it, but that the flashes or inspirations of true genius come quite unsought. Well, says Professor Ostwald, there is a certain amount of truth in both these theories. But they apply to different types of genius. There are in reality two distinct types, and not one. We have what might be called the "classical" type of genius, and we have the "romantic" type. Most of the well-known geniuses are of the classical type. They were masters of their genius, while, in the romantic type, their genius is master of them. The classical genius is centralized, and has purpose; he is intent upon producing, rather than upon recognition. He is not so flighty and passionate. He adopts the Greek motto: "Nothing in excess." * The classical geniuses, as a rule, live apart from people and work hard.

The romantic geniuses, on the other hand, are more "fluid" in type—as against the more "solid" type of the classical geniuses. They get their ideas with less

* Robert Louis Stevenson said that Art consists largely in "knowing what to leave out."

effort. They live in the fire of enthusiasm, while the classical genius does not get so fired or excited. The romantic genius is more intuitional. As a rule, the classical genius produces his work relatively late in life (40 to 50), and the romantic genius early in life. The romantic genius is the suffering type—melancholy, excitable, erratic, etc.

The romantic genius works in fits and starts, while the classical genius works more continuously. Hence, it is only of the classical genius type that it may be said that "genius is nine-tenths hard work." Work is not the *cause* of genius, but the *result*. So, the "capacity for taking infinite pains" is due to the fact that the genius *must* work, and is naturally industrious. The genius of the classical type cannot be lazy. The genius of the romantic type, even when he is working, can be lazy *when the mood is on*. The old adage "genius is born and not made" is only partially true: the genius is born *and* made. The cause of work is the genius. The great artist is absorbed in his work; the lesser artist, or pseudo-genius, in the product.

### Genius and Talent

What is the essential difference between them? *Work* is the key. Genius makes a man work; talent does not. Talent is the *result* of work, while genius is the *cause* of it. The work of the true genius is unconscious; the work of the talented is conscious. Thus, the true genius may be said to be in the grip of a higher power of spirit. The genius sees associations which other people do not see; he combines old things in new ways; he blazes new trails.

Talent is subject to training and can be cultivated.

Talent grows by external accretion, like a crystal; while genius springs from within, like true growth.

While it is probably true that "every genius is a crank," not every crank is a genius! Mrs. Carlyle remarked that "no woman should ever marry a genius," which may be true from her point-of-view, but may perhaps be set against Nietzsche's remark that "a married philosopher is ridiculous!"

The genius runs counter to the traditions of the times in which he lives; he is "different." Therefore, we make him suffer—because of his differences! The romantic genius loves *beauty* most, while the classical genius loves *truth* most. Hence, philosophers and scientists are of the classical genius type, while artists and poets are of the romantic genius type.

The romantic geniuses are the ones who often verge on insanity, and supply the majority of cases which have been quoted. Possibly, this theory is a half-truth. Classical geniuses are probably *further* from insanity than the average person. Lombroso contended that the "inspiration of genius" resembles an epileptic fit, characterized by unconsciousness, visions (usually weird) and exhaustion. St. Paul, Mohammed, Napoleon, Cæsar, Peter the Hermit, Swift, Molière, Handel, etc., were all epileptics. Lombroso's theory applies, at best, to a few representatives of the romantic type of genius. Examples of this could certainly be found: Coleridge was a drug fiend; Mozart had delusions of persecution; Swift became insane, and prophesied on the streets of Dublin, where the people came to consult him like an oracle; Baudelaire dyed his hair green and wrote erotic poems to a negress, etc.

This theory of the relations of genius and insanity

did not, of course, originate with Lombroso. Aristotle pointed out that men of genius were usually sad, and were of the melancholic temperament. Horace said that a natural genius either becomes insane or a poet! He becomes either a genius or a fool! He does not become *both,* as we have been told. While it may be true that many geniuses are sad, this may be due to temperament—or because they see more of the truth than other people!

We are inclined to class together the half-witted and the one-and-a-half witted. In the latter case, we see only a third of their wits, their powers. Hence, we tend to class them with the half-witted.

Genius and insanity are both egotistical. Precocity occurs in the romantic genius type; rarely in the classical genius type. In both genius and insanity we find erotic irregularities; they are both original; both different; both suffer from *wanderlust;* both are fearless (we speak of insane courage); both are passionate; both are awkward; both are insufficiently adapted to their surroundings; both believe themselves inspired— but the genius produces original work, while the insane man does not!

Genius, then, is not a form of insanity—though the genius may become insane. When the central control is lost, this occurs. The mind of the genius is more complex (as opposed to simple) in structure, and hence more easily destroyed. Geniuses are the advance-guards of civilization; they forge ahead, they make original experiments and try out new theories. They take risks and develop themselves further along certain lines. They are more highly strung, and "the tauter the string, the more readily it breaks."

The genius has to repress himself more than the majority of people, to fit into his environment; hence there is a greater "pressure" on him, as psycho-analysis has shown us. This, of course, is especially true of the romantic genius type.

Every normal child is to a certain extent a potential genius, inasmuch as he could give one new idea to the world, one original suggestion, if he were properly trained. We often bring up children in a way calculated to squash and stifle all originality, and hence all genius. For "differences" make genius. Hence, we should let the child develop and cultivate any "differences" which he may exhibit, allowing him to be original, within the bounds of rationality.

### Precocity and Genius

At what age does ordinary genius begin to manifest itself? The answers to this question are difficult and contradictory. But, as a general rule, genius of the romantic type begins to manifest at an early age, while genius of the classical type only becomes pronounced fairly late in life. Thus, to take but a few examples:

Aristophanes, the great comic poet of Greece, gained his first prize when but nineteen years of age. Cowley received the applause of the great at eleven, and Pope at twelve. Byron's general information, as a boy, was unusually large and varied, and the list of works, in divers compartments of literature, which he had perused before his fifteenth year, is astonishing. His first known poetical effusion was penned at twelve, and at eighteen he published his first volume of poems. Burns was a poet at sixteen, his first recorded poem having been written in memory of a fair girl companion of the harvest fields, from whose hands he was wont to re-move nettle-stings and thistles. Henry Kirke White was but seventeen when his first volume of poems was given to the public; Schiller published a poem on Moses when only fourteen; Klopstock began his "Messiah" at seventeen; at eighteen Tasso wrote "Rinaldo"; Calderon, the famous Spanish dramatist, penned his first play at fourteen; Goethe composed dialogues when only six or seven; Alfred de Musset wrote poems when only fourteen; Victor Hugo, called the "infant sublime," versified when a school boy, and at sixteen produced work of permanent value; Beaumont composed tragedies at twelve; Coleridge revealed his poetic genius at sixteen; Mrs. Browning began writing poetry at eight, and published an epic at twelve, while Mrs. Hemans published a volume of poems at fourteen.

Leonardo da Vinci, the most comprehensive and versatile of all the great Italian masters of art, when but a small boy, puzzled his teachers by his original remarks and searching inquiries. In his first effort at drawing, he surpassed in grace and naturalness of outline the models of his experienced instructor. When Michælangelo was placed at a grammar school, preparatory to his entering one of the learned professions, he spent his time chiefly in drawing, much to his father's disgust! Apprenticed to an eminent artist, his progress was so rapid as to excite the latter's jealousy, and to compel the confession that his pupil had no further need of him. Raphael, before he was sixteen, copied the illustrations of Perugino's designs so perfectly that his copies were frequently mistaken for the originals. Gainsborough became a painter at twelve, and Turner exhibited creditable work at fifteen. Sir

Christopher Wren, at the age of thirteen, had invented an astronomical apparatus, a pneumatic machine, and several curious, if not useful, instruments.

At the age of nine years, Handel composed "motets" and other pieces which were sung in the Cathedral; and, when only two years older, he provoked the mingled applause and envy of the foremost composer and organist of Berlin by his astonishing instrumentation. When but a choir boy at St. Stephen's, Haydn composed a mass, and was only twelve years old when he wrote his first opera.

Mozart, when barely able to reach up to the keyboard of the piano, would pick out thirds and other chords while his older sister was taking her lesson, and at the age of four began to compose. At nine he wrote sonatas for violin, viola, 'cello, horn, oboe, bassoon and harpsichord; also a small oratorio; and at twelve, in the presence of the whole imperial family of Austria, he wielded the conductor's baton at the performance of a mass composed by himself for the consecration of a new church.

Charles Dickens, when but a small boy, became famous among his playmates as the writer of a tragedy called "Misnar," and also as the relator of impromptu stories. Bonaparte was very young when he displayed his extraordinary military genius. Alexander the Great was only twelve when he assumed the head of the Macedonian government; Peter the Great became Czar at seventeen.

Many similar instances could be cited, showing that numerous great men displayed their genius at an early age. On the other hand, many of the world's greatest geniuses did not become famous until they were long past middle age. To mention but a few cases of this character:

### Age and Genius

The world-famed Cervantes developed no special brilliancy as a student, and was fifty-eight years of age when the first part of *Don Quixote* was given to the public. Bunyan did not write *Pilgrim's Progress* until he was more than forty years of age. Virgil's *Æneid* was written between his forty-third and fiftieth years. Æschylus, the founder of the drama, won his first prize at forty-one. Dante was thirty-five when he began the composition of his *Divine Comedy*. Chaucer's *Canterbury Tales* were the product of his old age. Wordsworth did not gain renown until after forty.

Scott was forty-three before he began to attract attention by his writings. Daniel DeFoe was fifty-eight when he produced his masterpiece *Robinson Crusoe;* Milton was sixty when he began to compose his famous "Paradise Lost." Bach did not compose until he was past forty. Columbus was fifty-six when he planted his flag on San Salvador. Franklin was more than forty when he began his investigation of electricity. Harvey published his discovery of the circulation of the blood at fifty. Darwin did not begin to write his *Origin* until long past forty, and his *Descent of Man* was published some ten years later. Descartes and Leibnitz, the great philosophers, did not achieve distinction until they were past fifty; and Kant was forty-six. "Had Cromwell died at forty-three, England would never have known a Commonwealth."

It is obvious, therefore, that genius—and particularly genius of the classical type—often does not manifest itself until late in life, and that the age-expressions of genius are extraordinarily elastic, extending from the earliest years to advanced age.

### Musical and Arithmetical Prodigies

It will be observed that, in the above discussion, I carefully limited myself to the manifestations of *normal* genius—meaning by that, mental output of some sort of a high order, bearing the stamp of originality and brilliance. And, while several of the musical and poetic geniuses (especially) began composing at a very early age, hardly any of them (with the exception of Mozart) could rightly be defined as "infant prodigies." Curiously enough, this seems to be the rule rather than the exception, in cases of arithmetical prodigies, where one would expect the result to show much later on in life! Yet this is not the case. Mr. F. W. H. Myers compiled a Table (with the help of Dr. Scripture's collection) in which he showed that, in thirteen cases of the sort, the gift was first observed, in all instances, before the tenth year, and in several at three or four years of age. Thus, in the cases of Colburn, Prolongeau, Safford and Van R., it was noted at six; in Mangiamele and Mondeux at ten; in Whately at three; in Bidder at ten; in Ampère at four; in Gauss at three; and in the other cases in early boyhood. In practically all instances, the gift lasted but a few years, then disappeared. In some of these cases the adult intelligence was good, in others average, and in still others low. In after years, none of these men could remember the means they employed to solve the problems set them. The answers "just seemed to come into their heads";

they gave them, and they turned out to be right! So, of Van R., it is said:

"He did not retain the slightest idea of the manner in which he performed his calculations in childhood."

Of Colburn it was stated:

"He positively declared that he did not know how the answers came into his mind." And so on. Thus of Bidder:

"He had an almost miraculous power of seeing, as it were, intuitively what factors would divide any large number, not a prime. Thus, if he were given the number 17,861, he would immediately remark it was $337 \times 53$. . . . He could not, he said, explain *how* he did this; it seemed a natural instinct to him." *

(These cases of arithmetical prodigies, of course, in which the results are obtained quite without the co-operation of the conscious mind, have an interesting bearing upon the reported cases of calculating animals, such as the Mannheim dogs, the horses of Elberfeld, etc. The literature upon this subject is already fairly voluminous, but, inasmuch as it is not the province of this book to touch upon this question, I shall not do more than refer to it in passing.)

In addition to these arithmetical prodigies, however, there are, as we know, prodigies of other types—

---

* It is true that there are many ingenious "systems" and short-cuts by which a number of apparently complicated problems may be solved; see, *e.g., The Master System of Short Method Arithmetic,* by Joe Bond, Chicago, 1924. These are doubtless known to expert mathematicians. It may be taken as certain, however, that such methods are quite unknown to mathematical prodigies—partly because many of these systems have only been evolved of late years, and partly because a thorough knowledge of arithmetical principles is necessitated before these short-cut systems become intelligible; and, in the majority of cases, the subjects themselves had no idea as to *how* the given results were obtained.

artistic, musical, etc. Nowhere have I been enabled to find a psychological analysis of any of these cases which would prove illuminating or helpful in solving the problem in hand. A late work of the kind, *The Psychology of a Musical Genius,* by G. Révész (1925), I found most disappointing. Aside from the fact that the young genius in question (Erwin Nyiregyházi) was shown to be some three years more advanced, mentally, than his age would warrant (as shown by the Terman tests) I can find nothing of much value in the book, from the psychological point-of-view. And, as against this, we have such cases as "Blind Tom," who was practically an imbecile, yet, when placed at the piano, played like an angel. It can hardly be contended, therefore, that Erwin's mental precocity proves anything, since, in other instances, this was notoriously lacking. The explanation of these cases is obviously yet to find; * they form part and parcel of the general problem of genius, and we shall accordingly have occasion to refer to them again when we come to our discussion of the mechanism of genius—how genius *works.* Before doing so, however, a further discussion of the peculiarities and general psychological characteristics of genius will be in order.

## Environment, and Other Factors

The environmental influences which might be thought to have some influence upon the development of genius are, probably, (1) Early training, home and school; (2) Geographical surroundings; (3) The race to which one belongs, and (4) The age in which one lives.

* It need hardly be pointed out, perhaps, that the Theosophists and many others see in such cases clear evidence of the theory of "reincarnation."

(1) One would be inclined to believe that this might have a profound influence upon the budding genius; such, however, does not appear to be the case; many of the world's greatest geniuses have come from poor families, and have risen to great heights despite educational and social handicaps. They were, moreover, trained for some trade or profession utterly different from that in which they ultimately made their mark. Paradoxical as it may seem, this influence seems to be very slight, in the majority of cases.

(2) This, on the other hand, appears to be considerable—beauty of surroundings and an equitable temperature seeming essential factors. Royse indeed goes so far as to assert that "no genius has ever been known to have sprung up in a country of pronouncedly unfavorable physical conditions." It is possible, of course, that this may be due, in large part, to the lack of educational facilities and the need of devoting all the energies to the practical affairs of living.

(3) Race again has an important influence upon genius; the best and most progressive stock has as a rule produced geniuses—which represent the best of that stock. But race itself is, in great part, the natural outcome of geographical environment; and so the influence of race upon genius resolves itself ultimately into the prior consideration of the influence of geographical conditions upon genius.

(4) The enormous influence upon the genius of the age in which he lives has long been recognized. Macaulay, in his essay on Dryden, goes so far as to say that "it is the age that forms the man, not the man that forms the age. Great minds do indeed react upon the society which has made them what they are; but

they only pay with interest what they have received." The scientific genius flourishes only in a scientific age; the artistic genius in an artistic age; the literary genius in a literary age, etc. There is doubtless a great truth here; but it must be remembered that many of the world's greatest geniuses (witness Roger Bacon) expressed themselves in a spirit directly contrary to their age, and in opposition to it. Progress has certainly been rendered possible by reason of scientific discoveries, but more particularly because of intellectual freedom, in ridding the mind of grotesque beliefs and fears. It may be largely true that "great geniuses and great epochs go together," but the mainsprings of the individual genius seem just as hard to find as ever, even granting the greater facilities for its expression. And it must never be forgotten that the genius, in turn, helps to mold the environment in which he lives. In the words of William James: "Both factors are essential to change. The community stagnates without the impulse of the individual. The impulse dies away without the sympathy of the community."

Many facts which have in the past been held to be proofs of hereditary genius may thus doubtless be explained by environmental influences and the spirit of the age in which such men dwell. Many geniuses have been driven into their ultimate career as the result of pure accident. Having thus discovered the vital center of their lives, they have henceforth devoted themselves to it with passionate devotion.

While it is true that many men have only achieved greatness as the result of continuous mental effort, it is also true that many others have done so with but slight conscious direction. With them, ideas seem to spring up spontaneously in the mind, being flashed into it with lightning-like speed and clarity. At the same time, a certain devotion to work is always necessary— giving objectivity to the ideas thus implanted. When this is *not* the case, the man remains nothing more than a dreamer, a visionary. He may be truly inspired, but he must give expression or external form to his inner conceptions. This necessitates *application,* and the driving force back of this is usually the power of genius itself.

### Racial Experiences and Memories

In her book *Everyman's Genius*, Mary Austin attempts to account for genius by the theory of "racial experiences." She says:

"Genius is primarily a type of psychological activity. ... Genius itself is an inborn capacity for utilizing racial experience in meeting immediate exigencies. ... It is the free play of man's inheritance...."

This idea of some sort of a racial memory has played a large part in modern psycho-analytic literature, as we know—Dr. C. G. Jung dealing with it extensively in his book *The Psychology of the Unconscious.* Dr. Eugenio Rignano has also discussed it from a totally different angle in his *Biological Memory.* How this can be held to account for genius, however, I cannot see. The outstanding and essential characteristic of the genius is that he is *different* from the rest of humanity, and does *not* share with them a common viewpoint. To take one tentative definition of genius, as "a man who sees similarities which other men do not," how can racial experience account for that? The composition of masses, operas and sonatas, the instantaneous solution of complicated mathematical problems, the discovery of new scientific truths, the sublime rendition of music by a man totally devoid of mentality—how can racial memory account for these things? This theory has, it seems to me, been pushed to absurd extremes by various investigators, even to the extent of accounting for our "flying dreams" by supposing that they represent a sort of memory, inherited from our ape-like ancestors, when they lived in trees! Much of Jung's material is purely fantastic. There is undoubtedly a grain of truth in this idea of a racial memory; we probably inherit a set of mental patterns, a sort of psychological groundwork, just as we inherit certain physiological stabilities, or even peculiarities, but this in no wise serves to explain genius. Such racial memories would tend to make all men very much alike (as indeed they are) but the essence of the true genius is that he is different from other men, this constituting the basic quality of his genius. It is doubtless true that a large percentage of our conscious mentation is rooted in the subconscious mind; but not all that rises into the conscious mind is of equal value; some of it is good, while some of it is the veriest rubbish. That is a mistake which many spiritualists are inclined to make: they believe that just *because* writings or messages have been obtained, by automatic writing or otherwise, that therefore these messages must necessarily come from some higher spiritual source, and are to be believed in consequence. Precisely the reverse of this is usually the case; they emanate from a lower level of mind than the normal consciousness, in many instances, and are accepted as revelations from the beyond merely because the subjects have hypnotized themselves into the belief that they must necessarily be so! If they used ordinary common sense, in estimating the value of these revelations, they would at once see that this is a fact. It is, of course, true that many striking communications have been received in this manner, apparently beyond the power of the individual to produce normally, in which information is given unknown to the scribe, but these cases must be judged on their own merits. They represent apparently supernormal phenomena, and are not characteristic of the normal output, or manifestations of genius in the ordinary acceptation of that word. We shall have occasion to return to this aspect of the problem later on, however, when discussing the mechanism of genius and its possible causation.

### Physiology and Genius

Inasmuch as the mind is in some manner undoubtedly dependent upon the brain for its manifestations in this life, various daring and ingenious theories have been advanced, from time to time in the past, to explain genius from a semi-physiological standpoint. One of these is that advanced by Mr. Aleister Crowley, in an article entitled "Energised Enthusiasm" in Volume IX of *The Equinox*. The theory is there advanced that, in addition to the gross secretion of the sex glands, there may also be formed (provided the suitable "magnetic relations" be established) a more subtle, secondary secretion, which is poured into the blood stream, stimulating the nerve cells, and particularly the brain cells, thus constituting, as it were, *the physical basis of genius*. It is to be observed that, at the time when this article was written, next to nothing was known of the endocrine glands. Today, this secondary secretion is known to exist—though its functions have not been finally determined. There is doubtless much material of interest in this connection, which might be obtained by making a careful, systematic and comparative study of the whole subject. Inasmuch as so little is known of this aspect of the question, however, it would be useless to discuss it further. I mention it here mainly for the sake of historical completeness, and because of the ingenuity of the idea.*

## Genius and Talent

Before coming to our final discussion of the nature of genius, a few words must be said as to the essential differences between true genius and mere talent—a topic which has been touched upon before, but only in a superficial manner. Frequently they are confused, but there is a great difference between them, from our present standpoint. Many men have possessed and developed great talent; relatively few of them have been great geniuses! Thus, in those ages of the world's history when wars were of almost constant occurrence, there were many expert generals; they possessed undoubted talent, which was developed by the spirit of the age in which they lived. Cæsar, Napoleon and Alex-

---

* In his *Goetia of Solomon the King*, Crowley has pursued this line of suggestive inquiry, particularly with regard to magical ceremonies and invocations, and he there says:—

"What is the cause of my illusion of seeing a spirit in the triangle of Art? Every smatterer, every expert in psychology, will answer: 'That cause lies in your brain....' These unusual impressions, then, produce unusual brain changes; hence their summary is of unusual kind. Its projection back into the apparently phenomenal world is therefore unusual. The spirits of the *Goetia* are portions of the human brain.... Our Ceremonial Magic fines down, then, to a series of minute, though of course empirical, physiological experiments...." He elsewhere speaks of "inflaming the brain" by means of magical ceremonies, etc.

ander the Great were, however, military geniuses. Many men have written upon evolution, but there was only one Darwin. Tens of thousands of men have composed music, written poetry and painted pictures, but the great geniuses in all these fields stand out like beacon lights, and have become household words. The same is true in any department of human endeavor. The output, intellectual or artistic, of the merely talented man is easily understood by us, and requires no stretching of ordinary psychological theories in order to account for his results. The same cannot be said of the products of true genius—particularly if we take into account, as we must, the results obtained by the various musical, arithmetical and other prodigies. For, in their cases, as we have seen, no intellectual background or training has usually been present: "Blind Tom," a virtual idiot, who could nevertheless play the most difficult musical compositions divinely, when placed at the piano; children extracting cube-roots and stating the number of seconds they had lived, almost before knowing their mathematical tables; veritable infants composing great music before being taught the elements of harmony and composition. *These* are the cases which are difficult to explain by means of normal psychological principles, and these are the cases which represent, in the $n^{th}$ degree, those flashes of inspiration which constitute the essence of true genius. In practically all these cases, the conscious mind does not seem to participate in the results, the ideas being seemingly flashed into it with lightning-like celerity, from some apparently external source. What is this source, and how may we explain genius of this character?

## Myers's Theory of Genius

The credit for the original attack upon this problem must be given to Mr. F. W. H. Myers who, in July, 1892, published his article on "The Mechanism of Genius" in the *Proceedings* S.P.R. (Vol. VIII, pp. 333-61). At the time when Myers wrote, practically nothing of value had been written upon the subject, and the daring originality of his views must always be given due credit. His article constituted one of a series of nine brilliant papers on "The Subliminal Consciousness," contributed to the publications of the Society. Myers' views may be summarized, in his own words, as follows:

"I suggest that Genius ... should be regarded as a power of utilizing a wider range than other men can utilize of faculties in some degree innate in all; a power of appropriating the results of subliminal mentation to subserve the supraliminal stream of thought; so that an 'inspiration of genius' will be in truth a *subliminal uprush,* an emergence into the current of ideas which the man is consciously manipulating of other ideas which he has not consciously originated, but which have shaped themselves beyond his will, in profounder regions of his being. I shall urge that there is here no real departure from normality; no abnormality, at least in the sense of degeneration; but rather a fulfillment of the true norm of man, with suggestions, it may be, of something *supernormal;* of something which transcends existing normality as an advanced stage of evolutionary progress transcends an earlier stage. ... The differentia of genius lies in an increased control over subliminal mentation. . . . When the subliminal mentation forces itself up through the supraliminal, without amalgamation, as in crystal-vision, automatic writing, etc., we have sensory or motor automatism. . . ."

### Genius and the Supernormal

Myers's theory of genius is not only original and ingenious, not only does it enable us to understand much of the mechanism actually involved, but it also dovetails nicely into a series of supernormal facts. Assume a stream of subconscious intellection of a far-reaching character—a subliminal consciousness—rushing along and maturing ideas of its own.* Normally, this process remains unconscious; occasionally, however, the final end-products, so to say, are flashed into the conscious mind, by reason of the pressure of the psychic energy lying behind these ideas. They then emerge into consciousness, much as a bubble might burst upon the surface of water, when liberated from some reservoir in the depths beneath. The finished product is thus brought vividly into consciousness, in the form of the solution of some problem, the explanation of some puzzling question, etc., constituting an inspiration of genius, or some intuition, or hunch, and so on, as the case may be. The elaboration or working-out of the problem has been effected in the depths beneath, and the product of the subliminal mentation has emerged into consciousness in some more or less clearly defined form.

This final product may take one of various forms—visual, auditory, etc., if it emerges in the form of some

---

* It is hardly necessary, at this late date, to adduce evidence that such subconscious mentation goes on; the literature of normal and abnormal psychology is filled with such material, aside from any evidences furnished by purely psychic phenomena.

"*sensory* automatism;" automatic writing, typtology, etc., if in some *motor* form. Or it may appear as a purely mental product—as some "idea" which emerges into consciousness. In all these cases, the result is given, but not the means by which this result is obtained. The intermediate steps, the working-out of the problem, has all been purely subconscious.

It is right and normal that our subconscious functions should remain such; too easy access to these depths of our being is not usually to be desired. Just as there is a physical diaphragm across the middle of our body, separating the lungs and heart from the viscera below, so there seems to be a sort of "psychical diaphragm," if I may so express it, separating the conscious from the subconscious mind. In the majority of normal, healthy individuals, this psychic diaphragm is more or less thick or impervious, preventing a too-ready flow, back and forth, of this mental material; but, in some cases, this barrier seems to become thinned or pervious, or overly porous, allowing a relatively free flow between these two streams of mentation. When this is the case, more extensive portions of the subconscious mind are tapped, or overflow into the conscious mind. The result is an influx of new material, good or bad, as the case may be. For it must be remembered that, as Mr. Myers put it:

"Hidden in the deep of our being is a rubbish-heap as well as a treasure house; degenerations and insanities as well as beginnings of higher development; and any prospectus which insists on the amount of gold to be had for the washing should describe also the mass of detritus in which the bright grains lie concealed. . . ."

The quality of the output will therefore depend upon

the layer of subconsciousness which has been tapped, whether this be normal and healthy, or the reverse. In the one case, we get the inspirations of genius; in the other abnormalities and insanities. The close connection between the two is thus evident, and we are enabled to see *why* these connections should exist. If mere rambling thoughts emerge, semi-personalized and loosely held together, we obtain the rubbish characteristic of insanity and many of the so-called spiritualistic "messages." If, on the other hand, some portion of a well-ordered stream emerges, we obtain meaningful, clear-cut communications, flashed from the subconscious to the conscious mind, which may take one or other form, as outlined above.

It all depends upon the *stratum* of the subconscious mind from which these thoughts originate, and the character and activity of that stratum. Thus, to take a typical example: *Ulysses,* by James Joyce. Read as an ordinary book, it is a more or less meaningless jumble of erotic inanities; looked at from another point-of-view, it is a most remarkable psychological document. As I regard it, the book represents the output of a morbid subconscious mind, the author having unusual access to that mind, and viewing what is taking place within it. His "psychical diaphragm" was evidently extremely porous, allowing a relatively free flow, through it, of these subconscious thoughts and ideas. *That* is the unusual factor. We can readily assume that we should only have to descend the slope a little further in order to reach the level of sheer insanity. The revelations of Blake and many others of his type indicate the borderland realm from which their inspirations were obviously derived.

On the other hand we find, fortunately, many instances in which helpful and lofty messages have been given—the true inspirations of genius. These emerge from a wholesome, normal stratum of the mind, which is active and integrated within itself. The end-products of this subliminal mentation have been flashed into the conscious mind, either as original ideas, or as some form of automatism. The former, of course, are the more common. The latter border upon other supernormal phenomena. These messages from the subconscious mind may take one of various forms, as before stated, and Mr. Myers must again be given the credit for showing just how this may come about, and showing the relationship between all sorts of apparently unrelated phenomena. Dreams, ghosts, premonitions, clairvoyance, automatic writing, crystal-gazing, warning voices, ghostly touches, hysteria, genius, hallucinations, telepathy—what an apparent chaos from which to bring order! Yet Myers showed that all these were in some way related; that many of these curious phenomena had a common source, and he succeeded in showing what that source was.

Thus, said Myers, automatisms may be either *motor* or *sensory*. If motor, we find the subconscious expressing itself in automatic writing, or in radiating energy, as exemplified in certain cures, or in the movements of objects without contact, etc. If sensory, this may take various forms, or methods of externalization, according to the sense affected. Thus, supposing an individual be walking across a dark moor at night; suddenly an apparition rises before him, with uplifted hand, and as suddenly vanishes. Investigation proves that another step would have carried the voyager over the edge of a precipice. Need we assume that this was some guardian angel sent to warn him in time? By no means! We may assume that the subconscious mind perceived the danger, and expressed its knowledge in this dramatic and symbolical form. In this case, the impression was visual in character. But again, the subject may hear a voice, warning him not to proceed. In such case, the sense of hearing had been appealed to. Or the subject might have felt a restraining hand. Here, the sense of touch was affected. These are but the various ways in which the subconscious mind expressed or externalized its knowledge. And similarly, throughout the whole realm of these phenomena, Myers showed that the subconscious mind might be the primary factor at work, inter-connecting and blending them all into a harmonious whole. As Professor James expressed it: "Whatever the judgment of the future may be on Mr. Myers's speculations, the credit will always remain to them of being the first attempt in any language to consider the phenomena of hallucination, automatism, double personality, and mediumship as connected parts of one whole subject." (*The Will to Believe*, p. 316.) It will thus be seen that the subconscious mind and its problems form an integral part of all psychic investigation, and have thrown a flood of light upon the mechanism of many of these curious phenomena.

### Intuition and Inspiration

Intuition has been variously defined, from varying points-of-view. Perhaps one of the best definitions is that contained in Walter Newton Weston's book *Intuition*, namely, as "that sense or faculty in the human mind by which man knows (or may know) facts of which he would otherwise not be cognizant—facts which might not be apparent to him through process of reason or so-called scientific proof. This faculty is called intuition."

When we come to inquire into the *mechanism* of intuition, however, we discover that very little has been said upon the subject in the past of any real value. Nearly everything which has been written can be boiled-down into a single sentence: a prompting from the subconscious mind. But just how the subconscious mind *obtained its information* is not always clear! Sometimes, this is clearly traceable, it is true: slight incidents, unnoticed observations and comparisons, inferences, unconscious perceptions, etc., these all play a part in forming the ultimate product. However, there are many cases on record where such explanations do not explain, and in these instances we seem to have evidence of some supernormal faculty at work, acquiring the necessary information, and subsequently imparting it to the conscious mind, in some more or less vague manner. It is indeed hard to draw the line between intuition, as thus understood, and other supernormal faculties.

*Inspiration* may mean either one of two things: religious inspiration—which is the sense in which the word is generally used; or non-religious inspiration. With the former we are not concerned. The latter is more closely connected with our subject. But when we seek for a definition for this kind of inspiration, and find it expressed in such words as the following, "a belief in an inner or occult sphere of the mind which can be influenced in other ways than through the senses," * it is obvious that we are merely stating one

* *The Psychology of Inspiration,* by George L. Raymond, pp. 55-56.

of the many problems of psychical research in other words!

### The Source of the Information

Assuming, then, that the flashes or inspirations of genius represent uprushes from the subliminal consciousness, emerging into the conscious mind as finished products, the question still remains: Whence did the subliminal obtain this information, which was thus imparted? Here we come to the *crux* of the problem, and it must be admitted that any answer we may make to this question must be merely tentative and theoretical. It is possible that some of these ideas may have been telepathically acquired, from other living minds—as in those instances when two or more people have had the same idea (say for an invention) at the same time. The number of cases of this character would probably be unexpectedly large, if they could be collected; no sooner does an original idea strike one man than it strikes another also, and both begin working upon the problem at the same time. Others seem to have been acquired by some kind of clairvoyance—cryptæsthesia, in the larger sense. Others cannot be thus explained. It would seem, in many cases, as though some larger reservoir of mind were in some way tapped, and the vast storehouse of its potential knowledge drawn upon. This is doubtless what Myers meant when he spoke of the multiplication-table being, as it were, "in the air." All minds may perhaps ultimately be unified at some common source, this forming the common spiritual Soil of humanity. Thus: just as every tree of the forest is undoubtedly a separate living entity, (yet their roots are planted in a common soil, unifying them in Mother

Earth) so it is possible that humanity may be in some manner unified in some larger spiritual world, from which we draw our mental sustenance, and from which we emerge as seemingly separate beings, just as the sun's rays emanate from a central source. In this vaster Cosmic Mind, all knowledge, all wisdom, may be contained, and the individual human being has only to induce within himself, consciously or unconsciously, the proper mental attitude, in order to open the doors of his inner vision, and receive this influx of knowledge and power.

Were some process of this kind really involved (as the Yogis have long taught) it would but remain for us to discover the proper technic, in order to receive or command this Universal Knowledge at will. This is, perhaps, the state of Cosmic Consciousness, of which so many artists and poets have tried to tell us, in words which evidently fail to convey the true inner meaning and vastness of their experience.

One further theory must not be lost sight of, a theory which is indeed, to many, an obvious truth. This is the possibility that other minds, possessing superior knowledge, are indeed contacted telepathically, but minds no longer *in the flesh,* spiritual entities of a higher order, whose wisdom transcends our own, and whose knowledge is imparted to living beings, who have voluntarily or otherwise placed themselves in a suitable attitude for the reception of these truths. On this view, the flashes of inspirational genius would represent thoughts and ideas imparted from some other mind, in which they originated, the man of genius being, on this view, merely a *channel* through whom these externally initiated ideas might flow.

All is possible! We do not know the ultimate solution of the majority of problems which confront us in this complex living Universe. We must leave our minds open for the reception of all new truths. Certain it is that the central problems of genius still remain largely unsolved, and will probably only *be* solved when a clearer knowledge is obtained of the baffling problem of the connection of mind and matter. Possibly, as Myers suggested, these higher powers and faculties are not the product of terrene evolution, but are intended for use in some other sphere or world. Some day, perhaps, we shall know. Meanwhile, we can but continue our investigations, firm in our belief that the Universe must ultimately be rational, and that Truth, which is said to be mighty, shall at last prevail!

# V

# Personality and Personal Identity

IT would be impossible, within the limits of one Chapter, to summarize the various psychological and metaphysical views regarding such terms as "self," "personality," "soul," "ego," "consciousness," "personal identity," "individual," "mind," "subject," "psyche," etc., which have been advanced in the past. Some of these terms are now practically discarded by psychologists; some of them have been given specific meanings by differing schools of thought; some of them are vague and ambiguous, and are used in one sense by some men and in another sense by others. Thus, the word "soul" has been practically abandoned by psychologists (being left to the theologians) and is replaced by other terms which, it is contended, more accurately express the facts. Formerly, it was more or less synonymous with mind, and Aristotle speaks of a "vegetative soul," an "animal soul" and a "transcendental soul." * "Mind," again, was used to define "consciousness"; but it was found that mind, in its broadest sense, must mean much more than this since we have subconscious and unconscious minds, and we attribute mind to many of the lower animals, which certainly have no self-consciousness.

The word "consciousness" is itself discarded by the majority of our modern psychologists, who fiercely resent its use. The term "psyche" has been largely appropriated by the psychoanalytic school; the word "in-

* Cf. Hammond: *Aristotle's Psychology.*

dividual" is most frequently used as synonymous with "organism," while "personality," "the self," etc., either involve metaphysical discussion, or are resolved into other terms.

All in all, enormous difficulties at once present themselves the moment we begin to use any of these terms; and while the man-in-the-street may feel that he knows very well what he means when he speaks of his "personality," his "personal identity," etc., the psychologist does *not,* demanding a more accurate and up-to-date definition of his terms before discussing them.

We must first of all endeavor, therefore, to define our terms somewhat—enough for our present purposes —before proceeding to utilize them in connection with psychic phenomena; for if we speak of the survival of personality and the proof of personal identity we must know at least what we are talking about, and *what* is supposed to survive and *in what* personal identity consists. After we have come to some agreement on these points, it will be time to consider the evidence afforded by psychical research as bearing upon these problems.

In order to clear the air as rapidly and effectually as possible, I propose, first of all, to summarize very briefly what William James has to say upon these questions, in his *Psychology.* After doing so, some of the later views may be taken into account. James's masterly presentation is everywhere acknowledged to be the best up to that time, being embodied in his chapters on "The Stream of Thought," and "The Consciousness of Self." A brief epitome and a few quotations will doubtless serve to summarize his argument.

Five characteristics of thought at once present themselves, upon slight reflection. These are:

(1) Every thought tends to be part of a personal consciousness; thought tends to personal form; it is not merely *a* thought, it is *my* thought.

(2) Thought is in constant change. No mental state once gone can recur and be identical with what it was before.

(3) Within each personal consciousness, thought is sensibly continuous. Hence, we may call it a stream of thought.

(4) Human thought appears to deal with objects independent of itself; it possesses the function of knowing. Thought may, but need not, in knowing, discriminate between its object and itself. However complex the object may be, the thought of it is one undivided state of consciousness.

(5) It is always interested more in one part of its object than in another, and welcomes and rejects, or chooses, all the while it thinks.

This stream of thought, then, possessing these peculiar characteristics, constitutes the basic groundwork or substratum of consciousness and the Self—using these terms, for the present, in a purely popular sense. We must now analyze this consciousness of self in greater detail.

The *Empirical Self,* or *Me,* in its widest possible sense, "is the sum-total of all that a man can call his." This Self has certain feelings and emotions—self-feelings—and gives rise to certain actions: self-seeking and self-preservation. The Self also has certain constituents, which may be sub-divided as follows:

(a) The material self: the body, its possessions, etc.

(b) The social self: relations to other people.

(c) The Spiritual self, which may be called the "self of selves." This requires a more detailed analysis. It seems to be the *active* element of consciousness. This self is *felt*. But *what* is felt? In what does the feeling of this central, active self consist? James believes that, if introspection be carried on carefully enough, it will be found to consist in certain subtle bodily processes, mostly taking place in the head. So, concludes James, if this be true and sufficiently inclusive, "it would follow that our entire feeling of spiritual activity, or what commonly passes by that name, is merely a feeling of bodily activities whose exact nature is by most men overlooked."

However, over and above these, there is an obscurer feeling of something more. What this is may be left for the moment; nor need we stop to consider self-seeking, self-feeling or self-preservation. These all constitute part of the "Phenomenal Self." We accordingly turn to our greatest problem—that of the *Pure Ego*.

The first thing that strikes us here is the sense of *Personal Identity*—the feeling that "I am the same Self that I was yesterday." All thoughts which we have relating to this Ego have a certain warmth and intimacy which other thoughts do not. This feeling of sameness, however, is not unique; it is a frequent phenomenon. It is probable that the perception of sameness, with regard to personal identity, is like any other perception of sameness by the mind. Resemblance among the parts of a continuum of feelings . . . this constitutes the real and verifiable "Personal Identity" which we feel.

Consciousness, while fluent, nevertheless seems to

flow in a series of pulsations. Each of these pulses represents the passing thought, the thought of the moment. But each thought inherits or appropriates the previous thought, as it comes into being. "Each thought is thus born an owner, and dies owned, transmitting whatever it realized as its Self to its own later proprietor."

The passing thought then seems to be the Thinker; and, though there *may* be another non-phenomenal Thinker behind that, so far we do not seem to need him to express the facts. Consciousness, in short, is apparently made up of a series of passing thoughts, which are themselves the thinkers; and the sense of personal identity is felt because of the feelings of warmth and intimacy before mentioned, associated with these thoughts, which are connected with this Thinker. On this view, it will be seen, a transcendental Thinker is done away with; it is not needed, and we do not need any Consciousness, as such, behind and beyond these thoughts, since it is composed of them and nothing but them. (This theory has been elaborated in great detail by Dr. Henry Rutgers Marshall, in his work on *Consciousness,* and by other writers.)

Having arrived at the above conclusion, James then passes on to review the history of the theories which have been advanced as to the nature of the Pure Self, or inner principle of Personal Identity. These are three in number, viz.:

(1)  The Spiritualistic theory.
(2)  The Associationist theory.
(3)  The Transcendentalist theory.

Let us consider these in turn.

The first of these postulates a *Soul*—a non-material, thinking entity. We here encounter, of course, all the difficulties connected with the problem of the connection of mind and matter, into which it would be impossible to enter now. James concludes that "the soul is at all events needless for expressing the actual subjective phenomena of consciousness as they appear.... The soul-theory is a complete superfluity, so far as accounting for the actual verified facts of conscious experience goes.... The soul, when closely scrutinized, guarantees no immortality of a sort we care for.... My final conclusion... about the substantial Soul is that it explains nothing and guarantees nothing.... Its successive thoughts are the only intelligible and verifiable things about it...."

Coming, now, to the Associationist theory, this fares no better at his hands. James points out that consciousness cannot be a mosaic, merely stuck together, or tied together in some way, but is a unique, whole thing—explicable, he thinks, on the theory previously advanced. We need not stop to consider this highly controversial matter at length.

The Transcendentalist theory, due largely to Kant, is similarly disposed of by James—his conclusion being that it is unnecessary, in so far as it is intelligible. He concludes that, "we may sum-up by saying that personality implies the incessant presence of two elements, an objective person, known by a passing subjective thought and recognized as continuing in time.... Let us use the words ME and I for the empirical person and the judging Thought."

The ME constantly changes throughout life; there is only a relative identity maintained, while there is a slow shifting, in which some common ingredient is seemingly maintained. There are changes in the ME, recognized by the I. These changes may be slow and slight, or they may be rapid and grave. The latter may be called mutations of the self, and consist (a) of alterations of memory (lapses, diseases of memory, etc.); or (b) of actual alterations in the self. These in turn consist (i) of insanities; (ii) of alternating and multiple personalities; and (iii) of mediumships or possessions—which are thus regarded as types of alternating personalities. All these must of course be regarded as abnormal, though the last may merge into the supernormal.

This concludes James's argument and his lengthy discussion of the consciousness of self. He ends by saying, however, that the question of the "ultimate knower" remains a metaphysical question, and that "room for much future inquiry lies in this direction."

Illuminating as it is, this theory of James's has been severely criticized by several writers, e.g., Professor F. B. Jevons, in his *Personality*. I cannot do better, perhaps, than quote a few passages from his book, in which this criticism appears. He says:

"If proof be wanted to show that James does, without knowing it, postulate a subject or person, it can be found in his own words. The sense of our personal identity, he says, 'is grounded on the resemblance of the phenomena compared.' If phenomena are compared they must be compared by somebody. . . . A subject or person is simply indispensable. If nobody makes comparisons, no comparisons will be made. If nobody draws inferences, no inferences will be drawn. . . .

"It is, however, not our personality alone, but our personal identity which James seeks to explain away. He explains it first by substituting resemblance for identity; and next by seeking for it in the phenomena, and not in the mind to which the phenomena are presented and by which the phenomena are compared. But by the very meaning of the words 'resemblance' is not the same as 'identity.' Things which resemble one another are things which, though they resemble one another, are different. If they were not different, they would not resemble one another. They would be identical. What is asserted by the upholders of personal identity is not that the phenomena presented to the subject or person are identical, but that the subject or person to whom they are presented, and by whom they are compared, is identical. . . .

"It would seem to be quite plain that, if the passing thought is the thinker, then there are as many Thinkers as there are passing thoughts. . . . But if our personal consciousness is a stream of thought, a unity, and a whole, then all that psychology, or psychological analysis, can do is to attend to each of its various phases or parts separately. But though the psychologist may attend to them separately, the fact that he attends to them separately does not give them any separate existence. . . . Moments—separate moments—are pure abstractions: time is continuous and unbroken. And the momentary thinker, for that very reason, if for no other, is a pure abstraction, scientific—convenient and even necessary for scientific purposes—but to be found only in the domain of science, not in the actual world of fact" (pp. 49-77).

While all this may be true in one sense, it is certainly not true in another! If we desire to analyze *personality*, we obviously cannot take the whole life of a man into consideration, but only a very small fraction of it, and preferably the present moment. Immediately-past states, reproduced by recent memories, also constitute the subject of analysis. We are more or less limited to these, in any investigation which may be made. The object of any analysis of the Self is certainly to find out how it is composed or made-up, its essential constituents. And, just as some of our complex emotions have been shown to be compounded of simpler ones, so the more complex elements of the human mind may also be shown to be compounded, as it were, of similar mental material.

Thus, to illustrate, by way of the emotions. McDougall, in his *Social Psychology*, has shown that *Admiration* is compounded of wonder and negative self-feeling; *Awe*, of admiration and fear; *Reverence*, of awe and gratitude; *Scorn*, of disgust and anger; *Contempt*, of disgust and positive self-feeling; *Loathing*, of fear and disgust; *Hate*, of anger, fear and disgust; *Envy*, of negative self-feeling and anger; *Reproach*, of anger and tender emotion; *Anxiety*, of tender emotion, pain and anger; *Revenge*, of anger and positive self-feeling; *Sorrow*, of tender emotion and negative self-feeling; *Pity*, of tender emotion and sympathetically-induced pain; and so forth.*

Now, in the same way that our emotions can be split-up, and shown to be due to more primary and simple emotions, the complex structure of our mental life may also be similarly analyzed. Before attempting such an analysis, however, a few commonly-used words must first of all be defined, or explained, so that the

---

* This analysis has since been modified in various directions, but is left intact, inasmuch as it is only the *principle* which is involved, and not the psychological details.

reader may follow the jargon of the modern psychologist without undue difficulty. Only a few such definitions will be necessary for our present purposes.

An *affect* is a specific kind of feeling or emotion.

A *complex* is any group of factors in the mental constitution. As used especially by the psychoanalysts, a system of emotionally-toned ideas which have been "repressed"—thus frequently giving rise to morbid behavior.

A *sentiment* is an idea of an object, with which one or more emotions are organized. (Prince: *The Unconscious,* p. 449.)

*Cognition* may be defined as "any process by means of which one arrives at knowledge or awareness of an object." (English: *A Student's Dictionary of Psychological Terms.*)

*Conation.* When a present mental state tends by its intrinsic nature to develop into something else, we have conation.

*Organization.* An ensemble, formed of different parts which coöperate. This may apply to the body (as an *organism*) or to the mind.

With these preliminary definitions in mind, we may now briefly summarize Prof J. W. Bridge's article, "A Theory of Personality," published in the *Journal of Abnormal Psychology,* January, 1926. He says in part:

"Personality is a psycho-physiological concept. This is meant in the sense that consciousness and bodily response are subjective and objective aspects of the same thing, in accordance with the double-aspect theory of mind-body relation.* . . . The personality has three

* We shall come to a discussion of this point later on.

parts or divisions; cognition, affection and conation. . . . Some components of personality are original, some are acquired. The original components or elements are probably sensation and image. More complex, derived components are perception, memory, association, judgment, reasoning, etc. . . . From the standpoint of consciousness the basic element is probably *impulse* (urge or drive). . . . An important component of personality occurring in all three of its divisions is *intelligence,* or the capacity to learn, which on analysis is probably reducible to the capacity to form and to change associative bonds. . . . By *organization of personality* is meant the formation of associative bonds among the various elements and the arrangement of the various components into a hierarchy of more or less complex levels. . . .

"Cognitive organization may begin with simple sensations and images. These are organized into perceptions and ideas. These are further organized into cognitive attitudes, information, and systems of knowledge. . . . Affective organization may begin with simple feelings and emotions, which are modified, conditioned and organized into compound emotions, moods, affective attitudes, sentiments, loyalties, interests and aversions. . . . The organization of affective elements may be called the *temperament*. The temperament is thus the total affective make-up. . . . Cognitive organization may begin with simple impulses which are conditioned, modified and integrated into more and more complex impulses. . . . These are coördinated into motor attitudes and habits. . . . The organization of conative elements may be called *character*. . . .

"The personality as thus described varies greatly from individual to individual. . . . There is individual difference in the *complexity* of personality. . . . There is no doubt marked variation in the degree of *integration* of the personality. . . . Organization is a slow process, but it is a measure of the *strength* of the personality as a whole or in any of its parts. . . . Disorders of personality are merely extreme forms of variations. . . . Weakness of personality may be used to mean poor organization and development. . . . Since the development of personality depends in part upon environmental influences, it behooves education to assist in affective organization as well as in cognitive and motor. . . ." *

Dr. Harold I. Gosline, in an article on "Personality from the Introspective Viewpoint," (*Jo. Ab. Psy.*, April, 1920), asserts that: "Activities of the personality may all be grouped under the will, the attention and the thought process. The common factor in all of these is the feeling of impulse." Sidis, on the other hand, has contended † that the personality cannot be thus broken-up *ad lib.*, but that "mental life is not simply a series of mental states; it is an individuality in which the psychic series occurs." This position, it will be observed, is directly opposed to that of James, so that

---

* Cf. also Morton Prince: "The Structure and Dynamic Elements of Human Personality," *Journal of Abnormal Psychology*, Dec., 1920, wherein very similar views are expressed. Also his book *The Unconscious*. The "motor theory" of consciousness—monistic—will be found defended at length in E. B. Holt's *Concept of Consciousness;* while, as we know, the Behaviorists have tried to do away with it altogether, in a most radical form: see Watson, *Psychology from the Standpoint of a Behaviourist*, etc. Cf. also Berman: *The Glands Regulating Personality* for an exposition of the "glandular" view. It would be unprofitable to enter into a discussion of these theories now, since they would take us too far afield. Dorsey and many others express much the same views, in varying forms.

† *The Foundations of Normal and Abnormal Psychology.*

the views of these two psychologists may be set off one against the other.

Summing-up, now, these views of modern psychologists, regarding the nature of the human personality, they may I think be stated somewhat as follows: Instead of being a simple, indivisible thing (as Plato contended) it is rather a compound, a composite, an integration, something *achieved;* it represents the sum-total of our mental and bodily activities. As such, it is subject to splits, dissociations, mutations of all kinds. A good analogy would perhaps be a rope, the strands of which are normally held or bound together by attention, concentration, education—all those factors which tend to unify and integrate the self. At times, certain strands of the rope (as the result of illness, emotional shock, etc.) tend to split-off, forming independent selves, and then we have cases of alternating or multiple personality.

Consciousness represents one portion of the mind in action; in the words of Mr. Wakeman, it is a "go" and not a "thing." On this view, the older conception of consciousness is done away with. Similarly, the permanent and lasting nature of personality becomes questionable, if it is not altogether destroyed. Hence, the difficulty of the modern psychologist in accepting the hypothesis of survival! He wants to know *what* survives, and *what* can possibly survive!

Let us see what may be said in answer to these arguments.

In the first place, if consciousness is a "go" and not a "thing," as stated—that is, an action, an activity—

it must be something which acts, something which is *in activity*. One cannot have movement without something to move. A cannon-ball moves with great rapidity; but it is the ball which moves. Light travels more swiftly than anything in the Universe; but again something moves—ether waves, or corpuscles, or a combination of both! One cannot have action, in short, without postulating something *in* action; something which moves. Similarly, one cannot logically contend that the *activity* of the mind represents or explains the mind; rather, one would be forced to the conclusion that the mind in action represents, phenomenally, the activity we perceive.

Hence we seem driven to conclude that the mind is some sort of an entity, whose passing activities are noted. We may agree to discard the older conceptions of consciousness, but every one save the extreme Behaviorists would agree that *something* exists, corresponding to what used to be called consciousness. What that something *is* still has to be explained.

Our Personality, again, seems to be a composite thing. It is subject to fluctuations, mutations, changes, dissociations into various selves. There are certain types of spiritualists, it is true, who dispute this—contending that whenever such a self is noted, it is in very truth an independent spirit, seeking more or less vainly to express itself. Such a contention is of course preposterous. It is opposed to the whole massive data of modern psychopathology; and moreover many of these selves can be seen building themselves up, as it were, before our eyes.* In the majority of such cases, nothing in the

* Flournoy gives a pretty illustration of this, in his *Spiritism and Psychology*, p. 127 (note): "Here are the details of this little episode,

least suggestive of spirits is to be noted. Yet how can anything which is so apparently unstable have the quality of permanence? And how may it hope to survive the shock of death—since even minor accidents and mal-adjustments seem to upset it so completely?

Various answers have been suggested to this difficult question, by psychic students. Mr. F. W. H. Myers, for example, in his *Human Personality,* has said:

"In favor of the partisans of the unity of the Ego, the effect of the new evidence (*i.e.,* psychic phenomena) is to raise their claim to a far higher ground, and to substantiate it for the first time with the strongest presumptive proof which can be imagined for it:—a proof, namely, that the Ego can and does survive not only the minor disintegrations which affect it during earth-life but the crowning disintegration of bodily death.... For the conscious Self of each one of us, as we call it, does not comprise the whole of the consciousness or of the faculty within us. There exists a more comprehensive consciousness, a profounder faculty, which for the most part remains potential only so far as regards the life of earth, but from which the consciousness and the faculty of earth-life are mere selections, and which reasserts itself in its plenitude after the liberating

where we see, as often, the naïve subconsciousness, not at first giving itself to be a separate spirit, hastening, nevertheless, to accept the suggestion which was made to it by one of the company. M. Leduc says, 'Who is there?' (No reply.) 'Is it a spirit?' 'No.' M. Leduc keeps silent a moment, then asks, 'Are you always there?' 'Yes.' New silence. I request M. Leduc to ask if it is a part of himself, or an independent spirit. He appears a little astonished, and asks only the second part of the question, 'Are you an independent spirit?' 'Yes!' An amusing effect of this episode was the change of tone in the table toward M. Leduc. Before it had called him *thou,* but after it accepted the suggestion that it was an independent spirit it called him *you*—as if it were speaking to a strange person!"

change of death.... I conceive that no Self of which we can here have cognizance is in reality more than a fragment of a larger Self, revealed in a fashion at once shifting and limited through an organism not so framed as to afford it full manifestation."

Mr. Myers, it will be observed, here depends in the first place upon *facts* (psychic phenomena) tending to prove survival—contending, very rightly, that if these actually prove the continuity of personality, then the personality must be more stable than commonly supposed—even permitting it to withstand the shock of death. This is an appeal to actual fact, and cannot be gainsaid, or disposed of by any *a priori* argument. And, in the second place, Myers contends that our empirical self is somehow rooted in a deeper Self, of which it is a mere temporary expression; and, though mutations and dissociations may affect this empirical self, the larger Self is left relatively unaffected thereby—ultimately rectifying, synthesizing and unifying these disordered portions when the opportunity to do so presents itself, in some spiritual world. Naturally, the validity of his views would depend primarily upon the proof of survival.

Dr. William McDougall has, again, and from a different standpoint, met the various objections which have been raised to the unity of personality—based upon the observed cases of mutations, multiple personality, etc., in his book, *Body and Mind,* as follows:

"We must maintain that the soul is in some sense a unitary being or entity distinct from all others; for we found that prominent among the facts which compel us to accept the animistic hypothesis are the facts of psychical individuality—the fact that consciousness, as known to us, occurs only as individual coherent streams of personal consciousness, and all the facts summed-up in the phrase 'the unity of consciousness.' We found that these facts remain absolutely unintelligible, unless we postulate some ground of this unity and coherence and separateness of individual streams of consciousness, some ground other than the bodily organization. . . .

"It may be that the soul that thinks in each of us is but the chief of a hierarchy of similar beings, and that this one alone, owing to the favorable position it occupies, is able to actualize in any full measure its capacities for conscious activities; and it may be that, if the subordinated beings exercise in any degree their psychic capacities, the chief soul is able, by a direct or telepathic action, to utilize and in some measure control their activities. . . . These alternating personalities may, therefore, properly be regarded as formed, *not* by the splitting of the normal stream of consciousness, but by the alternation of two phases of the empirical self, or of the organic basis of personal consciousness, each of which brings back to consciousness only memories of experiences enjoyed during former periods of its dominance. . . . I submit that we have no sufficient ground for the assumption that the co-conscious personality is formed by splitting-off from the normal personality; that rather the facts justify the view that they are radically distinct. The facts may therefore be reconciled with the animistic hypothesis by assuming that a normally subordinate being obtains, through the weakening of the control of the normally dominant soul, an opportunity for exercising and developing its potentialities in an unusual degree...."

It will be seen, therefore, that we have, in these alternate possibilities, means of escape from the prevalent notion that such mutations of the self prove (1) its complete disintegration, and (2) its total dependence upon the brain. For, if the empirical self be regarded as but a fragmentary portion of the total Self, and it is this empirical self which suffers mutations, we obviously have no right to assert that the total self is thus affected; indeed, many facts might be cited to the contrary.

Again, as to the dependence of the mind upon the brain: The chief and most important part of the personality, let us say, consists in the feeling of personal identity; and James and others have attempted to show, as we have seen, that this feeling consists largely of subtle changes taking place within the head.

But *what* is felt at such times? Changes, it is true, but how caused? If mind were somehow *manipulating* the brain, and expressing itself *through* it, as an instrument, would not these changes be perceived also? As Prof. F. C. S. Schiller has expressed it: "If the material encasement be coarse and simple, as in the lower organisms, it permits only a little intelligence to permeate through it; if it is delicate and complex, it leaves more pores and exits, as it were, for the manifestations of consciousness." (*Riddles of the Sphinx,* p. 294.)

If something of this sort were going on, within the brain, surely changes would result, and these changes might be felt, upon attentive introspection; the sluice-gates would be felt on being opened. But these inner feelings would not by any means prove that consciousness, or the sense of personal identity, was actually being *produced* by these changes; that would be merely assuming the creation theory of consciousness, and thus begging the question! The process of the transmission or the manifestation of consciousness might indeed be felt, upon close introspection; but this would involve (a) an observer, and (b) the psycho-physiological facts, as such, without any particular theory as to the explanation of those facts.*

It will be seen, therefore, that the arguments which have been brought to bear upon survival, based upon the complex nature of human personality, while weighty within their own sphere, do not, nevertheless, prove by any means conclusive; for these arguments can be met by others—offering us alternative explanations of the observed facts. The feeling of the unity of self, and the feeling of personal identity, may not, then, be illusory; they may be based upon actual fact—and may be subject to scientific demonstration! The central core of our psychic being may thus be a permanent and abiding entity—possessing the consciousness of self, and knit together by a chain of memory which (innumerable observations seem to prove) is far more inclusive than any conscious self could possibly embrace. Indeed, the very essence of memory seems to be that it remains *un*conscious; we are never aware of more than an infinitesimal fraction of our memory-self. Yet somehow, somewhere, these memories are conserved!

* Compare Bergson, *Creative Evolution*, p. 270: "Consciousness is distinct from the organism it animates, though it must undergo its vicissitudes. As the possible actions which a state of consciousness indicates are at every instant beginning to be carried out in the nervous centers, *the brain undergoes at every instant the motor indications of the state of consciousness....*"

Mechanistic physiology contends that they are recorded in the brain. Against his view Bergson has vigorously protested (Cf. his *Matter and Memory*); and if conscious survival of any sort be proved, it is of course refuted by the actual facts. Memory would then be shown to reside in some mental reservoir (individual, not necessarily Cosmic), from which they could be drawn by the self-activity of the reflecting mind.

Psychic facts, then, once established, must settle and determine this question, as they would determine many another philosophical problem. For, if it be proved that the mind of man—his personality—actually survives bodily death, and continues its functions and activities in some spiritual world, then all theories as to the relation of brain and mind which have been advanced in the past, based upon this assumed and inevitable relationship, would have to be abandoned, and be replaced by some form of animism, or interactionism —as Dr. McDougall has so forcibly contended.

The monistic mind-body relationship (mentioned earlier in this Chapter) would thus be shown to be untrue.

As for *Parallelism,* which contends that mental and bodily activities are equally real, but run along without (as it were) ever touching one another, Hyslop has shown that this virtually admits the activity of the mind, in its own sphere, independent of the physical organism. (See his paper "Parallelism and Materialism," in *Proceedings* A.S.P.R., Vol. I, No. 1; and his *Problems of Philosophy*. See also, in this connection, Hans Driesch, *Mind and Body*.)

Mechanism, however—the materialistic conception that "thought is a function of the brain"—is, in the opinion of the majority, still the great stumbling-block to the acceptance of psychic phenomena: and it is interesting to note that Dr. McDougall admits that "psychical research has, in my judgment . . . established the occurrence of phenomena that are incompatible with the mechanistic assumption."

Let survival once be proved, then, and a world-view of an entirely different order will be possible. Human Personality will once again be raised to its position of dignity and value, and the Soul of man will once more be enthroned on its former seat of glory.

# VI

# Déjà Vu

*The Sense of the Already Seen.*

ALMOST every one, at some time or another in his life, has had the experience of suddenly feeling that he has lived through the present moment before—that he has seen the same sights, heard the same words, performed the same actions, etc.; that everything is somehow familiar to him, and that he can almost tell just what is about to happen next. Among psychologists, it is invariably assumed that this sense of familiarity is an *illusion;* they speak of "false recognition," and classify this feeling under the general heading of "paramnesia" (false memory), in opposition to "agnosia," which is a sense of the "never known."

There can be no doubt that, in the vast majority of cases, this explanation is the correct one; the apparent sense of familiarity is illusory, and can be very largely explained by known psychological principles. Here and there one encounters cases, however, which are not so readily interpreted, and these give us food for thought. They seem to embody supernormal information—facts which the subject could not possibly have known. These cases require some other explanation. However, the whole problem is a most interesting one, and it will be worth our while to review, very briefly, the various theories which have been advanced by way of explaining this odd phenomenon.

Dr. Alfred Gordon, in an article upon this subject in the *Journal of Abnormal Psychology,* (Vol. XV, Nos.

2-3), gives seven curious cases of this type which came under his own observation. In some of these, the illusion of the "already seen" and of the "never seen" were found in combination in the same individual. He also refers to cases observed by Hughlings-Jackson (*Brain*, XI, 1889), in which this illusion was associated with attacks of epilepsy; to an instructive case of "Petit Mal," with a paramnesic aura and illusion of false recognition cited by J. Seglas, (*Revue Neurol.*, 1909, No. I, p. 1); to a somewhat similar case reported by Collin (*ib.*, 1913, p. 147) and to observations by Ribot (*Diseases of Memory*) and Pierre Janet (*Les Obsessions et la Psychasthenie*). He concludes that:

"Irrespective of which of the two phenomena is present, there is a common characteristic in all the cases of this category, namely, an inability for the time being to distinguish reality from unreality, the objective from the subjective. On the other hand, a fundamental distinction is evident in both sets of phenomena. In the illusion of the "already seen," there is a transient and a very brief sensation of going over again a part of one's own life; the individual merely finds in the present his own personality of the past. There is consequently no fundamental alteration of judgment. In the illusion of false recognition, on the contrary, we are dealing with an erroneous belief of a continuous character, not with a vague impression. The perception is definite and determined, it concerns a person or group of persons, an object or group of objects, which of course implies a radical alteration of judgment.... The disturbance of the sense of 'recognition' in psychoses is a common phenomenon, and finds its *raison d'être* in a fundamental change of the personality...."

A frequently noted concomitant of illusions of this character is the sense of unreality, of dreaminess, in which the clear sense of personality is temporarily lost. Dr. Frederic H. Packard has an interesting paper on this subject, "The Feeling of Unreality," in the *Journal of Abnormal Psychology,* June, 1906. It is, of course, also characteristic of post-hypnotic states (Bramwell, *Hypnotism,* p. 111, etc.). It is also characteristic of many psychic experiences.*

The illusion of the "already seen" has been discussed at great length by psychologists and psychiatrists; an enormous number of articles having appeared in technical journals, etc., which it would be impossible even to enumerate. In addition to these Ribot, William James, Bergson, Bernard-Leroy, Sully, Janet, Kræpelin, Grasset, Wigan, Proctor, F. Myers, and others have discussed this question in books and monographs, and a few quotations from the more important of these will serve to show the various theories which have been advanced in the past in order to explain this curious phenomenon.

Dr. Wigan, in his famous work on *The Duality of the Mind,* was among the first to study this illusion. His explanation was purely physiological. He believed that there was some temporary dissociation of the action of the two hemispheres of the brain, and that one of them

* See in this connection the curious article by Dr. Hendrick Hensoldt, in the *Occult Review,* December, 1905, "Among the Adepts and Mystics of Hindustan," in which he tells of these strange alterations going on within himself, during the production of seemingly illusory phenomena.

became conscious of some fact a fraction of a second before the other. A somewhat similar view was also defended by R. H. Proctor. These theories are now, however, given up.

G. H. Lewes * suggested that the result noted might be produced by "the recurrent effect of a shock, the echo of a passing sensation," or else an actual experience, previously undergone and forgotten. It is obvious that these theories can explain only a very small percentage of the recorded cases. Ribot, in his *Diseases of Memory* (pp. 186-91), puts forward the theory that the sudden hallucinatory state is accepted as the real one, and the real impression is relegated into the past, as a recollection. Why this should be so is not at all clear, nor does Ribot make it so! James † says, "I have over and over again in my own case succeeded in resolving the phenomenon into a case of memory, so indistinct that, whilst some past circumstances are presented again, others are not. The dissimilar portions of the past do not rise completely enough at first for the date to be identified. All we get is the present scene with a general suggestion of pastness about it...." While it is true that the precise time of the supposed past experience is nearly always indefinite and impossible to locate, James's theory also certainly fails to account for a large number of recorded instances, in which the experience is far more vivid and striking than in the cases recorded in his own experience.

Kræpelin, Pick, Forel, Arnauld and others regard the phenomenon as purely pathological; but the cases quoted by them were all insane people, suffering from

* *Problems of Life and Mind,* Vol. V, pp. 129-31.
† *Psychology,* I, p. 676.

hallucinations and systematized delusions, and entirely different from ordinary cases of so-called paramnesia. Pierre Janet * contended that this illusion of memory was merely a symptom of more serious mental trouble —a view which certainly cannot be sustained. James Sully † attempted to prove that dream experiences might explain the facts—as indeed they might, a certain number of them. Hoffding, ‡ on the contrary, holds that past waking experiences serve to explain many such cases. Grasset rather vaguely places the past memory in "the unconscious mind"; while Myers § put forward the theory that this phenomenon might be accounted for by supposing that the subliminal consciousness noted a certain scene or event a fraction of a second before the conscious mind; so that, when the latter caught-up with it, as it were, the sense of having already having experienced the event would naturally result, since it had actually been already experienced only a fraction of a second before. This explanation of Myers doubtless serves to cover many cases of this type; but again, there are certainly others which cannot be thus accounted for.

The great difficulty we encounter, in all these theories, is why one impression should thus be thrown back into the past, constituting a pseudo-memory, and why the illusion should be continuous. Bernard-Leroy clearly pointed out these difficulties, and attempted to overcome them by supposing that, instead of a duality of images, we have merely an "intellectual feeling" of the "already seen," which is sometimes superadded to

* *Les Obsessions et la psychasthenie,* Vol. I, p. 287 ff.
† *Illusions,* p. 198.
‡ *Psychologie,* pp. 166-67.
§ *Proceedings* S.P.R., 1895, 343.

our perception of the present, making us think that it belongs to the past.* This feeling of vague familiarity is, however, quite different from those cases in which the subject feels that he has definitely lived through a certain experience before, and can almost predict what is about to happen, in view of the past events. These are the cases which are difficult to account for, on theories such as those outlined above.

Bergson in his *Mind Energy,* has attempted to account for this illusion of the "already seen" by means of his theory of memory, and a lowering of the psychical tone, accompanied by general inattention to life. He says, in part:

"I hold that memory is never posterior to the formation of perception; it is contemporaneous with it. Step by step, as perception is created, the memory of it is projected beside it, as the shadow falls behind the body. But, in the normal condition, there is no consciousness of it—just as we should be unconscious of our shadow, were our eyes to throw light on it each time they turn in that direction. . . . The memory will be seen to duplicate the perception at every moment, to arise with it, to be developed at the same time, and to survive it precisely because it is of a quite different nature. . . . The memory seems to be to the perception what the image reflected in the mirror is to the object in front of it. . . . It is of the past in its form and of the present in its matter. . . .

"I turn now to the problem why this memory is ordinarily concealed, and why it is revealed in extraordinary cases. In a general way, or by right, the past only

* *L'illusion de Fausse Reconnaissance,* 1898.

reappears to consciousness in the measure in which it can aid us to understand the present and to foresee the future. It is the forerunner of action.... We hardly notice the extent to which our present consists in an anticipation of our future. In these conditions, ought we not to look for the initial cause of false recognition in a momentary stop of the impulse of our consciousness?... Perception is less in the present than in the future. Suppose now the impulse suddenly to stop; memory rejoins perception, the present is cognized and recognized at the same time.... False recognition seems then to be, upon the whole, the most harmless form of inattention to life. A constant lowering of tone of the fundamental attention is expressed outwardly by actual disorder or disease.... As soon as the arrest occurs, false recognition results from the natural functioning of these two faculties, each allowed its own way. It would take place every moment if the will, unceasingly striving towards action, did not prevent the present falling back on itself by continually pressing it forward into the future. The darting forward of consciousness, which reveals the life-impetus, escapes analysis by its simplicity...."

It is probable that this theory of M. Bergson's will explain a large number of cases of déjà vu—probably the majority of which relate to incidents occurring in ordinary daily life. In all these cases, however, it is obvious that the explanation depends upon one primary fact: that the remembered experience has just been lived through actually, but a moment before. It does not at all serve to explain those cases in which descriptions are given, e.g., of places, scenes, etc., which are only verified subsequently. Here we verge into the supernormal; for such cases Myers proposed the term "promnesia"—"memory beforehand"—to express this paradox. M. Lalande (*Revue Philosophique,* Nov., 1893) quotes some striking cases of this character, suggesting that telepathy from other living minds might account for some of these incidents. As Myers pointed out at the time, however, there are not many of the more advanced promnesic cases which telepathy would explain. Generally there is no other mind apparently involved, and it simply seems as though the promnesic either enjoyed at the moment a wider than ordinary percipience, or had already visited in some supernormal way the scene which he feels that he remembers. These are actually two possibilities of which we have well-attested examples.

I have elsewhere * suggested that, in certain rare cases, the subject may perhaps have actually visited the locality in question in his "astral" body, while partially conscious. Some instances seem difficult to account for on any other theory. Thus, in one case known to me, the subject in question walked through a certain castle, and, while doing so, stated that a certain door had formerly been situated where there was now only a brick wall. Investigation proved that a door had been there, at one time, but had been built-up, years before. Cases such as these give us pause, since they are certainly not to be accounted for on the ordinary theories. If one might assume some supernormal mode of perception, however, a case such as this might be understood. A clairvoyant vision would hardly explain the facts. Retrocognition—supernormal knowledge of the past—seems

* *The Story of Psychic Science,* p. 100.

largely inter-blended with many of these cases of pre-cognition, and, while they usually apply to individual lives, they do not invariably do so.

Of this impersonal type of experience, one of the most striking cases on record is that contained in the book *An Adventure*. It was issued under the names of Elizabeth Morison and Frances Lamont, but the real names of the authors are well known to psychic students, and the accuracy and genuineness of the record was vouched for by the publishers (Macmillan & Co.).

Briefly, their experience was this: While visiting Versailles, in August, 1901, these ladies walked through the grounds, visiting especially the *Petit Trianon*. Everything seemed quiet and deserted to them; the trees and general landscape appeared flat, as though cut out of cardboard; they both felt dreamy and curious, though neither of them mentioned this to the other at the time. They saw people wearing old-fashioned clothing; ancient gardening tools lying about: an old wheel-barrow, a broken plow, guards in costume, a kiosk, a bridge, a water-fall, a cottage, a cascade, a small wood, etc. Now, subsequent investigation showed that none of these things were in existence at the time of their visit! When next they examined the grounds, everything was different; visitors and tourists were everywhere about; there was no kiosk, no cottage, no bridge, no guards, no cascade, etc. Exploration and inquiry revealed no such places. Initiating a thorough historical research, they then discovered that they had seen the *Petit Trianon* and the grounds not as they are today, but exactly as they had been in the time of Marie Antoinette! The account should be read in full to be appreciated.

Here, then, we seem to have an extraordinary case of knowledge of the past, supernormally acquired— just as, in cases of precognitions, we have instances of supernormal knowledge of the future. This is not the place in which to summarize any of the material which has been collected with regard to premonitions in general. I am merely referring to certain incidents which seem to indicate supernormal knowledge both of the past and of the future; and drawing attention to the fact that, if this wider and more extensive fore-knowledge be evidenced in such cases, it might certainly be employed as an explanatory hypothesis in those simpler cases in which some knowledge of the future seems to be evidenced. Flashes of genuine premonition may in fact be operative in such cases—just as Mr. J. W. Dunne may have induced supernormal knowledge of both past and future by experimental means.

My suggestion is, then, that while many of these reported cases of the "already seen" may be accounted for along purely psychological lines, and by known principles, some of them suggest genuinely premonitory flashes, in which knowledge of the future is supernormally acquired, being then vaguely perceived by the conscious mind as a sort of hazy memory, which event is actually lived-through subsequently. This fore-knowledge might be of some scene or event but a few moments in the future, or of some event which is only realized hours, days or weeks after the premonitory warning. It is merely a question of degree, not of kind. Granted the reality and genuineness of premonitory experiences it is, after all, less strain upon our credulity to believe that the immediate future can thus at times be perceived rather than the distant future—since these cases are far more difficult to understand! There are, however, as we know, a number of well-attested cases of this character on record; and, this being so, we may well invoke the same supernormal premonitory faculty to explain the simpler cases also. We should then no longer deal with an illusion, but with reality.

# VII

## The Psychology of "Spirit Communication"

*(Some suggestive facts, drawn from the field of Psychopathology, which may serve to throw light upon this alleged process, and upon the mental state of the "Communicator," while communicating.)*

BOTH Dr. Hodgson and Dr. Hyslop were, as we know, firm believers in the idea that a spirit entity, during the actual process of communication, was in a more or less abnormal mental condition—this fact accounting for much of the error and confusion noted during the sittings. Both men were quite convinced of the persistence of human personality, and of the actual *fact* of spirit-communication. To them, there was no longer the slightest doubt upon *that* point. Dr. Hyslop, particularly, had declared, some years before his death, that he regarded the matter as settled, and that he intended devoting the remaining years of his life, so far as possible, to the study of the problems and difficulties involved in the process. He had, as we know, already written quite extensively upon this topic; but he was doubtless prevented, by the pressure of work and by his lingering illness, from devoting the time he would have liked to this particular question, which was so near his heart. The object of the present chapter is to continue this line of investigation—so far as I am enabled to do so—in the spirit and from the point-of-view from which he would probably have carried it on. I shall not, therefore, stop to question the validity of the spiritistic hypothesis, but shall assume that this has been taken for granted; that the accumulated evidence is now sufficiently strong to force adhesion to this belief, and that actual communication has been established between the two worlds. With this as a starting-point, innumerable fascinating problems at once present themselves for solution; and of these the most interesting are probably those connected with the actual process involved—the mechanism employed—and the probable difficulties which would be encountered, and would have to be overcome, by any spirit attempting to send or communicate messages to those still living. It is this series of problems with which the present chapter deals.

In order to obtain a suitable perspective, however, it will be necessary for us, first of all, to go back to certain fundamentals. There are, normally, three ways only in which living, human minds communicate with one another. These are (1) Air vibrations—sound, speech; (2) Marks made upon paper—writing, printing; and (3) Sign language—gestures, etc. It is to be noted that these are all roundabout, indirect and symbolic. We never come into contact with another mind *directly,* so to say. If the man to whom we are speaking reacts in a certain manner to our words, we merely *infer* that he has a mind, that we have somehow reached and influenced it, and that the meaning of our thought has been conveyed to his mind, by reason of his reaction to our remarks. He may show some visible emotion (a subtle sign language), or he may respond by a series of sentences, which in some manner reach and influence *our* mind, in the same way that ours reached his. It will be seen at once that, even in the normal interchange of thought between living human beings, the process is by no means so simple and obvious as had been supposed; but that a number of assumptions must be made, and a certain amount of metaphysical speculation indulged in, before we can begin to grasp what is apparently actually taking place before our very eyes. Consider, with Professor Bowne, what happens when two people converse together and know each other's mind.*

"No thoughts leave the mind of one and cross into the mind of the other. When we speak of an exchange of thought, even the crudest mind knows that this is a mere figure of speech.... To perceive another's thought, we must construct his thought within ourselves; this thought is our own and is strictly original with us. At the same time we owe it to the other; and if it had not originated with him, it would probably not have originated with us. But what has the other done? This: by an entirely mysterious world-order, the speaker is enabled to produce a series of signs which are totally unlike (the) thought, but which, by virtue of the same mysterious order, act as a series of incitements upon the hearer, so that he constructs within himself the corresponding mental state. The act of the speaker consists in availing himself of the proper incitements. The act of the hearer is immediately only the reaction of the soul against the incitement.... All communion between finite minds is of this sort.... Probably no reflecting person would deny this conclusion, but when we say that what is thus true of per-

* B. P. Bowne: *Metaphysics*, pp. 407-10; Cf. also Lotze: *Logik*, pp. 308, 326-27, etc.

ception of another's thought is equally true of the perception of the outer world in general, many minds will be disposed to question, and not a few will deny it outright. Yet there is no alternative but to affirm that to perceive the universe we must construct it in thought, and that our knowledge of the universe is but the unfolding of the mind's inner nature. . . . By describing the mind as a waxen tablet, and things as impressing themselves upon it, we seem to get some insight until we think to ask ourselves where this extended tablet is, and *how* things stamp themselves on it, and how the perceptive act would be explained even if they did. . . ."

The immediate antecedents of sensation and perception are a series of nervous changes in the brain. Whatever we know of the outer world is revealed only in and through these nervous changes. But these are totally unlike the objects assumed to exist as their causes. If we might conceive the mind as in the light, and in direct contact with its objects, the imagination at least would be comforted; but when we conceive the mind as coming in contact with the outer world only in the dark chamber of the skull, and then not in contact with the objects perceived, but only with a series of nerve-changes of which, moreover, it knows nothing, it is plain that the object is a long way off. All talk of pictures, impressions, etc., ceases because of the lack of all the conditions necessary to give such figures any meaning. It is not even clear that we shall ever find our way out of the darkness into the world of light and reality again. We began with complete trust in physics and the senses, and are forthwith led away from the object into a nervous labyrinth, where the object is entirely displaced by a set of nervous changes which are totally unlike anything but themselves. Finally, we land in the dark chamber of the skull. The object has gone completely, and knowledge has not yet appeared. Nervous signs are the raw material of all knowledge of the outer world, according to the most decided realism. But in order to pass beyond these signs into a knowledge of the outer world, we must posit an Interpreter who shall read back these signs into their objective meanings. But that Interpreter, again, must implicitly contain the meaning of the Universe within itself, and these signs are really but excitations which cause the soul to unfold what is within itself. Inasmuch as by common consent the soul communicates with the outer world only through these signs, and never comes nearer to the object than such signs can bring it, it follows that the principles of interpretation must be in the mind itself, and that the resulting construction is primarily only an expression of the mind's own nature. All reaction is of this sort; it expresses the nature of the reacting agent, and knowledge comes under the same head. This fact makes it necessary for us either to admit a preëstablished harmony between the laws of nature and the laws of thought, or else to allow that the objects of perception, the universe as it appears, are purely phenomenal—being but the way in which the mind reacts against the ground of sensations.

A certain *working* dualism must, therefore, be granted—no matter what view of the universe one may ultimately hold. This, it would seem, cannot be escaped.

It is to be understood, of course, that the above refers only to *normal* methods of perception, and *normal* methods of communication between living minds and takes no cognizance of *supernormal* methods, such as telepathy, on the one hand, and clairvoyance, on the other. In the former, we seem to have direct communication of thought, independent of the recognized channels of sense; and in the latter, direct perception of the outer world, likewise independent of the senses. Whether or no the material brain coöperates in these processes we do not know; they may be functions of the astral senses—that is, the sense-organs of the astral body—or they may be purely mental or psychic, as Myers believed. These are problems which remain as yet absolutely unsolved.

It will not be necessary, for our present purposes, to deal with general biological or psychological problems, or of the evolution of mind, self-consciousness, speech, etc.—though much of considerable interest could be said in this connection, bearing upon the matters in hand. Here, it need only be pointed out that the general physiological objection to mind existing as "an independent variable in the world," apart from brain activity, has been met, theoretically, by William James's "transmissive theory" of consciousness (advanced in his *Human Immortality*), in which he showed that the alternate possibility is always open to us—the brain being, on this view, an organ for the *transmission* rather than the *creation* of thought; and by Dr. William McDougall's contention that the *meaning* of thought probably has no physiological correlate (*Body and Mind*). These alternatives leave the field open, so to say, permitting the question to be settled by *fact*. If facts can be produced, showing that consciousness does indeed exist apart from brain-activity, then all physiological and metaphysical theories will have to be adjusted to them in consequence. It is merely a question of evidence, of fact, as to whether or not the spirit of man continues to live after the destruction of the physical brain. For our present purposes, as we have said, we shall assume that this is a fact; also that communication with it has been established. The actual problems and difficulties involved in the process must now be considered. We have already seen the roundabout and symbolic method by which communication between minds is carried on, and we know that this normal process is frequently subjected to difficulties and impediments, even in this life. We may now turn our attention, with these facts in mind, to the possible difficulties which may exist during the process of spirit communication.

I began this chapter by stating that, in the opinion of both Dr. Hodgson and Dr. Hyslop, the communicator, during the actual process of communicating, was in a more or less dreamy, hazy or abnormal mental state. This would not, of course, imply that these individuals were necessarily in this condition all the time—during their normal lives, so to say. They might be perfectly clear and rational at all times, save during the actual process of communication. Only on such occasions would they tend to lapse into this peculiar mental condition; and there are, certainly, many analogies which might be drawn in this connection.

To take one, of a simple and obvious character. A man is being swept along the middle of a river, and in imminent danger of drowning. He spies a floating log, and clings to it for dear life. As he is thus being carried down-stream, his whole mental energy would be concentrated upon the simple process of hanging on to that log. Certainly his mind would be in no condition to evolve some new scientific truth or indulge in metaphysical theories. However fine a mind he might have, at other times, he would be in no fit state to display it now. He would be intent, merely, upon clinging to that life-saving log.

Similarly, if the mere process of governing and controlling the medium's organism be exhausting and confusing (as we have been told *is* the case), there is every reason to believe that this would more or less absorb the mental energies of the communicator, and render his mind incapable, for the time being, of remembering past details, responding to rapid-fire questions, or bringing into evidence the whole force of his personality. He would tend to become hazy and confused, to drift away from the organism, lose control of it, and finally, perhaps to leave it altogether for the time being, in order to collect his thoughts and gather his mental energies together, for a further attempt at communicating.

Let us recall Dr. Hodgson's description of what actually happens (or is alleged to happen) during the production of automatic writing through Mrs. Piper's hand. He says:

"The consciousness controlling the hand holds a conversation with the sitter by writing, but, so far as I have been able to ascertain, it is *not directly conscious of the act of writing*. The writing seems to be an automatic registering which is produced by the nervous mechanism of Mrs. Piper's organism, and of which the consciousness communicating is as little aware as the ordinary person talking into a phonographic mouthpiece is aware of the registration on the revolving cylinder.... The statements of the communicators as to what occurs on the physical side may be put in brief general terms as follows. We all have bodies composed of 'luminiferous ether' enclosed in our flesh and blood bodies. The relation of Mrs. Piper's ethereal body to the ethereal world, in which the communicators claim to dwell, is such that a special store of peculiar energy is accumulated in connection with her organism, and this appears to them as a 'light.' Mrs. Piper's ethereal body is removed by them, and her ordinary body appears as a shell filled with this 'light.' Several 'communicators' may in turn be in contact with this 'light' at the same time.... If the communicator gets into contact with the 'light' and thinks his thoughts, they tend to be reproduced by movements in Mrs. Piper's organism. Upon the amount and brightness of this 'light,' *caeteris paribus,* the communications depend. When Mrs. Piper is in ill health, the 'light' is feebler, and the communications tend to be less coherent. It also gets used-up during a sitting, and when it gets dim there is a tendency to incoherence even in otherwise clear communicators. In all cases, coming into contact with the 'light' tends to produce bewilderment, and if the contact is continued too long, or the 'light' becomes very dim, the consciousness of the communicator tends to lapse completely." *

The communicator would tend, in other words, to lose his grasp on the 'light,' and drift away—only regaining his normal faculties after a period of partial or complete rest; he would then be enabled to return, communicate clearly again for a certain time, and then

* *Proceedings* S.P.R., Vol. XIII, pp. 398, 400.

undergo the same process of gradual confusion, until he once more lost contact with the organism and drifted away, as before. This might be repeated several times during a single sitting.

Were some such process as this actually undergone, during trance communications, (and it is stated that such is the case), it would enable us to understand, very largely, the confusion and haziness so often noted during these communications. It must always be remembered that, on any theory, the shock of death must be the greatest shock which the living consciousness can ever undergo. It is suddenly wrenched from its physical moorings, and plunged into a new environment, a new world—which, on any theory, must be a *mental* world, as opposed to the physical world, in which we now live.

A simple analogy will help make this clear. Suppose you are traveling in a railway train. The train is wrecked, and you are *almost* killed—being knocked unconscious in the collision. As you gradually recovered consciousness, your vision would at first be blurred and uncertain; you would "see men as trees walking." These dim figures would gradually resolve themselves into recognized entities. Similarly, you would hear vague and meaningless sounds; these would, in turn, ultimately become intelligible words and sentences, finally reaching your consciousness as meaningful expressions. As you slowly regained possession of your faculties, the outer world would once more take-on its normal aspect, and you would become oriented to your surroundings; your memory of past events would gradually return. A few moments and (provided you had not been seriously injured in the mishap) you would be yourself once again.

At death, very much the same experience must be undergone. But, on recovering, you would find yourself in a *new world,* instead of the one familiar to you. Everything would at first appear strange and somehow different to you. If the death had been sudden, this initial shock would certainly be all the greater—and it has frequently been stated that *suicides* suffer from a prolonged period of mental confusion before becoming adjusted to their new environment. Further, the mind would doubtless tend to suffer from delusions and hallucinations—owing to the greater creative power of thought—until these were realized and overcome. All this was fully perceived by the Tibetans hundreds of years ago, and was dealt with very fully in their *Book of the Dead.* Unlike the Egyptian work (of the same title) it is a most suggestive psychological treatise. For in it we read that the dying man is constantly warned that he will be liable to illusions of all kinds, and that he must rid his mind of these, so that he may pass through the Vale of Illusion, and emerge into the Clear Light of the Void. Once there, he will realize that what he has seen were merely thought-forms, having no substantial reality—being but the creations of his own mind. The analogy of *dreams* must strike every one reading these accounts; in fact the next sphere has been described by one eminent authority as a "rationalized dream world."

Dr. Hodgson, in his Second Report on Mrs. Piper (1898) said:

"That persons just deceased should be extremely confused and unable to communicate directly, or even at all, seems perfectly natural after the shock and wrench of death. Thus, in the case of Hart, he was unable to write the second day after his death. In another case, a friend of mine, whom I will call D., wrote, with what appeared to be much difficulty, his name and the words, 'I am all right now, Adieu,' within two or three days after his death. In another case, F., a near relative of Madame Elisa, was unable to write on the morning after his death. On the second day after, when a stranger was present with me for a sitting, he wrote two or three sentences, saying, 'I am too weak to articulate clearly,' and not many days later he wrote fairly well and clearly, and dictated also to Madame Elisa, as amanuensis, an account of his feelings at finding himself in his new surroundings. Both D. and F. became very clear in a short time. D. communicated later on frequently, both by writing and speech."

From any point-of-view, it must be obvious that, in view of the relative rarity of evidential messages, the difficulties in the way of their reception must be great. It is quite possible that every deceased person is not a good communicator; it may be that the ability to *send* clear messages is just as rare as the ability to receive them on this side. Indeed, there is a certain amount of direct evidence that such *is* the case—some individuals constituting good communicators, while others would always be relatively bad ones. Precisely what factors would go to make a good or bad communicator we do not know—any more than we know the essential constituents of mediumship. Probably very much the same essentials which would be required in the one case would be required in the other also. It is highly probable that health, morals, mentality, etc., have little or nothing to do with the matter; but that this ability consists primarily in some vital factor, just as it does in the case of mediumship. Perhaps some light may be thrown upon this in our subsequent discussion.

There is considerable evidence, in any case, that those on the other side do not come into *direct* contact with our material world, any more than we do with theirs. We can glimpse a spiritual world only occasionally, fitfully, through the instrumentality of specially gifted seers; and it is possible that something corresponding to mediumship may be required by those on the other side to enable them to come into any sort of contact with our world, and communicate with it.

Even when they do, it would seem probable that the conditions are so different, on the other side, that communicating intelligences would find it difficult, if not impossible, to describe things to us as they are, or to make us understand and appreciate them. Were a deaf man to try and explain the physical world to a blind man, or the blind man the nature of sound to a deaf man, each would find his task next to an impossibility. He would have no language with which to express his thoughts and ideas: and, however hard he might try, it is improbable that the other would ever have any real conception of that which the former described. It is probably the same in this case. When spirits undertake to explain to us the nature of the next life, and what it is that goes on there, they have no language with which they can express their thoughts, and thus we can never get a clear idea of what their world may be like. Again and again this is stated to be the case by those communicating, and it is certainly possible that such is the case.

Still another difficulty, in communicating, would be the fact that the nervous mechanism of the medium, which the spirit supposedly controls, more or less indirectly, is unfamiliar to the operating intelligence; and he or she has to learn to use it before any clear and systematic messages can be sent or received. We find no difficulty (normally) in operating *our own* nervous mechanism, when in health, because it is educated to our needs, and we understand it thoroughly; but it must be remembered that, even in this life, such education is a long and tedious process, and that very little is required to bring about a condition which prevents the proper operation of that nervous mechanism. How much greater must be the difficulty experienced by a spirit in working, or operating, the nervous mechanism of *another* organism entirely! Little habits, checks, inhibitions, etc., to which we are unaccustomed, would be noted, and would prevent the free expression of thought through the organism being manipulated. Some etheric intermediary doubtless exists between the mind and the brain, and this would require manipulation, consciously or unconsciously, also. It seems highly probable that the flow of thought is far more automatic and spontaneous with them than it is with us, and that the function of the physical brain may be largely that of a checking or inhibiting organ. Suggestive analogies here are those cases in which men, while drowning, have lived through years of their lives in a few seconds—seeming to show that, when the mind is partially detached from the control of the brain, it can think with extreme celerity. And there is considerable evidence tending to show that these spontaneous or automatic thoughts and ideas all tend to be registered on this side—being unconsciously registered by and through the medium's organism, and expressed in automatic speech or writing here.

It must also be remembered that the communicating entity does not only have to deal with the physical organism of the medium, but also with his subconscious mind, which keeps intruding itself into the stream of thought projected by the communicator (coloring and influencing it) and also, in all probability, with the telepathically conveyed thoughts of the sitter which, consciously or unconsciously, are being introjected into the mental stream. It has been stated, indeed, that one of the chief functions of "Rector," Mrs. Piper's main Control, was to shut-off this telepathic influence from the sitter, so as to allow a more unimpeded flow of thought from the communicator, without this mental interference from the living mind. All sorts of subtle influences would thus be brought to bear, during the process, of which we can have only the faintest conception, but all of which would tend to complicate the results and render the actual process of communication more difficult.

Certain it is that the subconscious mind of the medium plays a part in all these communications—no matter how direct they may appear to be, and it seems highly probable that all such messages come more or less directly *through* the subconscious mind of the medium, just as they must be expressed through the bodily organism of the medium. And, just as there are physiological traits, habits, tricks, inhibitions, etc., connected with the functioning of the nervous mechanism, so there must also be trends of thought, memories, associations, mental habits, etc., connected with and constituting an integral part of the mentality of the medium, which would tend to be incorporated in the messages—just as our dream-consciousness would pick-up a sense impression, resulting from some external stimulus, and weave it into a dream.

This was Professor William James's theory of communication: that a series of "dips down," so to say, were made by the external intelligence, imparting supernormal information, making contacts at a series of "points," which were immediately gathered-in by the medium's subconscious mind, and elaborated and dramatized therein—so that, while we should have, in truth, a series of actual communications, these communications would not be so consecutive and systematic as generally supposed, but on the other hand relatively disjointed and fragmentary. And it must be said that this is the appearance of the facts, in a large number of cases, where the fragmentary nature of the messages is most marked, and is interspersed by a large amount of chaff, which is obviously of subconscious origin.

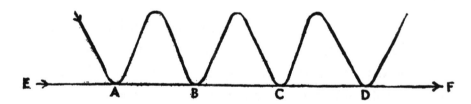

*William James's Theory—graphically illustrated.*

X = Potential Communicator (spirit entity): A, B, C, D = Points of "contact" with the subconscious mind of the Medium, E, F, which is functioning, in time, in the direction of the arrows. At the points A, B, C, D, etc., supernormal information is imparted. Between A and B, B and C, etc., however, the subconscious mind of the medium continues to function, picking-up the supernormal knowledge imparted at A, B, etc., and elaborating and dramatizing it—as we do every night in our dreams.

Were some such process as this indeed involved, it would enable us to understand, at least in part, the curious fusion of genuine supernormal knowledge and subconscious chaff which we see in so many of these communications.

Shortly before his death, Dr. Hyslop arrived at the conclusion that a very important difficulty consisted in the nature or structure of the mind which was said to be communicating at the time. Thus, we know that certain types are good visualizers, others poor; some are what are known as natural audiles, etc. Now, if the communicator be a good visualizer, and the medium a poor one, there might be great difficulty in conveying messages of the visual type through such a mind. The communicator might attempt to give his message in pictorial form—what is known as the pictographic method. These the medium might be enabled to sense only very imperfectly or not at all; and, if seen in part, might be very fragmentary and hazy, and their symbolism might be quite misunderstood and thus misinterpreted. Erroneous statements might thus be made by the medium, while the communicator himself might have been quite clear as to what was meant, and may have given the message correctly.

The alleged unusual or abnormal mental state of the communicator, at the time of communicating, is however the most fundamental of all difficulties, and doubtless the one most responsible for the confusions and errors so often noted. A very good illustration of this is to be found in an incident recorded by Dr. Hodgson, occurring in one of Mrs. Piper's sittings. Here the communicator told a number of facts (supposedly) relating to his past life. Inquiry showed that these statements were entirely false—but it turned out that *he had made the same statements in the delirium of death!* Hence it would appear that very much the same sort of mental confusion which had supervened in the former case had supervened in the latter also; and that there was a certain resemblance between the state of the man's mind during his last delirium and the confusion attendant upon his efforts at communication. Dr. Hyslop says, in this connection:

"It is especially noticeable in certain forms of communication of the 'possession' type that the last scenes of the deceased are acted over again in their first attempts to control or communicate. The mental confusion relevant to the death of my father was apparent in his first attempt to communicate through Mrs. Piper, and when I recalled this period of his dying experience, this confusion was repeated in a remarkable manner, with several evidential features in the messages. Twice an uncle lost the sense of personal identity in the attempt to communicate. His communications were in fact so confused that it was two years before he became at all clear in his efforts. He had died as the result of a sudden accident. Once my father, after mentioning the illness of my living sister, and her name, lost his personal identity long enough to confuse incidents relating to himself and his early life with those that applied to my sister and not to himself. The interesting feature of the incident was that, having failed to complete his messages a few minutes previously, when he came back the second time to try it again, Rector, the control, warned me that he was a little confused, but that what he wanted to tell me certainly related to my sister Lida.

Then came the message, claiming experiences for himself, when living, that were verifiable as my sister's. On any theory of the facts, a confused state of mind is the only explanation of them, and when associated with incidents of a supernormal and evidential character they afford reasonable attestation of the hypothesis here suggested."

We may well suppose, therefore, that the process of coming back produces an effect similar to the amnesia which so often accompanies a short or sudden interference with the normal stream of consciousness. The effect seems to be the same as that of certain kinds of dissociation, and this is the disturbance of memory which makes it difficult or impossible to recall in one mental state the events which have been experienced in another. The various disturbances of the normal consciousness or personality in the living offer clear illustrations of the psychological phenomena which are advanced as evidence of spirits when these phenomena are supernormally produced.

But there are other factors also which might tend to produce confusion in the mind of the communicator, at the time. One of these is the more or less unusual condition of the medium, mental and physical. The medium through whom the messages purport to come is in a trance condition, and when not in a trance the condition is one which is not usual, and perhaps in the broad sense may be called abnormal, though not technically so. This condition offers many obstacles to perfect transmission of messages. It is illustrated in many cases of somnambulism, in which the stream of consciousness goes on uninhibited, and when this is suppressed, as it is in deep trances, the difficulty is to get systematic communications through it. Add to this the frequent similar condition of the communicator, according to the hypothesis, and we can well imagine what causes triviality and confusion. We should have here a condition totally unlike that which we are accustomed to associate with the transmission of intelligent messages, telepathically or otherwise. The mental limitations of the medium would similarly have considerable influence.

This modifying influence of the medium's mind must never be lost sight of, as it is an important factor, and accounts for words, expressions, etc., which may be employed, but which would be quite uncharacteristic of the alleged communicator, were he normally active, and freely communicating in a state of clear consciousness. Characteristic phrases employed by the medium frequently crop up, and are sometimes repudiated by the communicator afterwards, as not expressing his thought! Thus, Dr. Hyslop's father invariably referred to Sunday as Sabbath, and never anything else, but the word Sunday was twice put in his mouth by G. P.—who was communicating for him at the time— to Mr. Hyslop's evident annoyance! Similarly, in the case of Mrs. Chenoweth, a communicator once remarked: "I don't like those 'whys'; they are hers, not mine."

It must also be remembered that, even in normal life, many people suffer from lapses of memory, temporary confusion, etc., just as these communicators apparently do while communicating. Many people are easily confused by sudden questions, or interruptions, which tend to interfere with the easy flow of unbroken thought. When such occurs, their whole chain of thinking is broken and disrupted. If the flow of thought, with those on the other side, is more fluent and automatic than it is here—as certain facts would seem to indicate —it is quite understandable how a series of rapid-fire questions aimed at the communicator might so confuse him as to render any rational replies and clear thinking on his part temporarily impossible. We find instances of this very thing occurring among living individuals.

In cases of abstraction, day-dreaming, etc., we see how the mind frequently flows along in a trivial and erratic manner, when the central control has been removed, and the current of thought is allowed to take its own spontaneous course. Sensory experiences, seemingly trivial incidents, etc., frequently come to the fore, for no apparent reason, since they have been completely forgotten by the conscious mind, and represent totally unimportant events. They are events, nevertheless, which have somehow made an indelible impression upon the subconscious mind, and which might easily come to the fore, when the subject began to lapse into an unusual mental condition. These facts, often trivial in the last degree, might then be communicated perhaps quite without the knowledge of the communicator, and be repudiated by the sitter as having no real value, and quite uncharacteristic of the person said to be communicating at the time. Mr. Bird and I both published instances of this character, drawn from our own memories, in the *Journal* S.P.R., Sept., 1929.*

Finally, it must be remembered that the medium is, during these communications, in a trance state, or some other peculiar mental condition; and that the process involved is probably some indirect telepathic method,

* See NOTE at end of Chapter.

with which the communicator is not familiar. Taking all these difficulties into consideration, therefore, it cannot be wondered at that the messages so often received are fragmentary and confused; it would be miraculous, indeed, if they were not! Were difficulties such as those above outlined actually operative, we can only wonder that some of the communicators have done as well as they have!

In the *Journal* S.P.R., May, 1925, Miss G. Tubby printed an account of the various attempts made by Dr. Hyslop, during the last weeks of his life, to pronounce certain words, and his failure to do so. His memory was perfectly clear at the time, but his physical organism would not respond to his thought. Thus, when trying to say *Smead,* he would say instead, *Sithin;* instead of *Carrington, Sitheneer;* instead of *Friend, Presen;* instead of *Hodgson, Chonson, Choneer* or *Hodgman;* instead of *Huxley, Shupney;* instead of *Myers, Maynard;* instead of *endowment, sivener,* etc. Commenting on this "Dr. Hyslop" said: "No one could understand what I meant. And *this was my own organism.* I wasn't guessing at all, not for one instant.... My mind was perfectly clear.... What if I had been a poor medium? some outside influence trying to express the same thing through another's organism might have fared the same way.... Tell them that, tell them that! It's a pretty illustration."

As Miss Tubby remarked at the time: "This should throw a flood of light on mediumship and proper name-getting."

The inability of the organism to express thought is therefore a most important factor to be taken into consideration, as well as the mental state of the communicator at the time. Both are essential aspects of this problem, and both of them must be taken into account. Any analogies which may be drawn here, between the seeming difficulties of communication and the difficulties of expressing thought, through a living organism, cannot fail to be of interest; and a number of striking and suggestive parallels may be drawn in this way. With this in mind, I made a search through the literature of abnormal psychology, and propose to epitomize here some interesting analogies which have been unearthed in consequence. These all bear more or less directly upon the problem in hand. In doing so, I wish to mention especially Dr. C. S. Bluemel's *Stammering, and Cognate Defects of Speech,* in two volumes, from which several of the following passages have been drawn.

As Ribot has appropriately remarked, we have *memories* rather than memory. We have, as it were, a number of separate and individual minds—an auditory mind, a visual mind, a kinæsthetic mind, a tactile mind, and so on. A person possessed of all the different senses is able to experience sensations of every type. It does not follow, however, that he can *think* equally well in all types of mental imagery. One man is eye-minded, thinking in terms of sight; another is ear-minded, thinking in terms of sound; still another is motor-minded, thinking in terms of muscular movements. The eye-minded man is called a visile, visual, or visionaire; the ear-minded man, an audile, an auditaire, or auditeur; the motor-minded man is a motile, moteur, or motaire. There is also a type called the tactile. This type is found frequently among the blind. One who can recall one type of image readily may find it very difficult to recall an image of another type. Rarely, words are remembered in visual or kinæsthetic terms. The average person is of the audito-moteur type. "Muscular movements are controlled indirectly.... Whatever views be held concerning the *fiat*—the decision to act—the admission must still be made that the mental imagery alone determines the nature of the performance...."

Auditory imagery is an important factor—though again never the sole factor—in mimetic performances. Frequently the ear-minded person can give faithful imitations of a brogue or a dialect, or he may be able to imitate the timbre of another person's voice.

"A lesion in the angular gyrus annihilates the visual images of printed and written words.... When the injury is profound, the patient is unable to *recognize* words that he sees, and the resulting condition is one of word-blindness,* in addition to the visual verbal amnesia and agraphia (inability to write) ... In *agraphia* while attempting to write, the patient may produce a jumble of letters. This perversion of the faculty of writing is called *paragraphia.*"

We now come to the consideration of cerebral disturbances that more directly affect the faculty of oral speech. *Aphemia* is a disturbance of speech due to lesion of the purely exterior motor mechanism. It usually manifests itself in complete mutism. There is, however, no disturbance of internal language—either visual, auditory or kinæsthetic. There is no word-deafness or word-blindness.

*Motor aphasia* is due to the total or partial obliteration of the kinæsthetic images or articulatory move-

---

* Word-blindness is sometimes called *alexia.*

ments. It is caused by lesion of the posterior part of the third frontal convolution of the left hemisphere. In this form of aphasia, it is to be noted that articulation is somewhat labored and spasmodic; but there is no similitude between the sounds uttered and those appropriate for the expression of the thought. The speaker can tell at once whether or not the sounds uttered are appropriate. The amount of amnesia that exists with a lesion in the auditory or kinæsthetic memory-center varies with the prominence of the different types of imagery in verbal thought.

A peculiar condition known as *optic aphasia* is produced by interruption of the fibers that convey stimuli from the visual memory-center to the verbal memory-centers. There is no object-blindness. The patient recognizes objects with facility; but the stimulus cannot pass to the verbal memory-centers; hence the patient is unable to recall the names of objects that he sees.

In *echolalia,* the patient reëchoes almost every word that he hears, frequently attaching no meaning to it. In the case of a woman seen at the Saltpétrière by Bateman, the mimetic tendency was very strong. She even reproduced foreign words with which she had never been familiar!

One patient could pronounce the word "cow" so long as he held his eye fixed upon the written letters; but the moment he shut his book it passed out of his memory and could not be recalled, although he recollected its initial, and could refer to it when necessary. He could not even recollect his own name unless he looked out for it, nor the name of any person of his acquaintance; but he was never at a loss for the initial of the word he wished to employ. [There is obviously an interesting analogy here with those cases in which mediums are enabled to secure an initial of a proper name, but no more.]

Lichtheim records a case,* in which the patient was able to read fluently, although he was aphasic for spontaneous speech. The patient could *repeat* quite accurately.

"In the case of the stammerer, inasmuch as his difficulty is to produce the vowel, and is not to produce voice *per se,* it is evident that his difficulty is to produce the *vowel-color,* or *vowel-quality....* The stammerer's difficulty is *transient auditory amnesia:* he is unable to recall the sound-image of the vowel that he wishes to enunciate.... The stammerer is an 'audito-moteur.' He relies for his speech-cues upon both kinæsthetic and auditory images. When he stammers in enunciating a word, it is because there is complete failure of the auditory image.... Stammering resembles aphasia in its mode or origin. Broadly, it may be stated that any cause that induces aphasia can also produce stammering.... Like aphasia, stammering often begins with a period of complete unconsciousness...."

In many cases of stammering, the impediment is in large part due to confusion or inhibition of thought.†

Dr. de Fursac, in his *Manual of Psychiatry,* says:

"A recollection of an occurrence, once evoked, is usually easily localized by us as to its position in the past. The power of localization disappears in certain psychoses. The patients cannot tell on what date or

* *Brain,* 1885.

† Speaking of inhibition in general, William James says: "Inhibition is not an occasional accident; it is an essential and unremitting element of our cerebral life."

even in what year some fact occurred, an impression of which they have, however, preserved."

Kræpelin, in his *Clinical Psychiatry* (p. 100), speaks of cases observed by him in which there was a "want of clearness in the ideas of time and place, with almost complete collectedness."

It would be possible to extend this list of references and suggestive analogies almost indefinitely; but enough has been said, perhaps, to establish the main point here made, viz., that there are interesting connections between abnormal mental states in the living, and those peculiar conditions into which the mind of man may also lapse *post mortem,* when temporarily suffering from the effects of shock, confusion, exhaustion, or the diminution of that psychic energy upon which clear-cut communications apparently depend. And that, just as we have cases of inability to recall names, dates, memories and events which should, theoretically, be clearly and forever lodged in the mind of the discarnate entity, so we have similar forgetfulness, confusion, loss of identity, inability to express one's thoughts, etc., on the part of living persons, whom we *know* to exist, and who are certainly still in possession of their physical brains, and living in a physical world to which they are accustomed.

If, therefore, the human mind is so delicately poised that slight physical, emotional or mental accidents tend to upset it, to interfere with its proper functionings and to prevent the free expression of normal thought, it seems only natural to suppose that, under novel and difficult circumstances, while attempting to communicate through an organism unfamiliar to it, like causes should produce similar results; and, were this the case, we should have, here, an explanation of the majority of those mistakes and confusions which have so frequently been noted in communications, seemingly emanating from the spiritual world.

Note:

### On the Uncertainties of Memory

In discussing the Margaret Veley case * M. Sudre made the remark that "the spirits of the dead, who, we are informed, are full of high thoughts, descend to very low ones in calling back memories of their terrestrial past." He cites, in support of this contention, a number of more or less trivial communications of the Margaret Veley personality. There is nothing unique in this, and many instances of like nature might be quoted. On the spiritistic theory, why should these things be?

Certain tentative suggestions may perhaps serve to throw light upon this difficult and vexed question. At all events, it may be of interest to see whether this may not be the case.

The anti-spiritistic critic always demands that the memory of an alleged communicator function with an accuracy exactly proportional to the importance of the material which is being remembered. It is my personal experience that memory does not behave in this way at all. I find a conspicuous tendency to retain various disconnected, trivial, meaningless incidents, while losing others of the same temporal period whose importance under any conceivable scale of measurement must have

* *Proceedings* S.P.R., 38, pp. 281-374.

been much greater. A few examples from my own experience will illustrate this. Take, e.g., the following.

I was about five years of age. Some athletic events for children had been arranged on the sands near Gorey, Jersey, where we were then living. I was running a race with another little boy about my own age. I accidentally put my foot into a hole in the sand, fell on my face, and of course lost the race; but afterwards I boasted to my father that I *would* have won it, if I had not caught my foot! Naturally, the things I remember from this period of my life are relatively few; but among them this episode stands out as a most vivid memory-picture. There seems no reason why it should do so; it was of no particular importance; it had no especial emotional value, since I was not immensely distressed over it. Why it should assume rank as a milestone of memory baffles me completely.

It will be understood that, when I speak of this episode as constituting today a vivid memory-picture, I mean just that. Plenty of things happened to me around my sixth year, of which I can now give some account. This one is not on any such flimsy basis. The complete sensorial picture of my fall, and my boasting to my father remains with me. I do not merely remember that I did this: *I remember doing it*. It is living memories of this sort with which I here deal, memories which exist in the form of detailed pictures constituting re-presentations of the past acts.

Another picture of this sort, from approximately my twelfth year. We were then living in Minneapolis, and after school my boy chum and I used to meet regularly. It is self-evident that of most of our specific meetings I retain no memory whatever. Of one such occasion, however, on which we encountered one another, running along Highland Avenue, and on which we shouted and waved our arms at each other, I retain the vivid type of memory-picture of which I am speaking.

Still another comes to me from about my sixteenth year. I was engaged in a football match, and was dribbling the ball, when a team-mate called out to me to pass, as he was clear of his field. This situation must have occurred repeatedly in such games—it is a commonplace in any game in which one confronts the choice between dribbling the ball and passing it. Why does the pictorial image of this particular occasion live on so vividly in my memory?

These are but three incidents out of a dozen comparable ones that I could mention, all of which are among the very clearest of the memory-pictures that I possess. Why? All are trivial incidents, meaningless in themselves, disconnected from any context of importance sufficiently commonplace to insure the fact that many similar episodes which I have forgotten must have occurred without even any outstanding emotional value to account on *this* basis for their preservation. Nevertheless they have been preserved: there they are. Why?

I think this question, with the answer that I have left hanging in the air because I do not know in what terms to give it, may have considerable bearing upon one of the major difficulties of the spiritistic hypothesis as an explanation for the conventional communication matter with which psychic research deals. For if it be true (as both Hodgson and Hyslop were inclined to believe) that the process of communicating is a most difficult and confusing one, and that the flow of thought becomes largely automatic at such times, then it seems quite reasonable to suppose that incidents such as the above might be automatically given and reproduced, while far more important and self-identifying material might fail to get through. In this connection, Hyslop has said (*Science and a Future Life,* p. 335):

"I do not say or imply that the past is not clearly recallable in the normal state beyond, but that as time elapses it seems that it cannot be recalled for 'communication.' We can well understand, therefore, why this recall involves a dream-like and delirious stream of trivial incidents, which usually characterize the automatic action of our minds when the stress of attention is removed and the current of thought has its own spontaneous course."

I have elsewhere emphasized the fact that a drowning man clinging to a floating log for dear life would hardly be in a good condition to discuss metaphysical subtleties or evolve new scientific truths! And it has been contended that the communicator, during the process of communicating, is in much the same situation; he is clinging onto the "light"—the medium's psycho-physical organism—and in danger every moment of becoming confused and slipping away. The process of thought, at such times, would certainly be largely unconscious and automatic, and would strongly tend to run in any grooves which might be established. If certain important elements out of the personal background tended not to come instantly and automatically to mind, and certain other sporadic unimportant ones tended to do so, we can easily understand that the same thing might occur on the other side, and that many trivial and disconnected incidents might thereby be communicated—perhaps without the communicator's knowledge. The particular incidents which I have cited from my own life—which are all of course unverifiable, and which I surely hope are below the level of communication which I should send from the other side, were I wholly conscious and in full control of the process of transmission—might naturally and inevitably flow through, in place of the things I should prefer to send.

At such times of stress or crisis as I have pictured, the functioning of the mind, living or dead, must certainly be for the larger part unconscious and automatic; and if, when communication from the other side is attempted, these are the conditions under which the communicator works, we can well understand that these sporadic thoughts from among his long-standing mental habits might tend to be automatically registered and reproduced on our side. Under these circumstances we can well see that many trivial and disconnected incidents might be thus communicated—without the knowledge of the communicator.

But it may be contended that, while all this is possible, it is nevertheless inconceivable that an individual could forget important and significant incidents in his life, while apparently conscious and wide-awake at the time. I may perhaps cite another incident which has some bearing upon this. Many years ago I induced my sister-in-law to write out for me and seal-up a letter, which was intended to be a *post mortem* test-message. Some years later, I asked her whether she remembered the contents of this letter. Not only had she forgotten it entirely, but she absolutely denied ever having written any such letter at all! Yet I have it in my possession today, still sealed and intact!

If an incident such as this can be completely forgotten, might not other less important incidents be forgotten also? Might it not be peculiarly plausible to imagine that such things as names and dates, whatever their importance, might, in view of their unpictorial character, fade into the background and be obscured behind pictorial memories of the sort I have been describing? And then, too, we must always remember that what seems important to one person at a given time might not seem half so important to another, or to the same individual at a different time and under different conditions; so that, of two persons knowing a given item, one might vividly remember it and give it a place of extreme importance, while the other would do neither of these things. As Gellett Burgess once remarked: "A woman remembereth an anniversary to the day thereof." Yet mere man proverbially forgets his anniversaries—to his great embarrassment—because, try as he will to assign them the same importance which they possess for the feminine mind, he cannot make them assume this place in his mental life.

So, incidents which might appear trivial and silly to us might have made a deep impression upon the alleged communicator for no reason at all, or for none that he himself could state, as I have tried to make clear in the above examples. If these tend to come to the surface of the mind, during the process of communication, and tend to be automatically registered on this side by virtue of that process, we have here I think an explanation of a common type of communication which has puzzled psychical researchers.

# VIII

## Animal Psychism

THERE are many cases on record which seem to prove that telepathic communication between animals frequently takes place, and that this may also occasionally be noted between animals and human beings. Rider Haggard, for example, reported a case which came under his own notice, in which he apparently perceived the apparition of his dog, Bob, at the very moment it was killed by a railway train. (*Journal* S.P.R., October, 1904.) Numerous instances could be quoted, again, in which animals have behaved in an extraordinary manner when taken to so-called haunted houses. They have whined, cowered under articles of furniture, slunk away, their hair has bristled with rage for no assignable cause, etc. A number of such cases might be quoted, which would constitute a collection of considerable interest. The object of the present chapter, however, is not to touch upon these points, but rather to deal with two seemingly neglected phases of the subject, namely, hypnotizing animals, and animal tricks—meaning by this various methods which have been devised to transfer information to animals in a manner undetected by the onlookers. Let us consider these, briefly, in turn.

### Hypnotizing Animals

So far as I can discover, very little has been written upon this subject in the past, though it is a topic of considerable interest. Carl Sextus, in his *Hypnotism*, has a brief chapter on "Animal Hypnotism," and Dr.

J. Milne Bramwell has offered a few speculations (in his *Hypnotism*) as to the various nervous centers probably involved or affected when animals feign death, hibernate, etc. But the literature on the subject is very scant, and I have been unable to find any account of the methods employed by stage hypnotists, or any study of the actual *modus operandi* involved.

It is generally known that music affects certain animals, and even reptiles, in a curious manner. The Hindu Fakirs make use of this in their exhibitions—charming cobras during the actual performance. Turtles are said to be influenced by the rhythmical beating of a tom-tom, and so on. Very few of the higher creatures seem to be seriously influenced by this means, however, and other more direct methods are resorted to.

Many of the lower animals can be rendered totally immovable merely by placing them on their backs. Ducks, chickens, rabbits, etc., can be influenced in this manner, and will stay put for some little time after being placed in this position. Dogs and cats are far more difficult to handle in this manner, though they will remain still for several seconds as a rule. Even wild birds such as owls, eagles, etc., will remain still when suddenly turned over onto their backs, in this manner. A slight tap on the top of the head will generally restore them immediately, and they will spring up, full of animation.

Chickens are readily influenced through the eye. An old experiment, very well known, is to place a hen with her head close to the ground and draw a chalk line on the floor directly outwards from the tip of the beak. The bird's eyes seemingly converge and it will remain still for as long as may be desired. Or, the bird may be held by the feet (in one hand) and gradually brought nearer and nearer the operator's face, keeping the eyes fixed intently on the eyes of the bird throughout. At first it will cluck and flap its wings wildly; these movements will gradually die-down, however, until it becomes quite still. It may then be grasped by both wings, with the other hand, and placed on its feet, where it will usually remain quietly, in a roosting position. As soon as it is picked up again, it will complain as loudly as before. This method is quite spectacular and effective, when well done.

Small alligators, when placed on their backs, will normally turn over instantly, showing great activity. Contrary to general belief, these creatures are by no means slow and sluggish, but on the contrary move with extreme rapidity when after food or when frightened. The feat of placing a small alligator on its back, and causing it to remain there for some time, is due to a trick device. Strong pressure is exerted on a certain spot in the neck, which serves to paralyze the creature for the time being. It then remains quite still until the finger is drawn smartly along the under surface of the body, when it will at once turn over onto its feet again.

Large crocodiles and alligators are handled in a different manner. The creature must first of all be caught! This is not always as easy as it sounds, especially if the alligator is a large one, as it has a powerful tail and moves with lightning-like rapidity when attacking. The safest method is to approach the creature from behind, and grasp the tail with the *right* hand, then immediately retreat a few paces, pulling the alligator along the ground as you go. The *left* front foot should then be grasped in the left hand and held securely. Held in this manner the creature is helpless. The right foot will not do. For some curious reason, the alligator is unable to turn round when held by the left foot, whereas it can if held on the other side. Grasped in the manner described, it may safely be lifted onto the table where the experiment is to be performed.

With a smaller and less powerful creature, the upper and lower jaws may now be grasped, thumb on one side and fingers on the other. The jaws are now pulled apart by main force, the head and upper part of the body being raised in the air for this purpose. Thus held, the open throat becomes visible. Watching it closely, the observer will note a certain physiological click take place in that region. As soon as this occurs, the left hand is immediately removed, the right hand still retaining its hold on the sides of the upper jaw. The alligator may now carefully be replaced on the table, when it will be found that it will remain there quite immobile, with its jaws wide open. This condition will last for the greater part of a minute. During that interval the operator has time to place a live guinea-pig or other small animal on its back, directly in front of the creature's mouth, leave it there for a few seconds, and again remove it, before the alligator returns to its normal condition. As soon as it does so, it will move and snap.

Larger and more powerful alligators cannot be handled in this manner, and pressure must be exerted on the sensitive spot on the side of the neck. This will produce temporary paralysis, as before explained, and the guinea-pig may be placed in front of its mouth, as in the last case. So long as the spell lasts, the alligator will remain quite immobile.

When placing the guinea-pig in position, and in removing it, the operator must exercise the utmost caution. So long as the alligator is under the influence, the pupils of the eyes will remain narrowed, like a cat's, visible as narrow lenses. The instant the normal condition is reëstablished, however, the pupils expand to their normal dimensions. The operator watches the pupils of the eyes while making all his movements, and the moment he sees them begin to expand, he must snatch his hand away instantly—otherwise the alligator, and not he, will possess it! Quickness of action and keenness of perception are his only salvation. As an added precaution, it is advisable to pull back the two front feet of the alligator, immediately the state is induced, so that it has to pull these into position before it can make a spring. When giving public performances, the operator usually makes a rapid downward stroke with his fingers over the creature's back, at the very moment the eyes expand. This tends to restore the alligator more rapidly, and at the same time gives the impression that the hypnotic pass was the real cause of the creature's return to a normal condition.

Performances of this kind with crocodiles and alligators are always dangerous, involving serious risk to the operator. They should never be attempted except under the supervision of an expert.

Lions, tigers, etc., cannot be hypnotized or influenced, in the true sense of the term. They can be soothed and quieted, but training must be depended upon for the rest. It should always be remembered, however, that wild animals of this type, "while they can be trained, are never tamed," in the words of Bostock, the famous animal trainer. The human eye certainly has an effect upon them, and they are keenly sensitive to human emotions, such as fear, etc. Nearly all wild animals seem to sense these states by a species of telepathy. It must be remembered, also, that there is a natural tendency on the part of all wild animals to chase anything which is moving or running away from them. The instant you run from an attacking animal, your fate is sealed!

Coming now to snakes, the python seems to be the one most easily handled. It is of course non-poisonous, since it kills by crushing. These snakes must always be carried in pairs, since a single male or female snake will die very shortly.

When attempting to hypnotize a snake of this sort, the operator removes it from the box and places it on the table. In doing so, he coils it up into three or four coils, intertwined as much as possible. The head of the snake should if possible face him. He should then immediately place the fingers of one hand below the snake's head and lift it a foot or more into the air, holding the head steady and looking intently into the eyes. The instant the snake moves its head away, it should be caught again by placing the fingers under the "chin," so to say, and held up as before. This immobilizes the upper part of the body, and the snake will have less tendency to move the lower part of it. If the head can be held stationary in this manner for a minute or two, it will be found that the snake has a tendency to remain rigid for some little time—since, as soon as a snake of this type is absolutely motionless, it will tend to remain so for a number of seconds. During this time, the operator has had time to place a live rabbit an inch or so in front of its mouth, hold it there for a few seconds, and then quickly remove it. The instant the snake moves, however, the rabbit must be snatched away, for the natural tendency of the snake would be for it to strike, and the effect of the hypnotic control would be visibly depreciated! A movement of any part of the snake's body is invariably followed by undulatory movements of the rest, and the whole process would then have to be gone through again—picking up the snake, coiling it on the table, and so on. Often this has to be done several times before it becomes still enough for the rabbit to be held before it a few seconds, as above described.

If, when the snake is coiled on the table, the head is *not* directly facing the operator (this cannot always be exactly gauged) it should be allowed to rest flat on the table, and the opened hand should be placed directly in front of its face, covering the head like a sort of cup. If the snake begins to move, the hand should be held in the same relative position, being moved backwards, so as to keep it an inch or so from the reptile's head. No fear need be felt that the snake will bite, for even if it does so no harm will result beyond a slight flesh wound (treated immediately with mercurochrome). Or, the fingers of the hand may be spread apart, and the hand placed over the snake's head like an inverted cup. The natural tendency of the snake would be to stop as soon as it saw some obstacle in its path (such as the grating formed by the fingers) and when once at rest it usually remains so for half a minute or more before moving again.

Hypnotic demonstrations with animals, reptiles,

birds, etc., are therefore based as a rule upon three fundamental principles: bodily posture; fixation of the eye; and pressure upon certain nerve-centers. It is only natural that any state into which these creatures may be thrown should be caused by physical and physiological, rather than psychological, means. Having practically no mind to which to appeal, any form of suggestion would be out of the question. The effect produced is, however, very striking, in many cases, and creates the impression in the mind of the audience that the animal has actually been hypnotized, in the strict sense of the term, and the effect is proportionately extraordinary.

### Animal Tricks

That many animals possess what might be termed a sixth sense has long been believed. Wild animals, particularly, are thought to show signs of this, and it is even manifest occasionally in our domestic animals, such as the dog and the horse. Bostock, in his book *Wild Animal Training,* has given several examples of this. One case is especially interesting—in which his lions and tigers all refused to eat, one evening, and some hours later, a fire broke out, in which a number of them perished. William J. Long, again, a practical naturalist, has cited several striking examples in his writings, which seem to indicate that there is some form of natural telepathy operative between wild animals, by means of which communication is established, and the alarm given, in times of danger. Even our cats and dogs show signs of possessing this higher sense, at times. The cases of Rolf, the Mannheim dog, and Lola, are well known, as are the talking horses of Elberfeld.

It is possible, therefore, that some such form of subtle communication exists, and we must certainly keep an open mind with regard to its possibility.

At the same time, it is undoubtedly true that the vast majority of performances given by animals are explicable by purely natural means, and that such exhibitions are rendered possible because a clever *code* has been worked-out, by the trainer, enabling the animal to perform seemingly miraculous feats. Whenever an animal is publicly exhibited, one may be fairly sure that such *is* the case. Real telepathic communication—granting that it exists—is not on tap in this manner. It is always uncertain in its operation. I now propose to explain just how these various code systems are employed, and how they operate. In this I shall be as brief as possible, merely indicating the *modus operandi* in each case, without going into unnecessary details. My notes for this have been gathered from various sources— talks with practical animal trainers, circus men, etc., as well as various articles upon the subject. I might particularly mention, in this connection, a valuable article by Charles H. Burlingame, published many years ago in the Chicago *Examiner* (1899).

A typical performing animal would doubtless be the dog. Cats are far harder to train; horses are unwieldy; other animals do not as a rule possess the necessary mentality and obedience. A certain psychological background is necessarily postulated, in all animal training; keen observation and perception, association, memory, simple reasoning, etc. Without this, training of any sort would be impossible. This is quite a different thing, however, from assuming that the animal possesses highly developed mathematical powers, or that it is normally capable of complicated intellectual flights! However, the simpler elements of mind are readily shown to exist. That a dog can remember many words is proved by the simplest training. For instance, when we say to a dog "stand up," "sit down," "shake hands," etc., he soon learns very well what is meant, and remembers his lessons. He will follow the glance of his master with surprising accuracy, and learn to interpret his bodily movements. He is a splendid judge of distance, and keenly sensitive to the emotions of any one near him at the time.

Let us consider the simplest method of training first. This is by means of the eye—the dog understanding what he is to do by following the glance of his master. In order to bring the dog, by means of eye-training, up to the point where he will find or pick-up any desired letter or number, from an alphabet or a series of numbers, it is first of all necessary that he be taught how to retrieve well. When he has learned this simple feat —and all clever dogs learn it quickly—he should be placed on a table with a row of cards in front of him. The cards should be of heavy cardboard, and one end of each card must be turned-up a little, in order that the dog may grasp it easily with his teeth.

At first, only five or six cards should be used. Accustom the dog to sit quietly on the table, his head well up and his eyes fixed on those of the trainer. In some cases, this will be a relatively easy matter; in others, it is more difficult, and will require patience on the part of the dog's master. The natural tendency is for the dog to turn his eyes away, after a few seconds; but every time he does so he must be lightly punished, while every time he keeps his eyes upon those of the trainer for some little time he should be rewarded. A scrap of meat or biscuit will serve this purpose best.

When the dog has succeeded in sitting still, and keeping his eyes fixed upon those of his trainer for some seconds, the latter should then cast a rapid but forceful look at one of the cards, without letting his eye-lids droop, and stare with immovable eyes at the selected card, at the same time giving a sharp word of command, such as "find it," or "fetch it." Inasmuch as the dog, in this respect, has a sharper eye than the man, he sees at once on which card or article the eye of his master is concentrated, and he accordingly picks it up. When the dog has learned that a glance or look is a sign to pick up the card, his training is nearly completed. It is now only necessary to add more cards, letters or numbers until words can be formed or examples solved. It is hardly necessary to say that this method is fairly obvious, and limited in its scope. It constitutes, however, excellent preliminary training for more complicated methods to follow later. Also, the dog can be taught by this means to bark any given number of times, in answer to questions. He merely continues to bark until he receives the cue to stop—by a slight change in his master's eyes or some slight facial movement.

The mnemonic or memory system is far more complicated, and necessitates great patience on the part of the trainer, coupled with considerable intelligence on the part of the dog. It is, however, well-nigh indetectable when well presented. It depends upon a set of cue words, or positions of the trainer's body, or both. The preliminary training—learning to sit still, to observe his master, to retrieve, etc., must first of all be taught, as in the last case.

The dog is seated on a large table, with a number of lettered or numbered cards in front of him, at a distance of about nine inches from his front paws. The trainer takes up his position directly in front of the first card, at a distance of about eighteen inches from it. The cue words for the first three cards, let us say, are "which," "where," and "quick."

When the trainer wishes one of the first three numbers picked up, he first of all points to it with his finger, to make the dog understand that in this position lies the article which is to be picked up. At the same time he speaks the first cue word "which." This is repeated several times, in a sharp tone of voice. In order to have a more perfect understanding with the dog, he stands directly in front of the card. After the dog has picked up this card several times, being rewarded each time, the trainer passes on to the second card, giving the cue word "where." If the dog attempts to pick up the first card, he must be reprimanded. As soon as he picks up the right card, he is rewarded with a small piece of meat. The trainer then passes on to the third card, giving the cue word "quick." He should then pass from one to the other, over and over again, until the dog has learned these three cards perfectly, so that every time he hears the word "where," for example, he will invariably pick up the right card.

After the first preliminary trials, these cue words may be incorporated into short sentences, such as, "Which is the right card, Carlo? Which is it? Which is it?" Or, "Quick, Carlo, give me number seven, quick." After the first few trials, it will be found that it is no longer necessary to point to the numbers. The dog will pick out the correct one when he hears the proper cue word. This must be repeated over and over again, using very few cards at first, and being careful not to tire the dog during these early lessons. A more substantial piece of meat and a little petting will soon have the effect of making the dog look forward to his lessons, instead of avoiding them.

More cards are now added to the first row, a suitable cue word being given to each, such as "can," "tell," "now," and so on. The dog should be trained to pick up these cards first of all, irrespective of the first ones laid down; then the cards of the entire first row should be given, jumping from one to the other. These should be learned thoroughly before any more cards are added. A few cards are now added to the second row. These should be placed directly above those in the first row, and about two inches from them. A string is tied loosely about the neck of the dog, the other end being held by the trainer, who should stand a few inches further away from the table than in the last case. The cue word for the first card is now given. The dog naturally attempts to pick up the customary card, but as he does so the trainer pulls the string, and the dog is compelled to pass over the first row of cards, and pick up the first card of the second row. He is suitably rewarded. After a number of trials, the dog will begin to understand that the distance of the trainer's body has something to do with this. Centering attention upon this first card, the trainer stands in position number 1, then in position number 2, giving the same cue word each time. Every time the dog makes a mistake he is punished, while every time he is correct he is rewarded.

After a time, it will be found that the string is no longer required as a prompter, for the dog will associate the distance of the trainer's body with the correct row of cards. The same thing must be gone through for each card in the second row.

A third row of cards is now added, and the same method employed—the trainer standing still further from the table, in position number 3. Finally a fourth row. This will be found sufficient to complete the letters of the alphabet, and any numbers which may be required. By picking them up one at a time, any given word may be spelled, or the result of any mathematical problem which has been set for the dog to work out. The question may sound complicated, but the answer is usually simple. Thus, if the trainer asks, "how many years has this gentleman been married?" and the dog picks up 13, it is only necessary for the dog to pick up first the 1 and then the 3. These numbers have been given him by means of the proper cues.

The principle of this system should now be clear. The relative distances of the trainer's body, together with the cue words, have supplied the dog with all the information necessary to enable him to spell out any answers that may be necessary, or the solution of any problem which may be set him. An intelligent dog or horse is a very good judge of distance, and soon learns just what his master wants, and what is expected of him, and will respond to his slightest wishes or movements. The dog can be trained to pick out flowers or small flags in the same way, by attaching these to wooden stands, so constructed that the dog can pick them up readily with his teeth.

This fundamental system can be extended in various

directions, and can be taught to an intelligent horse or pony also. It is, I believe, unquestionable that the feats accomplished by the vast majority of performing animals may be explained by means of such simple code signals. The horses of Elberfeld and the Mannheim dogs certainly remain a problem, and I am not contending that the above explanation covers their sensational accomplishments. I am merely endeavoring to summarize, very briefly, a few of the simple code systems which have been devised, and to show how they have been employed in the training of performing animals.

# IX

## Concerning Levitation

LEVITATION may be of two kinds: (1) the lifting of the human body from the earth or floor, or (2) the lifting of some inanimate object, such as a table. So far as I know, there are but few cases on record wherein the body of an animal, or some other living creature, has been thus levitated—except, of course, birds! Levitation, however, implies that the body thus lifted has been raised from the earth by some *supernormal* means.

As to the lifting of inanimate objects, we are here at once plunged into the much-disputed question of the physical phenomena of spiritualism. Personally, I have no doubt whatever that such phenomena exist, and that they are genuine. I have seen innumerable perfectly magnificent levitations in the presence of Eusapia Palladino, perfectly controlled, in good light, when every conceivable form of trickery was effectually eliminated. The armchair criticisms and polemics of no living man could shake my faith in *them!* Further, I feel quite assured that equally good phenomena have been observed in the presence of many other mediums. Telekinesis, however, is what we ordinarily observe; and telekinesis does not imply levitation, since objects may be merely moved in a horizontal direction, without actually being lifted from the surface on which they rest. A mere sliding, in other words, would constitute evidence for telekinesis, if genuinely supernormal. And it need hardly be pointed out that the evidence for telekinesis and the levitation of inanimate objects is very much stronger than the evidence for human levitation—the former phenomena having been observed far more frequently, and under far better conditions of control.

The question of the levitation of the human body has, however, again been brought to the front by the publication of M. Oliver Leroy's book upon this subject.* Being an orthodox Catholic, M. Leroy naturally discusses the evidence, historic and contemporary, from that point of view, and with special reference to instances of levitation in the lives of the saints. He makes a careful comparison, however, with cases of alleged levitation of certain mediums, wizards, demoniacs, magnetized persons, etc., as well as the reported cases of yogis, fakirs and holy men of the Orient. It may be said at once that, in many respects, M. Leroy has written an eminently fair, critical and judicial book, and the historic evidence which he has collected is of the utmost value. He has taken the pains to consult original documents and sources, and to publish the evidence of eye-witnesses, whenever possible. At the same time, of course, one cannot but feel the inevitable bias of the author, in his strained attempts to differentiate the levitations of Catholic saints from those of mediums, and to show that they are of quite a different nature or character. These arguments I shall presently discuss. First of all, however, a brief summary of the book is in order.

M. Leroy divides his book into three parts: dealing respectively with the *traditions*, the *facts* and the

* *Levitation: An Examination of the Evidence and Explanations.* By Oliver Leroy. London, 1928.

*theories.* The first section is again divided into two parts: *Non-Catholic Traditions,* and *Christian Hagiography.* In the former, he summarizes the older historic evidence to be found in the Greek beliefs, Buddhism, Taoism, Chinese Buddhism, Islamic Mysticism, among savages (the levitations of wizards and demoniacs), and of mediums and magnetized subjects. In dealing with Christian Hagiography he summarizes the evidence contained in the Old and New Testaments, in the Coptic Greek and Russian Churches, and finally in the Catholic Traditions. One remark of considerable interest should perhaps be quoted here (p. 35): "As regards the Protestant Churches, I have not found any traditions as to the levitation of their mystics. It may be noticed here, in this respect, that the ardent atmosphere of their revivals has not brought forth any belief of the kind—at least, to my knowledge."

Passing, then, to Part II, M. Leroy enters into a critical discussion of this evidence. He concludes—quite rightly, I think—that there is almost no scientific evidence for the levitation of savage wizards, demoniacs, etc. He thinks that the same is true of Oriental cases—yogis, fakirs, etc. Personally, I feel that the evidence here is considerably stronger than M. Leroy makes out, and this section of the book shows the least research and the poorest documentation. I know of several instances which seem to rest on good, first-hand evidence. However, I shall not stress the point. After a somewhat brief summary of the evidence for the levitation of certain mediums—Home, Stainton Moses, Eusapia Palladino, etc.—M. Leroy concludes that there is sufficient evidence here to warrant our belief, and that, while much of the evidence is poor, some of it is extremely good, resting as it does upon the first-hand testimony of men of science. A few typical instances of this character are quoted. I shall have more to say concerning this evidence later on.

Coming, now, to the evidence for the levitation of Catholic saints and mystics, M. Leroy has accumulated a mass of circumstantial data, and this portion of his book is by far the most valuable. He has enumerated dozens of instances, and has unearthed the testimony of eye-witnesses in a large number of these, thereby making immediately available a mass of material from the most widely scattered and inaccessible sources. Special attention is of course given to the cases of St. Theresa and St. Joseph of Copertino. It must be admitted that much of this evidence is very striking—the witnesses in many instances verifying the actuality of the levitation by passing their hands under the body of the levitated saint, as well as observing it carefully and without apparent emotional bias. Eliminating all doubtful cases, M. Leroy concludes that the evidence for the genuine levitation of many of these saints and mystics is undoubted and conclusive, and consequently that the occasional levitation of the human body is a fact.

Having arrived at this conclusion, M. Leroy then proceeds to compare the physical and psychological characteristics of levitation in the cases of (a) Catholic mystics, and (b) mediums. He concludes that there are certain analogies, but also certain differences. The principal analogies which he sees are: the upward or horizontal movement of the body; the fact that it can be lifted in any position; the fact that inanimate objects (such as chairs) are sometimes lifted with the body; the fact that the descent is usually slow and gentle; the fact that a peculiar organic state is generally noted; the fact that an invisible power seems to be present, producing the levitation. Further, the phenomenon is in both cases relatively rare.

Coming now to the alleged differences between the levitations of mediums and those noted in Catholic hagiography, M. Leroy has listed these in tabulated form; the most important being the following:

1. The levitations of mystics are conspicuous and intense, whereas those of mediums are coy and elusive.

2. In the cases of mystics, the body seems to have lost weight, while with mediums "the body seems to rest on some invisible support!"

3. The mystic's body is often irradiated during a levitation; this is never noted during the levitations of mediums.

4. The levitations of mystics are lasting; those of mediums brief and fleeting.

5. In the former the locality is immaterial; in the latter it is always in a séance room.

6. The one takes place in any degree of light; the other only in darkness or semi-darkness.

7. No change of temperature; frequent lowering of the temperature.

8. Illness no obstacle; illness inhibits the phenomena.

9. Spontaneous ecstasy; provoked trance condition.

10. No coöperation of those present; seeming vital coöperation.

11. Private demonstrations; public occurrences.

12. Personal faculty; alleged hereditary power.

13. Moral perfection of the life; indifferent morality.

14. Asceticism; no asceticism.

15. Repugnance to displaying power; eager display of power.

16. Unexpected; purposely invoked.

Such are the main differences which Mr. Leroy finds between the levitations of mystics, on the one hand, and mediums, on the other. It may be admitted that—judging from the relatively scant accounts available in both sets of instances—some of these differences seem to exist. Others, on the contrary, seem to be very forced, and impress one with the conviction that M. Leroy is trying to make out a case, by placing undue emphasis upon dubious or unessential details. After all, the levitation itself is the important phenomenon! The impression made upon me by this portion of the book is that, having been forced to admit that the evidence for the levitation of mediums is at least as good as that for the levitation of Catholic saints, M. Leroy feels himself bound to accentuate certain apparent differences, in the hope that the reader will be forced to conclude that the *modus operandi* is really different, though apparently similar. This, however, brings us to Part III of his book, devoted to theories.

After having disposed of the *a priori* objections of skeptics, M. Leroy summarizes the three types of theories which have been advanced in order to explain levitation. These are: the naturalistic, a "qualified supernaturalism," and absolute supernaturalism.

Considering, first, his qualified supernaturalism, we have (a) the view that levitation results from some unknown condition of the organism, depending in turn upon a special gift of the Holy Ghost. Aside from this latter element, it will be seen that this is merely a form of qualified naturalistic explanation. (b): The spiritualistic explanation—that disembodied spirits actually lift the body into the air. It is certainly problematical how many intelligent spiritualists would nowadays hold this crude view. M. Leroy naturally rejects both these theories—as well he might.

In the section devoted to absolute supernaturalism, M. Leroy gives the orthodox Catholic view of levitation—which is, to my mind, a beautiful example of the way in which word-juggling can be made to mean anything and nothing. Here it is, from p. 247:

"Levitation may be supposed to be a non-objective phenomenon, in the common acceptance of the word, but no less fraught with superior reality. It may be termed hallucination, but a divine one, infinitely truer than the short sight of the non-hallucinated people. According to this explanation, levitation is, in some cases, not a charisma of the levitated person, but of him who is granted the sight of it; and this interpretation accounts for some difficult cases ... where a very sincere and trustworthy testimony does not receive from other circumstances a satisfactory confirmation. ..."

If this means anything at all, it means that levitation is not to be considered a physical phenomenon, but a hallucination—the hallucinated person being in a peculiar psychological condition. Of course this view is directly contradicted by the facts that (a) in numerous instances, several individuals have witnessed a levitation at the same time; (b) in many instances the witnesses have actually placed their hands under the body and verified the levitation in question; (c) that such levitations have occasionally been photographed (Richet, *Thirty Years of Psychical Research,* p. 549); (d) these witnesses were, in the majority of cases, un-emotional scientific men, whose conduct at the time showed not the slightest trace of having been halluci-nated; and (e) in some instances, partial levitations have been registered by means of scales, balances and other laboratory apparatus. This theory of M. Leroy's, therefore, breaks down completely in the face of the available evidence, and we are forced to the conclusion that levitations are physical phenomena, that the body has actually been lifted from the floor or earth, either by normal or by supernormal means.

Contrary to the opinion of M. Leroy, I must re-gard the evidence for the levitation of mediums as in-finitely stronger than the evidence for the levitation of saints. It is newer, better attested, more circumstantial, and verified by men of science in a scientific age, rather than by religious enthusiasts in a superstitious age. I need not here enter into any summary of this evidence, some of which has been given by M. Leroy, but in far greater detail by Richet (*op. cit.*). I should like to quote one account, however, which seems to have been overlooked by nearly all writers upon this subject, though it is one of the most striking accounts on rec-ord. At a meeting of the English S.P.R., October 26, 1894, Sir Oliver Lodge read his paper upon the phe-nomena witnessed by himself, Richet, Myers and Ochorowicz in the presence of Eusapia Palladino, and at the conclusion of his paper Sir William Crookes made the following statements concerning the alleged phenomena he had witnessed in the presence of D. D. Home. He said:

"The best cases of Home's levitation I witnessed were in my own house. On one occasion he went to a clear part of the room, and, after standing quietly for a minute, told us he was rising. I saw him slowly rise up with a continuous gliding movement and remain about six inches off the ground for several seconds, when he slowly descended. On this occasion no one moved from their places. On another occasion I was invited to come to him, when he rose 18 inches off the ground, and I passed my hands under his feet, round him, and over his head when he was in the air....

"On several occasions Home and the chair in which he was sitting at the table rose off the ground. This was generally done very deliberately, and Home then sometimes tucked his feet on the seat of the chair and held up his hands in view of all of us. On such an occasion I have got down and seen and felt that all four legs were off the ground at the same time, Home's feet being on the chair. Less frequently the levitating power extended to those sitting next to him. Once my wife was thus raised off the ground in her chair...."

Now, in the first place, I challenge M. Leroy to produce any evidence equal to this in value, reported by an eminent man of science. And in the second place testimony such as this disposes of all theories of hallucination, divinely inspired or otherwise. Home, on this occasion, as on many other occasions, was very evidently raised from the floor by some means; and other mediums seem to have been levitated also, under excellent conditions of control, by what we must take to be the same means. There can be no question, I think, as to the genuine character of many of these levitations; they are well verified, supernormal physical phenomena. They actually *occur*. Such being the case, we are forced to seek some explanation, and are of necessity, as scientific investigators, forced to fall back upon some more or less naturalistic theory—which M. Leroy rejects.

In cases of bodily levitation, there is certainly no actual loss of weight, in the sense that the organs and tissues of the body are disintegrated, as they are asserted to be in certain cases of dematerialization. The human body remains intact. What seemingly occurs is that the pull of gravity is in some way partially or wholly neutralized or overcome for the time being. This must, seemingly, be due to some force generated within the medium's body, or the immediate environment, or both, counteracting in some way the gravitational pull. We must remember, in this connection, that weight is a relative, and not an absolute, thing. Weight is not an inherent attribute of an object, as most people think, but is solely due to the attraction of gravitation. Thus, a pound weight does not weigh the same at the equator and at the North Pole, for the simple reason that the weight is further from the center of gravity (the center of the earth) at the equator than it is at the pole, and hence is less. On the moon it would weigh somewhat less than three ounces, because of the moon's smaller mass; on the sun, nearly 28 pounds for a converse reason. Alone in a universe of chaos it would have no weight at all. Whatever particular numerical modification of the theory of gravitation we may ultimately be forced to accept, due to Einstein's views, and whatever theory we may ultimately adopt for the causation of gravitation, we must always admit that falling bodies act *as if* they were being subjected to some genuine pull—which is all that Newton claimed. If this pull, this attractive force, could be in some measure counteracted, therefore, the attracted body would appear to lose weight, and might actually float in the air, as though it had practically no weight for the time being. We should then have a levitation of the body in question.

Now we know that this can actually be accomplished experimentally, using a metal ball as the object to be raised. A sort of repulsive magnetism is generated in the metal plate on which the ball rests, and the ball is repelled from the plate, so that it floats some distance in the air above it. This is a simple physical experiment which has often been accomplished. I do not, of course, for one moment contend that there is a *direct* analogy here; the human body is *not* a metal object, and there is no known magnetic or electrical energy which would act upon it as it acted upon the metal ball, in the above experiment. It is possible, however, that we may have here an *indirect* analogy, which may afford us some clue as to what occurs when a human body is levitated.

Let us for the moment omit consideration of the Relativity theory, and assume that the weight of any body or object is due to an actual gravitational pull—to a force as postulated by Newton. This is constant and invariable, and the laws governing it are definitely known. Such being the case, there seem to be only two ways in which this pull could be neutralized or overcome: (1) Some screen must be introduced between the earth and the body, shielding it from the pull in question; or (2) some repulsive energy of force must be generated in the body itself, tending to offset the pull of gravity, in somewhat the same way that light-waves can neutralize each other, resulting in darkness. It is hardly necessary to emphasize the fact that such a hypothetical energy can be neither electricity nor magnetism, but some energy unknown to modern science and as such distinctly supernormal in character.

As to supposition Number 1: There is no known substance which is in any sense opaque to gravity, in the way that certain substances are opaque to other known forces or energies. Thus, glass is transparent to light while it is opaque for electricity, while a sheet of iron is opaque for light while it is transparent for electricity, etc. But there is no substance known which in any way screens or shuts-off the pull of gravity. Furthermore, in cases of levitation, no such screen was employed, the body being freely suspended in space. We may therefore disregard this supposition, and fall back upon Number 2, as the only conceivable one consistent with the older Newtonian theory of gravitation.

According to this view, some unknown force is spontaneously generated within the body, tending to offset or neutralize the attraction of gravitation, and hence causing it to lose weight. What the nature of this force may be we have not, of course, the slightest inkling. It is obviously supernormal, unknown and mysterious. If such a force exists, it is one of the duties of psychical researchers of the future to attempt to isolate and study it. Without entering into this theoretical question at greater length now, however, let us first of all consider one or two points which may be thought to have some bearing upon the problem under consideration.

It is probably fairly well known that the Fakirs and Yogis of India claim to be able to produce levitation experimentally by means of certain breathing exercises which (it is asserted) facilitate the intake and distribution of *prana*—the subtle, vital essence which is imbibed during the exercises in question. In my *Higher Psychical Development* (p. 57), I touched upon this question, remarking that:

"As you practice these breathing exercises, in connection with concentration, you are said to pass through four stages. (1) The body breaks out into perspiration; (2) everything appears to go black before you. That passes off, and then you experience the sensation of (3) hopping about like a frog. If you are sitting cross-legged, this is a curious feeling. Physically, people do not move—although apparently in some cases they *do*—but the theory is that you only hop about like this because the body is not properly balanced. If, they say, it were properly balanced, then, instead of hopping about, you would go straight up into the air—which is (4) levitation. ..."

The theory is, of course, that levitation is thus induced by breathing exercises, which increase the flow of prana through the body, which in turn neutralizes the pull of gravity.

Without, now, stopping to discuss this Oriental theory, let us pass on to certain facts more or less connected with it, which I myself have observed. These observations I included in my paper read before the

First International Psychical Congress: Copenhagen, 1921. I quote herewith a portion of this Report.

"You all know the old lifting game, in which four persons lift a fifth, by placing their fingers under the arms and knees of the fifth seated person. All four persons doing the lifting bend forward several times, in unison, inhaling and exhaling deeply together. The person seated in the chair also inhales and exhales at the same time. On the fifth count, say, all five persons hold their breath; the fingers of the four lifters are rapidly inserted under the arms and legs of the seated subject, and the lift is made. It is a fact, which practically every one will attest, that, under these circumstances, the person lifted seems to lose weight. A heavy man, whom it is found impossible to lift at first, will be lifted with apparent ease upon the lifters' four fingers, after the breathing and bending exercises have been undertaken. That is the subjective impression of the lifters. The question of course is: Is there really any loss of weight, or is this simply a subjective impression—an illusion?

"Although this test has been tried by many thousands of persons, it is curious that no one ever seems to have thought of putting the matter to the test by trying it upon registering scales, upon which the combined weight would, every moment, be in evidence. This test we undertook. On the afternoon of July 25 (1921), we tried this experiment a number of times upon the platform of one of the large, self-registering scales, manufactured by the Toledo Scales Co., built to register up to 2,000 pounds. This scale had been especially adjusted with the greatest exactitude for our test, and its accuracy was checked off before and after the experiment.

"Those doing the lifting were Mr. William Russell (electrical expert), Mr. Burling Hull (conjurer), Mr. Albert Poyner, of the Toledo Scales Company, and myself.... The reader of weights recorded during the various lifts was Mr. W. J. Mahnken, an expert engineer.

"A chair was placed in the center of the weighing platform. Upon this the subject to be lifted was seated. The four lifters took up their positions upon four corners of the platform. Our combined weight (five persons) was exactly 712 pounds. Movements upon our part produced only slight oscillations of the needle on the recording dial. Deep breathing produced almost no appreciable effect.

"Under these circumstances, the necessary bendings and breathings were undertaken. On the fifth count, the lift was made slowly, lasting about five seconds. The experiment was performed five times. On the first lift, the recorder stated that the needle on the dial had fallen to 660 pounds—a loss of 52 pounds. On the second lift, there was an apparent loss of 52 pounds. On the third lift, of 60 pounds. On the fourth lift, of 60 pounds. And on the fifth lift, of 60 pounds. These losses tallied with the subjective feelings of the lifters, who also felt that weight had been lost. How account for these remarkable results?

"If I lifted a chair, while standing upon the platform, the dial showed first of all a sudden increase of weight, then a lessened weight, and finally swung back to normal. If I squatted on my toes, and suddenly rose to an upright position, a similar gain and then loss of weight was observed. In our lifting tests, however, no gain of weight was at any time reported, invariably a loss, which however slowly returned to normal, as the subject was held for some considerable time in the air. ...I have no theory to offer as to these observations, which I cannot fully explain. I do not for a moment assume that any actual loss of weight occurred in the body of the lifted subject. I merely give you the facts as recorded, hoping that others may check off these results, and discover what freak in the laws of mechanics was responsible for the results we obtained...." *

It should perhaps be added that flash-light photographs of the dial were taken at the time, showing these losses; and also that I repeated these tests, some two years later, in Toledo, with more or less similar results, save that considerably smaller losses were then noted.

Let us compare these curious results with some obtained by the Milan Commission (1892), during their experiments with Eusapia Palladino. Here we read:

"Eusapia, seated on a chair, was placed on the platform of a weighing machine, and her feet were strongly bound together by a handkechief. One of us, M. Finzi, was told-off to read the weight. M. Schiaparelli and I employed ourselves in watching closely the balance and its surroundings, so as to be sure that Eusapia did not touch with hand or foot the ground, or any object in the neighborhood.

"Her weight with the chair was nearly 58 kilograms [nearly 128 pounds]; we placed on the scale a weight of 500 grams, at a point where it would be equivalent

---

* See my *Story of Psychic Science,* p. 228.

to 50 kilograms, and then the rider was placed at the figure eight. Eusapia's weight was thus exactly balanced. Then, though Eusapia did not move her chair, we had, in order to maintain equilibrium, to shift the rider first to six, then to four, and then to two, and finally to zero, and further, to obtain exact equilibrium, it would have been necessary to take away a little of the weight of 500 grams which represented 50 kilograms. It will be seen, therefore, that Eusapia diminished her weight in this experiment by at least 8 kilograms (17½ pounds). We are certain that she threw nothing away . . . and equally certain that she derived no support from any neighboring object. And finally, the movement was sufficiently slow—it occupied from ten to twenty seconds—to make it possible to attribute it to any jump, or quick movement of any kind. . . ."

It is true that the experimenters did not consider these tests conclusive, because of the crudeness of their scales, and later tests undertaken with more delicate balances yielded striking and positive, but not such remarkable, results. "Upon one occasion, when the balance was placed some ten inches behind Eusapia, in response to an urgent movement of her (controlled) hand, the rider oscillated violently, while the hands, feet and knees of the medium were being securely held. This effect, as of some heavy weight's being thrown into the scale, was however never repeated."

At the conclusion of our tenth séance in New York, I myself saw Eusapia step upon the platform of the scale, and apparently lose four pounds within a very few seconds. This occurred on December 9, 1909, and is noted in the (as yet unpublished) records of the

American Palladino séances. It may be stated, in passing, that I have frequently seen Eusapia make tables, stools, and other objects light or heavy, at will, merely by placing her hands over them, and willing them to become so.

Although these apparent losses of weight cannot, of course, be considered in any sense true levitations, they may perhaps be held to be *partial* levitations—effects which, if more pronounced, would have resulted in total levitations. The lifting of inanimate objects has interest, in this connection, because of the fact that the chair or stool on which the medium was sitting was occasionally said to have been levitated with his body, at the same time.

Now, we have more or less accustomed ourselves to the idea that telekinesis is effected by means of some externalization of energy from the medium's body, which can become sufficiently solid to affect matter. In other words, a sort of energized, invisible teleplasm. There is a great deal of direct and indirect evidence that this explanation is the true one. The vital energy issues from the medium's finger-tips, particularly, charging the material objects on which the hands are laid, affecting instruments and photographic plates, influencing the human body, and so on. Doubtless the cold breeze which issued from various spots on Eusapia's body was closely allied to this—a current which was certainly objective, as we verified to our complete satisfaction during the Naples experiments, when we observed that a small flag fluttered actively when placed in its path, notwithstanding the fact that the medium's mouth and nose were effectually held. Crawford apparently saw the process of the gradual condensation of this vital current into visible teleplasm. Finally, we have teleplasm itself, shaped and formed into definite materializations. Here, then, we seem to have a graduated series of stages all the way from invisible energy to solid matter. During normal dematerialization the reverse process apparently takes place; the visible substance returning to invisible energy, which is reabsorbed into the medium's organism.

Often this externalized energy seems to act as an attractive force, drawing objects toward the medium. More often, seemingly, it acts in the reverse manner, propelling objects from the medium. In the physical world, whenever such action is noted, there is always a corresponding reaction; whenever an apple falls to the ground, the earth also rises to meet the apple, the distance being proportional to the difference in mass between the earth and the apple. The same law doubtless applies whenever supernormal physical phenomena are produced. There is a reaction upon the body of the medium, and indeed such corresponding reactions have frequently been noted in muscular twitchings, contractions, etc., coincidental with the movement of the object. This was frequently noted in the case of Eusapia. In such cases, then, we have an invisible energy acting and reacting between the medium's body and a mass of matter—the object moved. Inasmuch as the object is generally much lighter than the body of the medium, the object is moved while the subject's body remains relatively stationary. But, supposing that the object were much *heavier* than the body of the medium, being practically immovable. Might not the reaction then have the effect of moving the medium's body *away* from the object, which would remain stationary? And if this outflowing of telekinetic energy were more or less constant and continuous, might not the medium's body be repelled backwards in space?

Suppose, now, that such an outpouring of telekinetic energy occurred, directed *downwards,* i.e., toward the *earth.* The latter would then act as an immovable body, while the medium would be propelled upwards into space—that is, levitated! This would continue as long as the expenditure of force continued, and, when it began to diminish, the medium's body would gradually sink to earth again, as is usually the case. A slight or sporadic externalization would thus result in lessening the weight of the subject, while a powerful and continuous exudation would induce a genuine levitation. No weight would actually be lost, from the physiological point of view; the attraction of gravitation would be just as uniform and law-abiding as ever, but a levitation would result nevertheless, because of this externalization of telekinetic force, powerful enough to offset it for the time being. We have here, perhaps, some faint clew as to the *modus operandi* of such levitations, enabling us to formulate in our minds some definite and not too irrational picture as to what may occur on such occasions. Granting their actuality, *some* explanation is certainly needed, and it seems to me that the theory formulated above covers the observed facts in a fairly satisfactory manner.

What is the nature of this telekinetic energy, and what are the factors which are instrumental in causing its externalization? As yet we know very little concerning it; still less of the conditions which facilitate or insure its exteriorization. It seems to be allied to, though not identical with, the neural energy of the body. It does not seem to be radiated from the plexuses or great vital centers, though it may be generated within them. It is probably connected, in some subtle way, with the sexual energies.* It can affect matter and the material world, and become more or less substantial or "solid,"† for the time being. It is sporadic and uncertain in its manifestations; it is occasionally externalized spontaneously (poltergeist phenomena), but more often voluntarily and experimentally. Its activities are usually associated with a peculiar psycho-physiological condition of the medium (trance, etc.), and it is the basis of physical mediumship. Beyond this we can hardly go.

Now, although there is at present no scientific basis for this belief, it is certainly conceivable that the human body may be at times "polarized," permitting a greater flow of energy through it than at other times. We have examples of this in the physical world. The copper wire does not generate the electricity which it carries; the electric energy merely flows through it (or around it). The magnetism in a bar-magnet is not generated within the magnet, but is permitted to flow through it, when all the atoms in the iron bar are pointed in the same direction. Heat the magnet red-hot, and it is no longer a magnet, since its contained atoms no longer point in one direction but in every direction. The flow of magnetism through it is thus prevented until the bar of iron is again magnetized, when it will be found that its atoms once more point in the same direction. Similarly, it has been contended, the human body can be

* See my *Story of Psychic Science,* pp. 145-47, for a discussion of this question of the possible connection between the Sexual Energies and Psychic Phenomena, on the one hand, and the Subtle Energies mentioned by the Yogis, on the other. Also later in the text.

† Eusapia was wont to say that she could move objects if her *will* were sufficiently *solid.*

thus polarized, to a certain extent, enabling a greater flow of vital energy through it to take place. Diet is said to facilitate this; * so does bodily posture; so do right feelings and emotions; while the Yogis claim that certain breathing exercises have an enormous influence in this direction. I am inclined to believe that *rhythm* also has a remarkable effect—the study of which has been almost entirely neglected. I will tell of a remarkable experience I once had, in this connection, when I was about eighteen years of age.

At that time in my life I was always in excellent physical condition, constantly engaged in cricket, football, tennis, gymnastics, boxing, running and so on. During one summer vacation, my chum and I walked from London to Exeter in a week—a distance, counting side-trips, etc., of approximately thirty miles a day. On the evening of the seventh day, we both of us had an identical experience: we both felt that we could rise into the air and float with only the slightest extra exertion; that we almost had difficulty in keeping on the ground! This feeling of physical ecstasy (for I can only call it that) lasted for about ten or twelve minutes; but it was noted by both of us at the same time, and lasted in both cases for about the same length of time. It was a unique and never-to-be-forgotten experience, unlike anything I have experienced before or since. It was not due to mere excellence of physical condition, as I have emphasized the fact that I was, at the time, nearly always in perfect training. We both of us attributed it, at the time, to the constant rhythm imparted to the body by the walking, and the deep breathing which we

* See my article on "The Occult Side of Diet," in the *Occult Review.*

frequently practiced in unison. Perhaps we were wiser than we knew!

It is all very well for the strictly scientific investigator to turn up his nose at these suggestions; but the fact remains that, if levitation is a genuine phenomenon, it is a most extraordinary one, and a phenomenon which no one has ever attempted to explain in any detail, so far as I know. The only recourse for such a critic is to assert that genuine levitation never occurs at all—which is certainly an easy way of disposing of the difficulty! But there is an enormous body of evidence tending to prove that genuine levitation of the human body does in fact occur; M. Leroy has accumulated much of this, and much more might easily be cited from spiritualistic sources. Many of these incidents are vouched for by eminent men of science, who have observed the phenomenon in a leisurely and dispassionate manner. Doubtless many cases have never been recorded. For instance, two acquaintances of mine have positively assured me that they have been levitated, while remaining perfectly rational and wide-awake. Both instances occurred in the afternoon, while they were dressed and more or less busily occupied. The evidence for many of Home's levitations seems incontestable. If, therefore, levitation be a fact, it requires *some* explanation, and I have attempted to suggest one in the preceding paragraphs, which may or may not contain within them some element of truth. As to this, time alone can tell!

Finally, it should be pointed out that I have discussed the problem of levitation purely from the point of view of Newtonian gravitation, and have said nothing concerning the relativity theory which, as we know, has thrown an entirely new light upon many physical problems, and especially upon the nature of gravity. I do not know to what extent some theory of levitation might be worked out from the relativistic point of view, which substitutes gravitational field, curvature of space-time, etc., for the traditional theory. Mr. J. M. Bird gave some attention to this idea (*Journal* A.S.P.R., March, 1928); I quite join him in leaving its detailed development to some more specialized investigator. I have merely attempted in the above to discuss this interesting problem from the psychical researcher's point of view, to offer some possible theoretic interpretation, and to call attention to the existing mass of evidence for genuine levitation, which seems to have been strangely overlooked.

# X

## Yoga Philosophy

Is there not much that psychical researchers **might learn** from the teachings of the Orient? I believe that there is. They have frequently returned disappointed, it is true, because they have sought objective and material miracles, paying little attention to the hidden and subjective phenomena—those mental and psychic phenomena which are rarely exhibited to strangers and mere mystery-mongers. They have witnessed certain conjuring tricks, snake-charming, and the feats of performing Fakirs, and concluded that nothing beyond these is to be found. The practitioners of Yoga are rarely accessible; but they have developed a remarkable system of metaphysics, and doubtless know much more concerning certain aspects of psychic phenomena than do we.

"East is East and West is West, and never the twain shall meet," wrote Kipling. The reason for this probably is that East and West hold such diametrically opposite views of life. To us Westerners, this material world is everything; this life is all. We are inclined to look upon the Hindus as visionaries, never in touch with reality, wrapped in transcendental vaporizings. To them, *we* are the dreamers, the visionaries, lost in a world of illusion; we are the ones who are devoting our lives to ephemeral baubles, just as a child might value its dolls. To them, this life is brief and fleeting; spirit is eternal; nothing else matters. To us, matter is the important thing—goods, chattels and possessions!

Here, then, is the basic reason for the lack of understanding and mutual appreciation between East and West. Is man essentially body or spirit? That is a very important question, and one which we are all called upon to solve. Is spirit as real, as actual, in its own sphere, as matter is in its? Experiments, observations, experiences, alone can prove this. Those who have traveled this Road say to us: "Do so and so, and you will see for yourself that what I say is true." The skeptic replies: "No, show me objectively, and I will believe." The other rejoins: "I cannot show you objectively; *experience* this state of which I speak, for yourself, and you will then realize its actuality." Thus the controversy rages! The only way to settle it is for the skeptic to experience enough of the mystical state to know that it exists, and that there is a great Truth here which is urging to be expressed.

Yoga Philosophy is built upon the fundamental postulate that there is an omnipotent, omniscient Intelligence, throughout the Universe, which is not, however, a personal Deity. It is Absolute Consciousness. With this Consciousness it is possible to merge. The object of Yoga is, very largely, to blend the individual consciousness with this Absolute Consciousness; then *Samadhi* is attained—unutterable bliss and peace. In this, however, the individual is not totally lost, as generally believed. The Drop is not poured into the Ocean; the Ocean is poured into the Drop. We acquire *its* powers and potentialities, while retaining the self as a sort of background of experience. We lose our individual consciousness, to a certain extent; but that is not the true man. This can best be exemplified by pointing out that when, *e.g.,* we are lost in excitement, or in some great emotion, we do not think "*I* am excited"; we feel the excitement. We are lost in something greater than ourselves; we become part of it; yet we experience it! We are greater than we know. . . .

This process of blending or merging the individual consciousness with the Absolute Consciousness is attained in eight steps or stages. It is a perfectly graduated system, and is so logical and systematic that one must acknowledge its theoretical perfection.

The first two steps are known, respectively, as *Yama* and *Niyama*. In these stages, a highly ethical mode of life is taught—control, indifference, detachment, renunciation, charity, etc., as well as such physical restraints as strict vegetarianism, abstemiousness, cleansing the body inside and out with water, etc. In these stages the man must learn to overcome the desires and temptations of this world—learn detachment—so that he may be prepared for the strenuous work that is to follow.

The third step deals with the body; it is known as *Asana*. It has to do with bodily posture. Any one who experiments will soon find that, after a very few minutes, the body will begin to make its presence known; it will become restless and irritable. This is bad for long-continued meditation, when absolute stillness and peace are required. So, the Yogis experimented for several hundred years, and finally settled upon eighty-four positions or postures, which can be retained almost indefinitely without interrupting the flow of thought. These are the *Asana* postures. Some of these are practically impossible for Europeans to assume; others can be attained with more or less practice. Once assumed, the body sinks into its required state of passivity, with the same sense of relief that a man might sink into a warm bath. The body can then be held immobile for hours. The flow of thought will proceed uninterruptedly. The body is steadied and poised. These are some results of *Asana*.

But there are other results. These positions are also favorable to the free circulation, within the body, of certain vital currents, which are said to circulate to and fro, from and to certain centers, which will be mentioned presently. The channels are left free and clear, so to say; this results from *Asana*.

The fourth stage also deals with the body; it is known as *pranayama*. The Yogis believe that, in addition to the chemical constituents of the air, there is also within it a vital fluid known as *prana*. This *prana* is imbibed when air is taken into the lungs, and circulated within the body, by means of suitable breathing exercises. *Pranayama* means literally prana control. Breathing exercises of various specific kinds are therefore a part of this system. By holding the breath, *prana* is said to be retained within the body, and it can be sent or directed to various parts of the body, by means of innumerable, vital channels known as the *nadi*. These *nadi* are not physical nerves, but analogous to them. They more nearly resemble vital currents. Hence we do not find them when dissecting the body. Slow, deep breaths accumulate more of this *prana* than a number of shallow ones. Hence the Yogis attempt to regulate the breath, and make the intervals between inhalation and exhalation as long as possible. There is much that might be termed mythical physiology in all this; but it should be remembered that subjective as well as objective phenomena are being portrayed in all such descriptions.

To return, however: there is another use for *prana*. There are said to be in the body certain vital centers, known as *Chakras,* or lotuses, which are inactive in undeveloped persons, but which can be stimulated into activity by means of *pranayama*. A current of *prana* is directed to one of these centers, which is aroused into activity. We shall come to these Centers presently.

Along with *pranayama,* in this stage, goes *Mantra-yoga,* or yoga by means of chants or mantras. *Mantras* are rhythmic sentences or words, the pronunciation of which is said to set-up a certain vibratory activity within the body and mind which facilitates psychic manifestations, and assists in further inner development. The translation of these mantras does not matter particularly; it is the pronunciation of the words themselves which counts. All languages have such rhythmic mantras. There are certain English words which are more or less similar. The Greeks and Romans also knew the power of words in this respect. The Mohammedans have several mantras—the most famous being "Ishhad la Allah illa 'llah,"—"there is no God but Allah," and so on.

The value of *Mantras* is therefore well known. The basis of nearly all the Yoga Mantras is the sacred word OM, or more properly AUM. There is much symbolism connected with this word; the A. is formed in the throat, the U. in the middle of the mouth, and the M. by the lips, symbolic of the creation, maintenance and destruction of the Universe. If properly pronounced, this word will be found to produce a peculiar effect upon the point between the eyes, at the root of the nose. It should be pronounced with a *hum* at the end, like the hum of a bee. It should be repeated many times, and as many times as possible with one breath. This number may be increased greatly by constant practice.

The word AUM is usually combined with others, so as to form complex *mantras*. Thus: "Aum Mani Padme Hum," "Aum Tat Sat Aum," etc. These *Mantras* are said to generate a real *power*, and the power of the Mantra is considered very great. It may be used for aggressive purposes, attacking a man by means of Mantras, using the term here as almost synonymous with spells. The Yogis are taught the power of such Spells, and also how to construct shields (*Grahana*) to protect themselves from Mantras thus directed at them.

These *Mantras* are pronounced continuously at certain stages of development; incense is sometimes burned to increase their effect.

We are now ready to begin the fifth stage of development, known as *Pratyahara*. We begin to work with the mind. The body having been stilled (*asana*), the vital forces circulating (*pranayama*), a definite rhythm of the body having been set-up (*mantrayoga*), the mind is free to turn its attention upon itself.

But before we can begin to do anything with the mind, it must first be cleared and steadied. If you close your eyes and turn your attention inward, you will probably find that your mind is turning and tossing about, like an angry sea-serpent; it is never still for one moment; and, further, that the senses keep impinging upon it, so as to keep it in constant agitation. For these reasons, silence is necessary; the eyes must be closed or fixed upon some immovable object (such as the tip of the nose, which also completes the "reflex arc") ; smell, taste and touch must be eliminated. With the sense-organs thus shut off, the attention is turned inward, and attempts must be made to still the mind, so that it may become quiet and calm. It must be made empty, to a certain extent. The Yogis contend that, if you wish to write anything upon a blackboard, the blackboard must be clean; if you wish to write in the sand, that sand must be quiet and still. Hence, before you can begin to use the mind, for purposes of concentration, etc., you must first make it still and quiet. This is accomplished by means of meditation—*pratyahara*. Rigid and prolonged self-analysis will enable one gradually to acquire this condition.

When this state has been reached, we are ready for the next step, *Dharana* which means Concentration. Holding the mind still, we begin to do something with it. An object of contemplation is held fixedly in the mind; it must not be allowed to waver, change its form, color, etc., as it will have a tendency to do. Interruptions of consciousness of this sort are technically known as "Breaks"—i.e., breaks in consciousness. A rigid self-analysis will reveal an astonishing number of such Breaks. Every time the mind is allowed to wander away from the object of contemplation, a check must be made, so as to enable the neophyte to ascertain how many Breaks there may have been, in a given length of time. A little check-mark may be made upon paper, or a bead pulled over by the fingers—which beads are threaded upon a string. (This is the origin of "telling the beads," which thus originated many hundreds of years B.C.).

Having trained the mind thus far, we are ready to begin the seventh stage of training, known as *Dhyana*. This means Unification. It now becomes increasingly difficult to express in few words the inner meaning of these practices. When we are looking at some object, we are aware of at least two things—the object, and one's self. This, however, is illusory, and is based upon the fatal Duality of the mind. All is ultimately *One;* the object and ourselves are but fractions of the Absolute Consciousness. We must realize this. Accordingly, an attempt is made to unify one's self with the object of concentration. Holding it in mind, this attempt at unification must be made; when suddenly an extraordinary phenomenon will take place. A sort of "click" will occur, and you and the object are no longer two, but one! You and the object have merged: *Dhyana* has been attained!

Various mental and spiritual results can be attained in *Dhyana;* but it is not the ultimate goal; that is *Samadhi,* the eighth stage. This consists essentially in unification with the Absolute Consciousness. Then Cosmic Consciousness is attained; ecstasy is reached; the Yogi is no longer of this earth; he dwells in a sphere apart; he is possessed of all the great *Siddhis* (psychic powers); he can free his spirit and exercise powers undreamed of. He is possessed of all knowledge, all wisdom, for he has the Absolute Consciousness to draw upon.*

This, then, is the goal of attainment: this is the climax towards which the Yogi has been steadily progressing. In this state, happiness and bliss are said to

---

* It must be understood that, in all this, I am merely summarizing the *teachings* of Yoga and not my own views regarding it.

exist; ecstasy is constant, beyond anything attained upon this earth.

But, in reaching this goal, several other phenomena have been noticed. Psychic powers have been incidentally gained. They are off-shoots, as it were, like the branches of a tree. We have been following the main trunk, up to the top, "where the bird perches"; but, branching from the tree, are big and little branches, psychic phenomena of various kinds, gained incidentally; and these powers are developed by the awakening of the *Kundalini,* and the arousing into activity of the various *Chakras.*

This *Kundalini* is a mysterious, secret Energy, which is said to reside in the lowest of the seven Centers, located at the base of the spine. It resembles a Serpent, in three-and-a-half coils, with its tail in its mouth. Hence it has been called the Serpent Power. It is doubtless closely related to the sexual energies, but is not identical with them.* This power is said to be resident in all of us, but is not aroused into activity except by the measures prescribed in Yoga. To arouse it, the *prana* must be directed forcibly against this lowest Center, striking it as one would strike a nail with a hammer. It then begins to move, to stir. Finally, it becomes aroused into vital activity. The lowest Center is then vivified; it becomes active. By continuing the process, each of the seven *Chakras* or lotus-centers is aroused in turn; and when all of them are aroused and active, all psychic powers are said to belong to the Yogi; he can command animals and control matter; he can leave his body at will; he can levitate himself; he can overcome illness and death; he is clairvoyant, telepathic; he is

* See Note, *ante.*

conscious of his dreams; he can create by thought; it is then that "miracles" are performed.

There are seven of these Chakras or vital Centers in the body. The first is the *Muladhara,* situated at the base of the spine, having four "petals." On these Petals are various Sanscrit letters. It is in this Center that *Kundalini* sleeps, until aroused.*

The second Chakra is known as *Svadisthana;* it is situated at the base of the sexual organ; it has six petals, and is blood-red.

The third Chakra is the *Manipura,* just below the Solar Plexus; it is of a golden color, and has ten petals. It is said to be "lustrous like a gem," and is the Seat of the "Lord of Fire."

The fourth Center is the *Anahata* Chakra, which is situated in the heart. It is blood-red, has twelve petals, and is the Seat of the Prana. The Yogis have a saying that "He who has awakened this Chakra can walk in the air"—that is, he experiences levitation. The mystics are supposed to have unconsciously aroused this Center; hence their ability to levitate. It is in the *Anahata* Chakra that the "Sound" is heard—the Pulse of Life. In this Center is the "Tree which grants all desires," and beneath it the "Jewelled Altar." This Chakra is the critical point in Yoga development.

The fifth Chakra is *Vishuddha.* This is situated in the throat, just below the larynx; it is of a golden

---

*A great deal of symbolism must be understood to exist in all this. There are not, of course, any actual Sanscrit letters on the Petals, because there are no physical Petals either. The vital Centers have been likened to lotuses—hence the number of Petals said to exist. They are doubtless thought to correspond to vital radiating-points. In all that follows, the reader must remember that these Centers are thought to correspond more to vitality or energy than to any definite anatomical structure.

color, has sixteen Petals, and is the Seat of the *Akasa Tattva* (Ether). In *Vishuddha* is the Moon, "the Gateway of the Great Liberation." Here, it is said, "the three forms of time" are perceived.

The sixth Chakra is *Ajna,* which is situated between the eyebrows. This has a connection with the Pineal Gland; it has two Petals, and is said to possess three Mystical Principles.

The seventh Chakra is *Sahasrara,* known as the sacred thousand-petaled lotus. It is situated at the top of the head, and is white-gold in color. Herein is achieved the "Great Bliss." Herein is the Supreme Light—the ultimate goal of Yoga.

Now, it must not be thought that these various Centers actually reside *in* the organs or parts of the body mentioned. They correspond to such organs or parts, but are actually *in* the spine—to the extent that they can be said to be *in* space at all. Up the center of the spine is said to be a hollow tube, the *Sushumna,* and up this the *Kundalini* passes. In its path are the various *Chakras.* On either side of the *Sushumna* are two other passages, *Ida* and *Pingala,* into the functionings of which we have not space to enter now.

Doubtless, the Allegory of Eve and the Serpent, the Tree of Life, etc., originated in this conception of the Hindus; for here we have the Serpent Power—*Kundalini,* and the various psychic powers (knowledge) which may produce disastrous results by reason of their premature awakening.

As one is practicing *pranayma,* and the necessary concentration, in order to arouse *Kundalini,* certain forces will begin to develop—certain phenomena will be observed. One of them is a peculiar internal sound;

this is known as the "Voice of the Nada." This is heard internally; it is the so-called "Soundless Sound," "The Voice of the Silence," etc., of which so much has been written. Various preliminary sounds are heard first of all: a nightingale, a cymbal, rushing waters, a flute, a trumpet-blast, thunder, etc., until finally all these die away, and the Silence reigns supreme. These sounds are doubtless associated with physiological phenomena, connected with the deep breathing exercises. Many other phenomena may also be noted in the various stages, which have been discussed in detail by numerous authorities upon Yoga.

Such, in briefest outline, is this system of training. It will be seen that it is at once systematic, clear, concise. It begins with the body and ends with the highest psychic and spiritual powers. Most of the development is inner; exterior manifestations are purely incidental. Thus, true Yoga has no connection with the feats of Fakirs, who torture their bodies, hold aloft their arms until they wither, etc. The true Yogi is one who maintains his body in perfect health and beauty; he does not despise it, for he realizes that upon it his powers largely depend. But it is completely subjected to the dictates of the Will. It is the slave, and not the master. By these means perfection is ultimately attained. . . .

Such is the system formulated by Patanjali, several hundreds of years B.C.—a system which has counted thousands of adherents, and has produced some of the most noted saints of India.

. . . . . . .

In this teaching, and the psychic phenomena which are said to result in consequence, there is assuredly a field for profound study. Various attempts have been made of late to correlate these teachings with normal anatomy and physiology; to discover the physical bases of the Kundali Yoga. In a work entitled *The Mysterious Kundalini,* Dr. Vasant G. Rele—amplifying a paper read before the Bombay Medical Union in July, 1926—attempted to show that the various *Chakras* correspond to the important plexuses in the body, and that *Kundalini* typifies the function of the right vagus nerve. With this conception Sir John Woodroffe ("Arthur Avalon"), who writes a Foreword to the book, cannot agree. He contends that it represents some superphysical force or power—which is, of course, the view taken by the Yogis themselves. However, the attempt to bring the phenomena of Kundali Yoga within the realm of orthodox science is an interesting step in the right direction, and a sign of the times. And Dr. Rele's further contention—that many of these phenomena are due to bringing under conscious control processes and functions normally unconscious— is a real contribution to the subject, and one which should be followed up by open-minded physiologists. Mrs. Alice Bailey, in her book *The Soul and its Mechanism,* has also attempted to show the relationship between the *Chakras* and the main nervous plexuses in the body, and the ductless glands.

For further information upon this interesting subject, the reader may be referred to the writings of Swamis Vivekananda and Abhedananda; Geraldine Coster's *Yoga and Western Psychology;* Felix Guyot's *Yoga for the West;* my own *Higher Psychical Development;* Dr. Evans-Wentz's *Tibetan Yoga and Secret Doctrines,* and Arthur Avalon's great work *The Serpent Power;* etc.

# PART II
## Psychic Phenomena Among Primitive Peoples

# Psychic Phenomena Among Primitive Peoples

*A Résumé of the Evidence for Genuine Psychic Man-
ifestations in Africa, India, China and the
Islands of the Eastern and Western
Hemispheres*

## Introductory

FEW modern students of these problems, who have
made a really careful, first-hand investigation of the
evidence, would doubt that genuine psychic phenomena
*occur,* that both mental and physical manifestations of
a supernormal character actually have been observed
and recorded. Scattered throughout the pages of history, they are as plentiful today as ever, despite the
mechanistic philosophy behind modern science which
is more or less directly opposed to such happenings. In
the great centers of our civilization, in London, New
York, Paris, Berlin, in our own critical and skeptical
age, these phenomena are now being observed, and are
being studied more intensively than ever, by the aid of
instrumental checks and psychological analysis. And if
this be true, if such manifestations actually occur, is it
not highly probable that similar phenomena have likewise occurred in so-called uncivilized countries, and
that many such instances might be noted among these
more primitive peoples, if pains were taken to observe
and record them impartially and accurately? We know
that many such accounts are to be found in the books
of explorers, who often "went to scoff and remained to

pray." Is there any valid reason for disregarding this evidence, merely because the alleged facts were noted in some far-off land and among primitive peoples? The uniformity of these accounts, and the apparent similarity of many of the phenomena to those observed in our very midst should at least give us pause, and make us wonder whether there must not be some fire where there is so much smoke.

As Mr. Andrew Lang remarked in an article on "Ancient Spiritualism" many years ago:

"Is it not stretching probability almost beyond what it will bear, to allege that all the phenomena, in the Arctic circle as in Australia, in ancient Alexandria as in modern London, are, always, the result of an imposture modeled on savage ideas of the supernatural? If so we are reduced to the choice between actual objective facts of unknown origin (frequently counterfeited of course) and collective hallucinations in given conditions. On either hypothesis the topic is certainly not without interest for the student of human nature. Even if we could, at most, establish the fact that people like Iamblichus, Mr. Crookes, Lord Crawford, Jesuits in Canada, professional conjurors in Zululand, Spaniards in early Peru, Australian blacks, Maoris, Eskimo, cardinals, ambassadors, are similarly hallucinated, as they declare, in the presence of priests, diviners, Home, Zulu magicians, Biraarks, Jossakeeds, *angakut, tohungas,* and saints, and Mr. Stainton Moses, still the identity of the false impressions is a topic for psychological study. Or, if we disbelieve this cloud of witnesses, if they voluntarily fabled, we ask, why do they all fable in exactly the same fashion? Even setting aside the animistic hypothesis, the subject is full of curious neglected problems."

Such is undoubtedly the case! And it is also true that many of these native rites and ceremonies are rapidly disappearing before the march of modern civilization, so that, unless they are studied soon, the opportunity to study them will have gone forever. As savages cease to be savages, our opportunities for learning their mystic lore must decrease. I have often thought what a wonderful experience it would be to organize an expedition to travel round the world, and study these native magicians, rain-makers, voodoo doctors and wizards in their native haunts, making notes, photographs and motion pictures of their magical ceremonies in actual operation! The resulting material would assuredly be of great value, scientifically, and also from the purely historic point-of-view. Perhaps, some day, such an expedition will be organized.

Meanwhile, it is admittedly difficult to obtain first-hand, accurate accounts of such happenings, partly because white men are seldom admitted to these ceremonies, and partly because they do not bother themselves to investigate the accounts which they do hear, being content, as a rule, to set down all such stories as mere superstition on the part of the natives. Then, too, there is the natural shrinking from appearing credulous and ridiculous in the eyes of one's fellows, so that it is more than probable that for every account which has been published there are a hundred which have been observed and secretly believed in by visiting Europeans. However, many such accounts *have* been published, and a number of these will be cited presently.

A few preliminary words may not be out of place, however, regarding the inherent difficulties often involved in securing such evidence, and the even greater difficulty in sifting and analyzing it, once secured. For, even assuming that genuine psychic phenomena may at times occur, it is also true that savage peoples are extraordinarily credulous, superstitious, and inclined to attribute any unusual natural happening to the agency of spirits, ghosts, gods or demons. They are often fear-ridden, priest-ridden and full believers in the most preposterous legends and traditions. All this must be taken into account in estimating the evidence. The line of demarcation is a most difficult one, and can only be drawn in a most tentative and uncertain manner. Reports which might call for serious consideration, if given by white men, must often be discredited entirely when given by credulous savages. At the same time, there is no reason to disbelieve them *a priori,* as many seem to think. They should be investigated impartially. And when that is done, it is often found that they rest upon a substantial foundation of fact. This has often been verified by open-minded investigators. Thus, there is no doubt that the American negro is extremely superstitious; he is also very psychic. It becomes our task to sift the wheat from the chaff. Our closest analogy probably lies in the phenomena of Witchcraft, which were reported in civilized communities, in relatively modern times, and at the same time in a highly uncritical and superstitious age. An impartial survey of the evidence might permit us to conclude that, while the vast bulk of the material can be accounted for by modern psychopathology and abnormal psychology, there nevertheless remains an inexplicable residuum, which seems to indicate very strongly the existence of genuine psychic phenomena; and I may add that this was the conclusion arrived at by Mr. Edmund Gurney, after perusing more than two hundred and sixty books on the subject, as he states in his celebrated "Note on Witchcraft," published in *Phantasms of the Living*, Vol. I, pp. 172-85. Here he said:

"The part of the case for witchcraft which is now an exploded superstition had never, even in its own day, any real evidential foundation; while the part which had a real foundation is now more firmly established than ever."

It is my belief that a very similar state of affairs will be found to exist with regard to psychic phenomena among primitive peoples.

Before entering into a summary of the available evidence, however, one or two further remarks are necessitated as to the character of the material itself. It is not my province to discuss in this paper any of the actual *beliefs* of primitives, such as their ideas of the soul, of a future life, demonology, etc. That would in itself necessitate an enormous treatise, and the subject has been ably covered by anthropologists before. Authorities such as Frazer may be consulted in this connection. Nor shall I attempt any outline of their various religious philosophies, their secret organizations nor the various schools of Occult training which flow from them as a natural consequence. Thus, in China we find the Golden Orchid Society, the Heaven-and-Earth Society, etc., which—while they are partly Masonic and Occult in character—are also largely political organizations. In Africa, the system of magic, demonology and witchcraft is extremely complicated, and the same may be said of the various islands scattered throughout the Indian and Pacific oceans. In Africa and among the natives of Haiti Voodoo is very prevalent—of which more later. In India there are three or four distinct categories of occult exponents, and a word or two may not be out of place with regard to these, as there seems to be so much confusion in the public mind with regard to them, jumbling them all together in one common class, whereas they are in reality quite distinct. We have in the first place three kinds of Fakirs: The first are little more than beggars who sit by the wayside and are fed by the credulous populace; the second torture their own bodies, lie upon beds of spikes, hold their arms aloft until they become withered, permit themselves to be buried alive while in a state of catalepsy, etc. The third are the traveling conjurers or magicians, who perform various tricks such as the mango tree trick, the basket trick, the rope trick, snake charming, and so forth. Lastly, we have the Yogis or holy men who are genuine ascetics and hard to approach. They are exponents of one of the various Yoga systems, prevalent in India, the object of which is to arouse latent psychic powers and ultimately to attain Cosmic Consciousness. The methods by which this is to be accomplished are detailed, complicated and laborious. For those who may be interested, I may perhaps state that I have given an epitome of this system in my *Higher Psychical Development,* while the various tricks of the Hindu Fakirs are explained in my little book on *Hindu Magic.* The feats of the Egyptian Fakirs are very similar, and it may be said that their control of the functions of the body is genuine and very remarkable, while the state of catalepsy (in which they are buried alive) is also real and worthy of prolonged physiological investigation. I have had the opportunity of studying several of these Fakirs at close range, and over considerable periods of time, and feel assured that the state of self-imposed catalepsy is a genuine and very extraordinary one. (See *The Story of Psychic Science*, pp.183-91.)

All these systems, however, are peculiar to the peoples involved, and would require extensive treatment in themselves. As before stated, it is not the province of this book to deal with these questions at length (though it would be improper to avoid mentioning them) but rather with instances of telepathy, clairvoyance, premonition, etc., which bear close analogy to similar cases reported and published by the various Societies for Psychical Research. We may then be in a better position to judge their points of similarity and their possible differences. These cases are all summarized or quoted from various sources, and in every instance seem to rest upon respectable authority. Confirmatory evidence is given wherever possible.

### Telepathy and Clairvoyance

Let us first of all consider certain cases of apparent telepathy and clairvoyance which have been reported, placing these together, because it is often difficult to distinguish them, owing to the nature of the accounts themselves. Indeed, it has often been found difficult even in new and well-attested cases, occurring in our midst, which are of visual or pictographic character, and Mr. Gurney, as we know, was often forced to speak of "telepathic clairvoyance," while as shrewd a critic of the evidence as Mr. Theodore Besterman came to the conclusion that much of the material commonly classed as telepathic may be in reality clairvoyant in character. These occurrences may all be distinguished, however, from prophetic or premonitory cases, on the one hand, and apparitional cases, on the other, while the mediumistic phenomena constitute a class in themselves. We may accordingly consider them somewhat in that order.

By way of introduction, I may perhaps quote a few sentences from an article by J. Shepley Part, M.D., Late Assistant to the Gold Coast Colony, who, in an article entitled "A Few Notes on Occultism in West Africa," says:

"When I first went to Africa, few men probably were more skeptical on such subjects as clairvoyance, apparitions and the so-called supernatural generally; I had of course heard the popular smatterings of these things and, when I did, had, in the usual style, put all down to fiction, over-excited brain, suggestion or auto-suggestion and the like. I hope to advance some evidence . . . that phenomena do at times occur that are not explainable by ordinary scientific methods, and that certain men can avail themselves of forces which are beyond the ken of the ordinary individual. It is certain that when I was first brought into contact with such things I was incredulous, and, as a consequence, put them on one side for a considerable time as not worth investigation—much to my subsequent regret. . . .

"I have repeatedly been told by well-educated and broadminded natives (and such do exist) that it is possible for certain trained individuals to 'project their consciousness' to a distance irrespective of time and space, and to do so while retaining a continuity of consciousness with that in their ordinary condition. We also hear the fact stated in this way: that the individual has the power to go to any place without regard to time or distance, etc., and it is not an uncommon remark to hear that so-and-so has been to such-and-such a place 'during the night,' or 'yesterday afternoon,' or 'this morning,' such journey being out of all possibility by ordinary means. . . .

"Towards the end of the last Ashantee expedition I happened to be stationed on the coast at the termination of the *shortest* route from Kumassi to the coast. A day *before* the expected entry of the expedition into Kumassi, I was informed by my boy that the Governor had entered the town at noon (this was about 1.30). About an hour later I was told the same thing in the town by an old chief, an educated man, who, when I laughed at it, remarked that native means of communication were much more rapid than ours. I may mention that the upper portion of the line was in charge of the Royal Engineers, and the coast lines under reserve for Government wires only. The news was confirmed the following evening by official wire. The head of the military wire was some 30 to 36 hours distance from Kumassi, so this excludes irresponsible chattering by the operators. As to runners, we were five days at the *shortest* for special runners from the front. The route is entirely through forest country, and, in regard to water transit of sound from drums, there is no direct access to the coast from Kumassi by water. . . . With regard to the means by which these phenomena are obtained—these are secret, and their professors are members of a secret society. But I was informed on good authority that the process gone through to obtain the power of clairvoyance as exemplified above is purely physical, and requires—when the means have been taught—but constant practice to bring the several stages to perfection, but that special means are used in each stage, initiation being necessary to each stage of development, and then only on approval of the chiefs of the order, which is very stringently guarded. Only a very few are initiated into the highest development.

"The stages may be divided as under:

"1. Simple clairvoyance.

"2. The paying of 'astral visits' or projection of the consciousness only.

"3. The same as 2, with power to materialize the entity projected or . . . to affect material objects. . . . In conclusion, I can only reiterate that, as to ways and means in detail, I am in the dark. . . ."

The first case is taken from Mr. R. W. Felkin's book *From Khartoum to the Source of the Nile.* He writes:

"I had not received any letters from Europe for a year, and was of course very anxious to get some. I knew quite well that a good many must be waiting for me somewhere, but it was hardly likely that they would come to hand for some time, because the Nile was blocked by the floating islands of grass. One morning, however, a man came into our tent in a state of great excitement. The local *m'logo,* or wizard, he said, had been roaming up the country the night before in the form of a jackal. He had, the messenger went on, visited a place called *Meschera-er-Rek* (which was some 550 miles distant from Lado, our camping place) and had seen two steamers, one of them with mails for our party. Also, the steamers were commanded by a white pasha, who was minutely described. Now, in the ordinary course of nature the man could not possibly have covered so vast a stretch of country in one night nor even in twenty nights. I ridiculed the whole thing as absolutely absurd. We were having our coffee at the time, and Emin seemed inclined to give credence to the story, for he suddenly rose up and said he would have the man brought before him. In due time the wizard ... was marched into our tent, and Emin at once addressed him in Arabic saying, 'Where did you go last night?'

" 'I was at Meschera-er-Rek,' he replied in the same tongue.

" 'What were you doing there?'

" 'I went to see some friends.'

" 'What did you see?'

" 'I saw two steamers arriving from Khartoum.'

" 'Oh, this is nonsense! You could not possibly have been at Meschera-er-Rek last night.'

" 'I *was* there,' came the tacit rejoinder, 'and with the steamer was an Englishman—a short man with a big beard.'

" 'Well, what was he doing—what was his mission?'

" 'He says that the great Pasha at Khartoum has sent him, and he has got some papers for you. He is starting overland tomorrow to come to you, bringing the papers with him, and he will be here about thirty days from now.'

"As a matter of fact ... the *m'logo's* statement

proved absolutely correct. In thirty-two days an Englishman *did* arrive in our camp, bringing letters for us from Khartoum. More than this, we knew from the wizard's description that Lupton Bey, and none other, was the man who was coming."

The next case was reported by Mr. David Leslie, S.A., a well-known hunter and explorer, to Cyril Campbell, former war correspondent of the London *Times* during the Balkan troubles. Mr. Leslie says:

"I had sent out my native elephant hunters with instructions to meet me on a certain date at a selected spot. I arrived there at the appointed time; but none of my hunters had put in an appearance. Having nothing much to do, I went to a native doctor who had a great reputation, just to amuse myself and see what the man would say. At first the doctor refused to tell anything because, he said, he had no knowledge of white men's affairs. At last he consented and said he would 'open the gate of distance and would travel through it,' even though it would cost him his life. He then demanded the names and number of the hunters. I demurred at first but finally did as he requested. The doctor then made eight fires, one for each hunter, and cast into them roots which burned with a sickly-smelling smoke. The man took some medicine and fell into a trance for about ten minutes, his limbs moving all the time. When he came round from the trance, he raked out the ashes of his first fire, and described the appearance of the man represented by it, and said 'This man has died of fever and his gun is lost.' He then said the second hunter had killed four elephants, and described the shape and size of the tusks. He said the next had been killed by an elephant, but that the gun was coming home all right. Then he described the appearance and fortunes of the next, adding that the survivors would not be home for three months, and would travel by a route different from that agreed upon. The affair turned out correct in every particular, and, as the hunters were scattered over a country over two hundred miles away, the man could hardly have obtained news of them from other natives. Nor did the diviner know that he was going to be consulted. . . ."

Here is another example of native clairvoyance.*

"An English wild-rubber buyer lost a dispatch box, containing business papers of great importance. It disappeared in the course of a day's march. The trader made inquiries, searched the trail, but found nothing. The box had evidently been stolen. At the sea-port he confided in an English friend and he suggested consulting a witch-doctor. The magician was produced: he was taken to the district where he placed the palms of his hands over the boy's eyes. Both stood up. The witch doctor lifted a hot pot and placed it on the subject's head. Neither seemed to feel the heat—apparently sufficient to sear flesh. The old man then proceeded to grip the boy's hands firmly over the pot's rim, then smear his face with the simmering mixture. It cooled and hardened, and apparently closed the boy's eyes, nostrils and mouth. No breathing was discernible. The old man began to talk, the youth to sway. No one understood his words, which were uttered with emo-

* *Occult Review,* March, 1909.

tional enthusiasm. A final shout and the boy suddenly became alive, ran three times round the ring, and brought the pot down on the head of an inconspicuous negro in the crowd. The victim fell moaning; the pot-bearer started running to the near-by woods, followed by all. He stumbled, fell head-long, tore his skin on briars, careened against tree trunks, but kept on. For three hours he ran. At last, still in a state of trance, and faint from exhaustion, he fell prostrate over a log at the edge of the swamp, and did not get up. Under his head, half buried in the mud, was the dispatch box. ... Thief, witch-doctor and boy all denied collusion. To the Englishman's queries, he replied with the empty word he had learned from the white men—magic!"

Under the title of "Extraordinary News Transference," Mr. R. M. Bloch records the following experience which occurred in his own life (*Occult Review,* December, 1918):

"Some years ago I was up in the interior of Ashanti, a goodish distance from civilization, as represented even by a stray magistrate. On the Monday evening I and my partner had a difference of opinion, and we agreed to part, so next morning I made tracks for Cape Coast Castle, about 150 miles distant. Now, with the exception of Government runners, a white man, traveling light, i.e., without much baggage or a hammock, covers the ground considerably faster than any native, and I got down to the little town shortly after Saturday noon. I dropped into the first store and had a drink, when to my surprise the man in charge remarked, 'Sorry to hear your partner pegged out.' I replied it was nonsense, since I had left him only five days before perfectly fit, but the store-keeper assured me the news had come through on the Thursday evening, X having died the day before. And within a week his boys struggled down with his kit.

"The amazing part of this case is the fact of the news coming down to the coast, without filtering through to the boys who accompanied me, for, had they known it, they would infallibly have told me, and I naturally would have turned back. This obviously precludes the possibility of runners carrying the news, while even if we postulate drums or other forms of signaling, it seems strange that I should only hear of the tragedy at the end of the journey, and not at any of the intermediate villages where I stopped the night. ... I am at a loss to explain the incident."

The following are two or three instances of the same character which were investigated by Mr. Blackburn of Johannesburg, and sent to the same periodical. While I can see no reason for doubting the sincerity or accuracy of any of these accounts, they are perhaps less-well evidenced, and I shall accordingly be content to summarize them briefly:

1. A magistrate at King Williamstown during the border wars stated that one day the son of the chief we were fighting against came into court with his head shaved. (This native was a clerk in the office.) The magistrate quickly recognized the sign of mourning, and asked what relation was dead. The youth stated his father had at last been killed in the war, and even mentioned the spot where the body was lying. The magistrate thought the whole thing strange, for he had heard

nothing by telegraph: but soon after, a telegram came, giving details of the news, which fitted in with the description given by the native.

2. At 9 A.M. on a Monday, a Kafir herd-boy was attacked by a bull. He defended himself with a crowbar. Kafir and bull were dead by 10 A.M. At 12 the same day B, a farmer residing forty-two miles from the scene of the tragedy, appended this postscript to a business letter: "My Kafirs are saying your herd-boy stabbed your red Devon bull with a long knife and that both are dead. Hope it is only a Kafir yarn." The letter was dispatched by mounted messenger before 12.30 the same day.

3. A Kafir was being tried for manslaughter at Johannesburg. At 5 in the afternoon an old Kafir woman on a Boer's farm thirty-eight miles from Johannesburg stated that the boy had been acquitted, and that the principal witness against him had been taken to prison. As the Kafir had pleaded guilty at the preliminary hearing, and was to be undefended, this result seemed extremely improbable. Later it was learned that the Kafir was given counsel at the last moment, the plea of guilty withdrawn, and he was acquitted at 3.15 P.M. At 4 that afternoon the principal witness was knocked down by a cab in the street, and taken to the jail hospital, where he died. In each of these cases the accurate news traveled in less than half the time that would have been required by the fastest horse. Mr. Blackburn sums up as follows:

"That news is sometimes transmitted under conditions unknown to Europeans is, I am satisfied, a fact; but the explanation lies neither in the legs of a horse nor the lungs of a Kafir."

What is meant by the last remark is simply this. One of the "explanations" commonly advanced for cases of this type is that a native stands upon some hill-top and shouts aloud the news to a native upon the next hill-top, and so on over a great stretch of country. That natives can convey information over great distances in this way is undoubtedly true, and in times of great national excitement might well be the case. But such a system would require a pre-arranged chain of receivers, alert and ready, and to assume that such a chain exists for the transmission of trivial and unexpected incidents seems far-fetched indeed. Furthermore, the nature of the country itself often prevents any such system from operating; for example, the intervention of dense forest, etc. This explanation must be very limited in its scope. Normal methods of news-transmission, by men afoot or on horseback, have frequently been excluded, and their possibility denied by numerous careful investigators.

Doubtless, one of the commonest forms of news-transmission, and one of the most difficult to eliminate effectually, is that of signaling by means of drums or columns of smoke. It is well known that such means are frequently employed. However, experienced colonials assert that this is limited, almost exclusively, to matters of importance, such as native unrest or the passage of a white man through the country. To assume that, e.g., the news that a Kafir herd-boy had been hurt by a bull should have been transmitted in this manner seems incredible indeed, for such an event must be a common occurrence in that country. Further, details are often given which no amount of signaling could satisfactorily account for—such as the personal appearance of a man, what he was doing at the time, in what position his body was lying, etc. Such details would hardly be transmitted over hundreds of miles, since they would doubtless be considered of no consequence by the natives themselves. Finally, we have the specific assurance, in many cases, that no drums were available—as in the above instance of the lost elephant hunters. Doubtless, news is occasionally transmitted by this means, but to attempt to account for many of the recorded incidents, with all their details, by means of smoke columns, tom-toms, etc., seems little short of preposterous, and is an example of the lengths to which skeptics will go before admitting the possibility of some genuine telepathic faculty which may be evidenced at such times. That some sixth sense is employed by the natives, upon occasion, seems beyond reasonable doubt; and this is, indeed, their own explanation of such matters. They call this sixth sense "The Ear of the Great Mother."

Let us not wander too far afield, however, in theory, but rather continue our narration of specific instances. We shall come to explanations, and their own formulæ, later on.

Mr. Carveth Wells (in his *Six Years in the Malay Jungle,* pp. 205-6) has narrated an interesting case of experimental clairvoyance, in which he tested a native magician, Tok Sami, who accurately divined for him the colors of dice contained within a brass box—not once, but several times; and repeated the same feat for his wife some months later.

From Africa and Malay we turn to North America, and find similar incidents narrated about the American Indians. The following account, for example, is given by General Browne, of the U.S. Army, being originally published by him in the *Atlantic Monthly*, xviii, pp. 118 seq. (See also D. G. Brinton, *The Myths of the New World*, p. 270.)

"The medicine-man whom I knew best," says General Browne, "was Ma-qué-a-pos (the Wolf's Word), an ignorant and unintellectual person. I knew him perfectly well. His nature was simple, innocent, and harmless, devoid of cunning, and wanting in those fierce traits that make up the Indian character. His predictions were sometimes absolutely astounding.... On one occasion a party of voyageurs set out from Fort Benton, the remotest post of the American Fur Company, for the purpose of finding the Kaine, or Blood Band of the northern Blackfeet. Their route lay almost due north, crossing the British line near the Chief Mountain and the great lake Omax-een.... The expedition was perilous in its commencement, and the danger increased with each day's journey.... The party of adventurers soon found that they were in the thickest of the Cree war-party operations, and so full of danger was every day's travel that a council was called, and seven of the ten turned back....

"On the afternoon of the last day, four young Indians were seen who, after a cautious approach, made the sign of peace, laid down their arms, and came forward, announcing themselves to be Blackfeet of the Blood Band. They were sent out, they said, by Ma-qué-a-pos, to find three whites mounted on horses of a peculiar color, dressed in garments accurately described to them, and armed with weapons which they, without seeing them, minutely described. The whole history of the expedition had been detailed to them by Ma-qué-a-pos. The purpose of the journey, the *personnel* of the party, the exact locality at which to find the three who persevered, had been detailed by him with as much fidelity as could have been done by one of the whites themselves. And so convinced were the Indians of the truth of the old man's 'medicine,' that the four young men were sent to appoint a rendezvous, for four days later, at a spot a hundred miles distant. On arriving there, accompanied by the young Indians, the whites found the entire camp of Rising Head, a noted war chief awaiting them. The objects of the expedition were speedily accomplished, and the whites, after a few days' rest, returned to safer haunts. The writer of this paper was at the head of the party of whites, and himself met the Indian messengers.

"Upon questioning the chief men of the Indian camp, many of whom afterwards became my warm personal friends, and one of them my adopted brother, no suspicion of the facts, as narrated, could be sustained. Ma-qué-a-pos could give no explanation beyond the general one—that he 'saw us coming, and heard us talk on our journey.' He had not, during that time, been absent from the Indian camp.

"A subsequent intimate acquaintance with Ma-qué-a-pos disclosed a remarkable 'medicine' faculty as accurate as it was inexplicable. He was tested in every way and almost always stood the test successfully. Yet he never claimed that the gift entitled him to any particular regard, except as the instrument of a power he did not pretend to understand...."

Under the heading of "Savage Telepathy," an interesting case was published in the *Journal* S.P.R., January, 1926. It was reported by Commander R. Jukes Hughes, R.N., through Mr. Theodore Besterman. Commander Hughes says:

"In the year 1878, I happened to be serving under a Govt. Commission in the Transkei (S.A.). Our Chief was Col. J. T. Eustace, R.M., with Kreli the Chief of the Gealakas, and the third member was Capt. T. Sansom. At the time I am writing of, our work was near the right bank of the Bashee River.... The Geaike-Gealaka war was recently over and the Transkei was absolutely clear of natives. The Commission employed about a dozen natives, but their work for the same kept them from roaming the country.

"One day they came to us rather excited and announced that there had been a great disaster in Zululand, that our troops had been overwhelmed by the Zulus, who were pouring into Natal. We had an immediate consultation as to what we should do, as if the rumor was correct it was possible that a general rising of all the Kafirs west of the Tugela River would take place, in which case we should have to scuttle for the Old Colony with our horses and leave the wagons to their fate; but within a few hours we had further news through the same agency, stating that the strain had been relieved—this was the result of the noble stand made by the handful of troops at Rorke's Drift.

"News of the disaster did not reach us officially until two days after the event.

"We were roughly speaking some 300 miles (as the crow flies) from the scene of the disaster, with some very rough country between, including several rivers. For some years I lived under canvas in those parts, so had a fair knowledge of the difficulties of travel."

In reply to further questions, Commander Hughes states:

"The events occurring in Zululand were reported to us within an hour or so, if not quicker, of their occurrence.... In my opinion it was absolutely impossible for natives to have obtained the information by normal means, certainly not by water communication."

In his "International Notes," (*Journal,* A.S.P.R., April, 1926, pp. 233-36), Mr. Harry Price quoted an interesting article by General Sir James Willcocks entitled "Second Sight in the East," which appeared originally in the London *Evening News,* in which several cases are given of apparent clairvoyance. In one of these, a child was saved from premature burial by the advice of a Brahmin; in another a lost article was found, while the third is an example of the seeming glamour cast over spectators by the visiting Yogi.

This last instance is of particular interest because of its possible bearing upon one of the best-known and most-disputed feats performed by Oriental Fakirs: I refer to the celebrated "Rope Trick," in which a rope is thrown into the air, a boy climbs up and is lost to view, and (in some of the more dramatic versions) his limbs and trunk fall to earth, where they piece themselves together again, leaving him as smiling and happy as before! There seems to be hardly an individual who does not know this story, and narrate it with great gusto (however skeptical he may be otherwise) together with the still more incredible sequel, that a camera failed to record anything of the sort, when its exposed plates were developed! *Ergo,* the spectators were hallucinated!

Now, a number of investigators have tried in vain to see this performance, or even to obtain some first-hand evidence from those who claimed to have seen it, but always without success. My own father (who was quite interested in such things) lived for ten years in India, but while he saw the stock feats many times, he was never enabled to see the famous rope exploit, or to discover any one who had seen it. This, I may add, is the opinion of many competent observers, such as Kellar, Thurston, Bertram, Seeman, Major Branson, Dr. Richard Hodgson, and others. Hodgson, in his paper on "Indian Magic and the Testimony of Conjurers," traced back this story to the fourteenth century, and it has been repeated by many others since. The theory usually advanced is that the spectators were in some way hypnotized by the Fakir, and that what they thought they saw was merely the product of their own imagination. There is, however, scant evidence that collective or mass hypnotism of this sort is practicable; there is no analogy in the annals of hypnotism which would entitle us to believe such a thing possible. On the contrary, there are many indications that the traditional story is merely a yarn—such as the fact that some of the "photographs" which were published in support of the story turned out, upon investigation, to be woodcuts!

Since the above was written, however, it is only fair to say that one form of this famous exploit has been seen and photographed by Mr. Harry Price, and he has given us the details, together with an excellent photograph, in his book *Confessions of a Ghost Hunter,* pp. 344-54. The performer in this case, Karachi, was assisted by his son Kyder, and the demonstration was given in a large field at Wheathampstead, England, in January, 1935. A number of well-known persons witnessed the feat, in which a rope, about eight feet in length, apparently ascended of its own volition skyward, and was climbed by the magician's son, who was photographed in the act of doing so! To be sure, this was not the *traditional* rope trick, but it represented the nearest approach to it which has been seen under what might be called test conditions. I refer the reader to Mr. Price's interesting account for further details of this historic and fascinating episode. Below is appended a list of the more important references to this feat, in which the reader will find the subject thoroughly discussed.*

It may be thought that I have dwelt at undue length upon this famous rope exploit, but, as I have indicated, it is of extreme importance because it bears upon the question of collective hallucination, a theory which has from time to time been advanced to explain the phenomena observed in the presence of D. D. Home, Eusapia Palladino, and other mediums. From the above

---

*Indian Conjuring,* by Major L. H. Branson; *Around the World with a Magician and a Juggler,* by Baron Hartwig Seeman; *Up and Down and Round About the World,* by Harry Kellar; *Hindu Magic,* by Hereward Carrington; *Hindu Magic,* by Howard Thurston; *The Fraud of Theosophy Exposed,* by John Nevil Maskelyne; *The Confessions of a Ghost Hunter,* by Harry Price; *Indian Magic and the Testimony of Conjurers,* by Dr. Richard Hodgson; *Proceedings* S.P.R., Vol. IX, pp. 354-66; *Journal* S.P.R., Vol. IV, p. 107; V, 80, 84, 195; XIX, 124; XX, 401-2; XXIV, 124, 137-38, 311, 345; XXV, 179-80, etc.

it will be seen that there is little respectable evidence for such extraordinary mass hypnotism, and consequently that the objective character of the observed phenomena in the presence of these mediums receives an added, independent verification. The hallucination theory receives little support from our study of Oriental magic and mystery.

### Cases of Prediction

To return, however, from this digression to our account of apparently genuine psychic experiences among primitive peoples. I may next give a small group of cases of prediction, in which some future event was foretold, or supernormal knowledge was displayed of occurrences about to happen. Several interesting cases of the kind have been published by Mr. Theodore Besterman, in the *Occult Review,* November, 1926, and January, 1927, and I am indebted to him for several valuable references. Also to an article in the same periodical for February, 1923. It is interesting to note that such occurrences are scattered throughout the world—one being reported in Central Africa, another in India, a third in Australia, a fourth in Fiji, and so on. . . . Yet these accounts bear a striking similarity one to another! This only bears out what has been said above regarding the universality of such phenomena. Thus, in the cases which follow, it will be observed that the first is from South Africa, the second from Central Africa, the third from Mesopotamia; while others come to us from New Guinea, Borneo, Sumatra, Java, North America, India, the South Sea Islands, etc. Yet all these cases seem to be indicative of genuine supernormal occurrences of the same general type. Let us first take a case from South Africa.

The Rev. Canon (afterwards Bishop) Callaway, M.D., gives an interesting case in his book *The Religious System of the Amazulu,* thus summarized by Edward Lawrence, F.R.A.I.

A number of natives having a quarrel with their own tribe on the Tukela river settled with a relative among the Amahlongwa, and lived with him as dependents in his village. Soon after settling there, a young child was seized with convulsions, and, thoroughly alarmed at his condition, some young men, cousins of the child, were deputed to consult a "Witch," who divined correctly by the aid of "familiar spirits." After waiting in her hut a long time in dead silence a voice, as of a very little child, was heard, as if proceeding from the roof, and saluted them. Then "the spirits" began by saying: "You have come to inquire about something." The woman said: "Tell them. They say you have come to inquire about something." So they smote the ground in token of assent. The spirits declared that the matter which brought them there was of great importance; an omen had appeared in some one. Smiting the ground once again, the inquirers asked: "How big is the person in whom the omen has appeared?" The spirits answered: "It is a young person." Then the spirits went on to say that the omen was bodily; that the person affected was a boy, that the boy was still young—too young, in fact, to attend to the herds. "There he is, we see him; it is as if he had convulsions." The spirits then went on to detail in a most minute and correct manner the time when the first convulsion took place, and the character of the attack, and what was done and said by the mother and others. They declared the suffering boy was the only child of his father. He was their brother, but really not their brother but their real cousin. The cousins were told to return home and sacrifice a white he-goat and then pour its gall on the invalid, and give him a certain medicine to drink. The lads went home, sacrificed the goat, poured the gall over the child, and gave him the medicine. Dr. Callaway declared: "And the child never had an attack of convulsions after, and is living to this day, a strong, healthy young man." He adds that the wise woman lived a considerable distance from the kraal of those who inquired of her, and they had never seen her before.

Dr. Callaway also instanced the case of a native named Umpengula, who was in service at Pietermaritzburg. He had a dream and in it saw his brother Undayeni, dressed in his finest attire and dancing at a wedding. On awakening he had a strong impression that his brother had died. Unable to shake this impression off, he repeatedly burst into tears, and looked constantly in the direction by which a messenger must come with the news. During the morning the messenger came. On seeing him, he said, "I know why you are come. Undayeni is dead." He was dead!

Sir Harry Johnston, in his work on *British Central Africa,* relates that on one occasion his journey on Lake Nyasa was held up on account of the non-arrival of the steamer. To soothe his anxiety, "Jumbe" of Kotakota—a Coast Arab and Wali, or representative of the Sultan of Zanzibar—sent for his necromancer, who was to ascertain, by means of sand, what the future held in store for him as regards steamer communication. The necromancer informed them that the steamer the *Ilala*, had run aground on the rocks, but that another steamer, called the *Charles Janson*, would shortly call for the great traveler. Sir Harry Johnston states: "This information turned out to be perfectly correct," for eventually the *Charles Janson*, with Archdeacon Maples on board, came to fetch him and convey him on his journey.

The Reverend W. A. Wigram, D.D., lived for ten years with the tribes of Eastern Kurdistan, spoke their language, and understood their traditions and superstitions. From this out-of-the-way corner of the world, from the "Cradle of Mankind," as he called it, he has given us some remarkable illustrations of second sight. He mentions the case of a seer whom his fellow tribesmen consulted on all matters of importance, and who foretold a certain disaster that would befall them in a special raid which they contemplated. "If you go to battle now," said he, "you will flee seven ways before the Mussulmans; and, though you yourself, chief, will be saved by a willow tree, death will be my portion."

The raid took place, the Christians being routed by the Mohammedans and scattered. A random shot put an end to the life of the seer, whom the Kurds intended to spare; the chief himself took to flight, his own life being saved through clinging to a projecting branch of a willow which over-hung the river Zab he was attempting to swim.

Dr. Wigram narrates a still more remarkable case, in which a certain Nwiya, a Prophet, came running to him in the morning, telling him that two expected travelers would arrive that day, coming up a certain valley; that one of them would wear a black hat and the other a white one, and giving other details. That afternoon the two travelers arrived up the valley, one wearing an astrakhan fur cap, the other a sun-helmet. Dr. Wigram concludes: "Any suspicion of confederacy may be ruled out of the question without hesitation, for it was a physical impossibility; and clairvoyance, or some form of thought-transference, seems to be the most natural explanation of so strange a coincidence of statement and fact."

This, indeed, seems the conclusion to which many observers have been forced, after having obtained a first-hand knowledge of the facts. Thus, the late Samuel Pollard, who lived as a missionary among the aborigines of Western China for many years, states that he watched native mediums at work many times, only to be convinced that, in many cases, the phenomena were false and made to order. "But," he continues, "do what you will, you cannot *always* be sure that there is not some real phenomenon here, though you are not so sure that you can explain it."

Again, Mr. Edward Lawrence says (*Open Court,* February, 1919, p. 78):

"Travelers who relate these stories are unable to account for them or find any satisfactory explanation. But coincidences like those narrated continually occur, and make one think that there must exist a side to savage superstition which requires further elucidation, and which the white man has been unable to fathom."

The Reverend C. E. Fox, of San Cristobal, Solomon Islands, asserted that spiritualism in all its forms was much practiced by the natives. All sorts of phenomena—apparently well authenticated—had been reported. Levitation, movements of physical objects without human agency, mysterious lights, second sight, mediums, appearances of burns on a wizard when a brand was thrown at his wraith, ghostly smells and other startling manifestations were declared to have occurred. Mr. Carl Lumholt, M.A., gives an account of a prophecy by a native of Central Mexico, fulfilled four days later; and Mr. Joseph F. Woodroff, who spent eight years in the upper Amazon, narrates another, in which his boat was wrecked, as foretold by a native diviner.

Mr. Grahame Houblon has narrated a psychic incident in Mesopotamia, (*Occult Review*, March, 1925), in which a native named Balloo told him of a battle and who had been killed and injured. The account is, however, second-hand. Mr. Houblon concludes that: "Telepathy . . . would seem to be nature's first contrivance for the exchange of ideas, and what we see of it among civilized humans is an insignificant survival, just as the little tuatera lizard of New Zealand is the insignificant surviving representative of the once omnipresent order of dinosaurs."

### *Apparitions and Haunted Houses*

We now turn to a consideration of a small group of apparitional cases, in which a ghost has been seen under conditions which render ordinary explanations difficult if not impossible. Curious as it may seem, these are apparently the rarest of all—at least I have found it next to impossible to unearth well-authenticated cases. The reason for this is certainly not because of the paucity of material, since ghosts are so frequent among primitive peoples as to be taken almost as a matter-of-course.

However, occurrences of this type may usually be explained as due to hallucination, expectancy, suggestion, etc., and are different from our own well-authenticated cases of veridical apparitions. Coincidental cases of this type are hard to verify, even in our own country, and it is probable that white men have rarely deigned to investigate reported instances of this type, dismissing them off-hand as mere superstitions. Cases of clear-cut prediction are not so easily dismissed, and doubtless made a greater impression upon the white men present at the time. It is probably because of this fact that greater numbers of them are available.

The following account comes to us from New Guinea, giving the writer's experience in a haunted house. It contains several points of unusual interest, particularly the item of the visible foot-prints. The reader will, perhaps, be reminded of a similar incident in Bulwer Lytton's *The House and the Brain*.

Captain A. W. Monckton, F.R.G.S., F.Z.S., tells the following story in his book *Some Experiences of a New Guinea Resident Magistrate* (p. 109). "I tell the story for what it is worth," he writes, "and I leave my readers who are interested in psychical research to form what opinion they choose. All I say is that the story, as narrated, is absolutely true."

The author was staying alone in the house of a man named Moreton, at Samarai, Moreton being elsewhere at the time; he was Resident Magistrate of the Eastern Division.

Captain Monckton tells us that he was sitting, writing, one evening, busily engaged on his work, when he suddenly became aware that the doors leading onto the front and back verandas of the house were both wide open. Almost unconsciously, he got up and closed them. Soon thereafter he heard foot-steps on the coral walk outside, which crossed the palm-floored veranda, and stalked across the room. He glanced up, saw no one, but was so preoccupied that he paid no particular attention to them, thinking it was one of the native servants.

This, however, occurred a second time; the foot-steps first being heard on the walk, then on the veranda, and finally in the room in which he was writing. The steps seemed perfectly solid and natural, and it never occurred to Captain Monckton that they were in any sense supernormal. They squeaked on the palm-floored veranda and resounded on the boards in his room. This time they appeared to pass directly behind his chair.

More alert to the situation, Captain Monckton looked up, and noted with surprise that the doors were again open—the doors he had closed but a few moments before. This time he made *sure* that he shut them securely; nor could he see anything in the room or on the veranda to account for the foot-steps. No one was visible!

Thoroughly interested now, Captain Monckton called the servants, going out onto the porch to do so. While he was there, the foot-steps resounded in the room *behind* him, which was well lighted by the reading lamp. Still nothing visible!

The servants (who had also heard the steps) were told that they must find the intruder, as Captain Monckton did not wish to be disturbed in this manner! They said that they had seen no one but that they would look. Exploration of the house and surrounding grounds failed to disclose any one, or any reason for the disturbances.

A *third* time, the same thing was repeated. Despite the watchers, the foot-steps were heard advancing up the coral walk, across the veranda, and finally across the brilliantly lighted room! The most interesting feature of the case, however, is that, on this third occasion, the depressions made by the "invisible feet" could be distinctly *seen* on the palm-floored veranda, which "gave" slightly, under each step!

Whatever Captain Monckton may have thought, (and he offers no opinion or explanation) he moved to the ship for the night and slept on board. Nothing of the sort ever happened again, and a year later the house was pulled down. Before this, however, the author had sat up in it on purpose, with a man named Armit, Health Officer and Collector of Customs, but the investigation produced no results. Armit, on this occasion, mentioned that Moreton, the former occupant, had once or twice hinted at something queer having happened. Moreton himself was therefore interviewed on the subject. He also admitted hearing foot-steps on former occasions, when he occupied the house.

A somewhat similar case is narrated by Oscar Cook, late District Officer, North Borneo Civil Service, in his enchanting volume, *Borneo: Stealer of Hearts*. Here, also, foot-steps were heard walking about the house, but in this case the phantom was seen independently by two other witnesses—one of whom shot at the figure! No normal explanation was forthcoming.

## Poltergeist Cases

Our next case is a poltergeist, in which *physical* phenomena occurred, similar to our own instances of this type. In poltergeist cases, it will be remembered, bells are rung, crockery broken, objects thrown and moved about by no visible agency, and so on. The number of reported cases of this type is considerable—some of them being quite recent and well-authenticated.* One of the commonest phenomena, in cases of this sort, is the throwing of stones—frequently from outside the house, but often from within it also. This was the type of manifestation in the following case, where the phenomena seem to have been carefully observed at the time of their occurrence. It was reported in the *Journal* S.P.R., May, 1906, being witnessed by an Associate of the Society, Mr. W. G. Grottendieck, in Sumatra. He says:

"It was in September, 1903, that the following abnormal fact occurred to me. Every detail of it has been examined by me very carefully. I had been on a long journey through the jungle of Palembang and Djambi (Sumatra) with a gang of 50 Javanese coolies for exploring purposes. Coming back from the long trip, I found that my house had been occupied by somebody else, and I had to put up my bed in another house that was not yet ready, and had just been erected from wooden poles and *lalang* or *kadjang*. The roof was formed of great dry leaves. . . . I put my bullsack and mosquito curtain on the wooden floor and soon fell asleep. At about 1 o'clock at night I half awoke hearing something fall near my head, outside the mosquito curtain on the floor. After a couple of minutes I completely awoke and turned my head around to see what was

* See, in this connection, *Bulletin* II of The American Psychical Institute, wherein more than 300 such cases are summarized, dating back to the year 530 A.D.

falling down on the floor. They were *black stones* from ⅛ to ¾ of an inch long! I got out of the curtain and turned up the kerosene lamp, that was standing on the floor at the foot of my bed. I saw then that the stones were falling through the roof in a parabolic line. They fell on the floor close to my head-pillow. I went out and awoke the boy, a Malay-Palembang coolie, who was sleeping on the floor in the next room. I told him to go outside and to examine the jungle up to a certain distance. He did so whilst I lighted up the jungle a little by means of a small ever-ready electric lantern. At the same time that my boy was outside the stones did not stop falling. My boy came in again, and I told him to search the kitchen to see if anybody could be there. He went to the kitchen and I went inside the room again, to watch the stones falling down. I knelt down near the head of my bed and tried to catch the stones, while they were falling through the air toward me, but I could never catch them; it seemed to me that they *changed their direction* in the air as soon as I tried to get hold of them. I could not catch any of them before they fell on the floor.... They came right through the *kadjang*, but there were no holes in the *kadjang*. When I tried to catch them there, at the very spot of coming out, I also failed.... I did not notice anything particular about the stones except that they were *warmer* than they would have been under ordinary circumstances.... The next day, when awake again, I found the stones on the floor and everything as I had left it in the night.... Altogether there had been about 18 or 22 stones...."

In reply to questions, Mr. Grottendieck states that, "In the Dutch East Indies this phenomenon seems to happen pretty often; at least every now and then it is reported in the newspapers, generally concerning a house in the city."

Mr. Northcote W. Thomas gives an account of "A Javanese Poltergeist" in the *Occult Review,* for November, 1905; while an Egyptian case is reported in the same periodical, June, 1912.

## MEDIUMISTIC PHENOMENA

### (a). *Physical*

We now come to a group of cases, in which the phenomena were *experimentally induced*—as opposed to the spontaneous phenomena previously recorded. These, therefore, more closely resemble our own séance phenomena observed in the presence of mediums, rather than the sporadic cases reported by individuals, such as apparitions coincidental with death. We may consequently regard these phenomena as similar to those produced by native mediums.

When it comes to the citation of cases of physical phenomena really analogous to those of our Occidental mediums, it must be admitted that such cases are extremely rare. Indeed, I have been enabled to unearth only a few, as the result of a fairly lengthy and laborious research. Magical results, on the one hand, and spontaneous cases, such as poltergeist phenomena, on the other, do not come within this category. One of the most representative accounts is, perhaps, that contained in William Howitt's *History of the Supernatural,* Vol. I, pp. 429-31, where he says:

"The Indians have always been great spiritualists, ghost-seers, table-rappers, and perhaps, too, magnetizers. . . . The lodge which their jossakids or prophets, or, as the Canadians term them, jongleurs, erect for their incantations, is composed of stout posts, connected with basket-work, and covered with birch-bark. It is tall and narrow, and resembles a chimney; it is firmly built, and two men, even if exerting their utmost strength, would be unable to move, shake, or bend it; it is so narrow that a man who crawls in has scarcely room to move about in it.

" 'Thirty years ago,' a gentleman told me who had lived among the Indians, and was even related to them through his wife, 'I was present at the incantation and performance of a jossakid in one of these lodges; I saw the man creep into the hut, which was about ten feet high, after swallowing a mysterious potion made of a root. He immediately began singing and beating the drum in his basket-work chimney. The entire case began gradually trembling and shaking, and oscillating slowly amid great noise. The more the necromancer sang and drummed, the more violent the oscillations of the long case became. It bent backwards and forwards, up and down, like the mast of a vessel caught in a storm and tossed on the waves. I could not understand how these movements could be produced, by a man inside, as we could not have caused them from the exterior. . . .

"The drum ceased and the jossakid yelled that 'the spirits were coming over him.' We then heard through the noise, and crackling, and oscillations of the hut, *two* voices speaking inside, one above, the other below. The lower one asked questions, which the upper one answered. Both voices seemed entirely different, and I believed I could explain this by very clever ventriloquism. . . .

"Thirty years later, the Indian had become a Christian, and was on his death-bed. 'Uncle,' I said to him, recalling that circumstance, 'Uncle, dost thou remember prophesying to us in thy lodge thirty years ago, and astonishing us, not only by thy discourse, but by the movements of thy prophet-lodge?...Now thou art old, and hast become a Christian; thou art sick, and cannot live much longer; tell me, then, how and through what means thou didst deceive us?'

"My sick Indian replied, 'I have become a Christian, I am old, I am sick, I cannot live much longer, and I can do no other than speak the truth. Believe me, I did not deceive you; I did not move the lodge; it was shaken by the power of the spirits. Nor did I speak with a double tongue; I only replied to you what the spirits said to me. I heard their voices. The top of the lodge was full of them, and before me the sky and wide lands lay extended; I could see a great distance round me; and I believed I could recognize the most distant objects.' The old jossakid said this with such an expression of simple truth and firm conviction that it seemed to me, at least, that he did not believe himself a deceiver, but had full faith in the efficacy of his magic arts, and the reality of his visions."

From another part of the world entirely—India—accounts have been published of phenomena very similar to those witnessed in the presence of our own mediums. M. Louis Jacolliot, Chief Justice of Chandarnagar, in his *Occult Science in India* (pp. 199-274), gives an account of a number of curious manifestations produced in his presence by a native medium or Fakir named Covindasamy. Among other phenomena were raps, movements of objects without contact, lights, partial materializations and the levitation of the Fakir himself——on one occasion for eight minutes, as timed by Jacolliot——while the Fakir sat cross-legged on a low stool, both feet being well removed from the floor. All these manifestations were produced in Jacolliot's own home, in fair light. His account of the raps produced is particularly interesting. He says:

"The Fakir was . . . in position with both hands extended towards an immense bronze vase full of water. Within five minutes the vase commenced to rock to and fro upon its base, and approach the Fakir gently and with a regular motion. As the distance diminished, metallic sounds escaped from it, as if some one had struck it with a steel rod. At certain times the blows were so numerous and quick that they produced sound similar to that made by a hail-storm upon a metal roof. . . . At one time, at my command, the blows changed into a continuous roll, like that of a drum; at another, on the contrary, they succeeded each other with the slowness and regularity of the ticking of a clock. . . ."

Compare with this the account of Sir William Crookes (*Researches in Spiritualism*, p. 39):

"Presently percussive sounds were heard on the parchment, resembling the dropping of grains of sand on its surface. . . . At each percussion a fragment of graphite which I had placed on the membrane was seen to be projected upwards about 1-50th of an inch. . . . Sometimes the sounds were as rapid as those of an induction coil, whilst at others they were more than a second apart."

Take again the following account of certain materializations which were observed in Jacolliot's own house—he and the native medium alone being present.

"A slightly phosphorescent cloud seemed to have formed in the middle of my chamber, from which semblances of hands appeared to go and come with great rapidity. In a few minutes, several hands appeared to have lost their vaporous appearance and to resemble human hands; so much so, indeed, that they might readily have been mistaken for the latter. Singular to relate, while some became, as it were, more material, others became more luminous. Some became opaque, and cast a shadow in the light, while others became so transparent that an object behind them could be distinctly seen. I counted as many as sixteen. Asking the Fakir if I could touch them, I had hardly expressed a wish to that effect, when one of them, breaking away from the rest, flew toward me and pressed my outstretched hand. It was small, supple and moist, like the hand of a young woman. . . ."

Compare, again, the account given by Crookes (*ibid.* p. 92):

"The hands and fingers do not always appear to be solid and life-like. Sometimes, indeed, they are more like the appearance of a nebulous cloud partly condensed into the form of a hand. This is not equally visible to all present. For instance, a flower or a small object is seen to move; one person present will see a nebulous-looking hand, whilst others will see nothing at all but the moving flower. I have more than once seen, first an object move, then a luminous cloud appear to form about it, and lastly, the cloud condense into shape and become a perfectly-formed hand. At this stage, the hand is visible to all present. It is not always a mere form, but sometimes appears perfectly life-like and graceful, the fingers moving and the flesh apparently as human as that of any in the room. At the wrist, or arm, it becomes hazy, and fades off into a luminous cloud. To the touch, the hand sometimes appears icy-cold and dead, at other times, warm and life-like, grasping my own with the firm pressure of an old friend. I have retained one of these hands in my own, firmly resolved not to let it escape. There was no struggle or effort made to get loose, but it gradually seemed to resolve itself into vapor, and faded in that manner from my grasp...."

I may perhaps add that I myself have witnessed and experienced similar phenomena in the presence of Eusapia Palladino.

It will be seen, therefore, that there are many striking similarities between these phenomena, witnessed by Jacolliot in India, and those observed by psychical researchers in London and New York. That is one of the interesting and significant points which it is the intention of this chapter to emphasize and bring out more clearly, perhaps, than has been realized in the past.

Dowsing (i.e., water finding by means of the Divining Rod) has been utilized in the Orient for many years, and the Government of Bombay has now appointed an official water-finder, issuing an annual "Report" on his work, which has so far been eminently successful. In the "Report on the Work of the Water

Diviner" it is stated that, of 81 wells which have been sunk, water was found in 79 cases, and that "on 16 additional sites situated in 'precarious tracts,' preliminary bores were sunk. Every bore was successful, eight of them being certified by the engineer of the District Local Board, the others having apparently been made privately...." As Mr. Theodore Besterman says, in commenting upon these facts: "Subject to verification ... the figures given above undoubtedly make a considerable step forward in the regularity and reliability of the dowsing faculty...." (*Journal* S.P.R., July, 1929, pp. 129-30.)

.    .    .    .    .    .    .

Enough examples of various types of psychic phenomena have now been given, perhaps, to emphasize the fact that these are substantially the same all over the world; that, no matter where we may go, we shall find practically identical manifestations being observed and recorded (subject to slight local variations) and that these are more or less identical with those observed in our midst. Mr. Gerald Arundel, it is true, in his article on "Spiritualism in Tropical America," (*Occult Review*, February, 1914), attempted to prove that there are certain differences,—attributing these to the variations of temperature and climate. He says:

"Why is it that the psychic phenomena of the tropics are distinct from those of cold climates? In my opinion, one climate is, generally speaking, more favorable to a particular class of phenomena; and another climate to a different class; that psychic phenomena depend, not only on individual psychic force, not only on temperament, character and certain bodily peculiarities, but in a noticeable degree on locality and climate as well. . . ."

I am unable to discern any essential differences, however, either in the experience he himself relates, or in those of other investigators. On the contrary, I am constantly struck by their great similarity—the slight differences being due, as I have said, to local customs and traditions. We find the same bodily and mental conditions, the same phenomena, the same results, and the same causes. As Mr. Andrew Lang expressed it, in his *Cock Lane and Common Sense* (p. 356):

"All the world over . . . the same persons are credited with the rejected phenomena, clairvoyance, discerning of spirits, powers of voluntary telepathic and telekinetic impact. Thus we find that uniform and recurrent evidence vouches for a mass of phenomena which science scouts. Science has now accepted a portion of the mass but still rejects the stranger occurrences. . . . These facts, at the lowest estimate, must suggest that man may have faculties, and be surrounded by agencies, which physical science does not take into account in its theory of the universe and of human nature."

## (b). Mental

Turning, now, from these physical phenomena to those purely mental or psychic, we find many instances in which supernormal knowledge has apparently been displayed by a native medium, in trance, resembling the communications of our own mediums. Sometimes these are written automatically, in sand; more often they are spoken through the mouth of the entranced medium. Such communications may relate to the sitter's health, to some object he has lost, to some friend or relative, or may represent direct messages from the spirit of the dead man. These communications may be spoken automatically, or may be given by means of the direct voice, as in the instance cited above. The following is typical of the former method.

In the December (1929) number of *The Realist* an article appeared by Mr. B. Malinowski, dealing with psychic phenomena in the South Sea Islands. He says:

"The distance between living men and ghosts is not so great in Melanesia. To the Trobriand Islander the spirit world is quite near at hand.... I was interested to know in what form the medium was transported to the spirit world. I received the following answer: '*T-yoseuo*, the fallow part of me remains here; I myself go out. I, the man, go away....' On one occasion, the chief of a tribe happened to die while I was in the vicinity, and when night came every one (including the visitors) had to prepare to join in the vigil. I sat with a number of other travelers to overlook the scene, and near at hand was a reputed medium, of whom it was said 'great things were expected that night.' I tried to exchange a few words with the medium, who was sitting next to me, but he was by no means talkative. He was not himself, but in a state of excitement, mumbling words, at times twitching, at times falling into a rigid trance, his eyes glistening and fixed.... As the night wore on, the natives became more and more excited, and the medium slowly went under control.... Suddenly, he stood up, and with a powerful, full-throated voice I never expected him possessing, he began to intone the song. He paused, and then came an answer through the medium, spoken in an entirely different voice. At times there was a strange effect as of several voices striving for an audience; his sentences became shorter, more and more jerky, ending in gasping, gurgling sounds, until at last he sank back on the platform, evidently exhausted. Only afterwards did I learn that the dead man's spirit had spoken through Tomwaya (the medium), and everybody present had unmistakably and unhesitatingly recognized his voice— stronger and somewhat different, yet fundamentally the same. . . ."

The parallel here between this savage séance and the séances given by our so-called voice mediums is evident; it is also characteristic of many direct-message mediums, in which a change of voice and personality is noted, corresponding to the alleged change of communicator. In the majority of instances, when independent voice phenomena are noted, it has usually been assumed that ventriloquism was employed—the medium "throwing his voice" and merely impersonating the dead man or god supposedly communicating at the time. There are, however—as we have seen—certain cases in which this explanation seemingly fails to cover the facts, cases in which definite supernormal knowledge is shown—of events, languages, etc., unknown to the medium at the time. Were these instances more numerous and better authenticated, they would doubtless constitute a striking body of evidence. However, here as elsewhere, accurately recorded, first-hand accounts are few and far between; and we must be content, for the time being, to leave this question still *sub judice*. The time will come, it is to be hoped, when occurrences of this type will receive the attention they deserve.

Turning, now, to other psychic phenomena analogous to our own: An interesting case of crystal-gazing in Tahiti is reported by M. Jean Dorsenne, in the *Revue Metapsychique* (1926, No. 3, p. 226) in which he was enabled to see in the crystal used by the sorcerer a vision already seen by a native *consultante*.

Let us now turn, for a few moments, to certain countries, and endeavor to ascertain, so far as possible, the particular *types* of psychic manifestation peculiar to them. It is to be noted that, while the characteristics of these psychic phenomena are everywhere *fundamentally* the same, they nevertheless differ from one another in striking and interesting ways, with regard to their *details*. These dissimilarities seem to be due to differing environmental psychological settings or peculiarities, giving to the resultant phenomena characteristics essentially their own. We may first of all consider China, Japan, Siberia and Malay, as examples of this, before passing on to more general considerations.

### Psychic Phenomena in China

Many years ago, Lafcadio Hearn wrote a charming little book entitled *Chinese Ghosts*. The stories were of course entirely fiction, but were based upon current beliefs and superstitions of the people, much as our own ghost stories are! The interesting point about the book, which I wish to emphasize, however, is this: that the *type* of ghost story in China and Japan is entirely different from our own. Instead of the fleeting, nebulous visitant with which we are familiar, in our own ghost stories, Chinese ghosts stay materialized for considerable periods of time; or else they are grotesque, monstrous and horrible. Doubtless, there are many instances of veridical hallucinations, similar to ours, could such be obtained; but the *traditional* ghost story is certainly very different in character from our own; and this is, to a certain extent, true of the ghost stories of many primitive peoples.

Writing of psychic and occult matters generally among the Chinese, Dr. Herbert A. Giles, Professor of Chinese in the University of Cambridge, and sometime H. B. M. Consul at Ningpo, says, in his *Civilization of China* (pp. 65-71):

"Divination and fortune-telling have always played a conspicuous part in ordinary Chinese life. Wise men, of the magician type, sit in stalls in street and marketplace, ready for a small fee to advise those who consult them on any enterprise to be undertaken, even of the most trivial kind. . . . The omens can be taken in various ways, as by calculation based upon books, of which there is quite a literature, or by drawing lots inscribed with mystic signs, to be interpreted by the fortune-teller. . . .

"Of all Chinese superstitions, the one that has been most persistent, and has exerted the greatest influence upon national life, is the famous Wind-and-Water system (*feng shui*) of geomancy. According to the principles which govern this system, and of which quite a special literature exists, the good or evil fortunes of individuals and the communities are determined by the various physical aspects and conditions which surround their everyday life.

"In some parts of China, *planchette* is frequently resorted to as a means of reading the future, and adapting one's actions accordingly. It is a purely professional performance, being carried through publicly before some altar in a temple, and payment made for the response. The question is written down on a piece of paper, which is burnt at the altar apparently before any one could gather knowledge of its contents; and the answer from the god is forthwith traced on a tray of sand, word for word, each word being obliterated to make room for the next, by two men, supposed to be ignorant of the question, who hold the ends of a V-shaped instrument from the point of which a little wooden pencil projects at right angles.

"Another method of abstracting information from the spirits of the unseen world is nothing more nor less than hypnotism, which has long been known to the Chinese, and is mentioned in literature as far back as the middle of the seventeenth century. With all the paraphernalia of altar, candles, incense, etc., a medium is thrown into a hypnotic condition, during which his body is supposed to be possessed by a spirit, and every word he may utter to be divinely inspired. . . .

"This same influence is also used in cases of serious illness, but always secretly, for such practices, as well as dark séances for communicating with spirits, are strictly forbidden by the Chinese authorities, who regard the employment of occult means as more likely to be subversive of morality than to do any good whatever to a sick person, or to any one else. All secret societies of any sort or kind are equally under the ban of the law...."

The subject of obsession or possession by evil entities in China has been made the subject of an extensive work by Dr. John L. Nevins (*Demon Possession and Allied Themes*) who came to the conclusion, after an extensive investigation of the subject, that genuine possession was a fact, and that the occurrences could be explained in no other way. Dr. Nevins was, for forty years, a missionary to the Chinese, and while we must grant his thorough familiarity with the people, it is questionable to what extent his theological bias influenced his judgment of the facts.

### Occult Phenomena in Japan

Probably in no country in the world is the saying "the old order changeth" as true as it is of Japan, which country has, in a few years, transmuted itself from a relatively primitive state to a powerful, modern nation, equipped with all implements of modern science. Whatever may be said here, therefore, relates not to the modern country, but to the older Japan of fifty years ago and more, when many of these practices were still in existence, as they probably still are in rural communities, just as we find all sorts of odd superstitions and beliefs in our own remote hamlets.

Some forty years ago, Mr. Percival Lowell, the eminent astronomer, visited Japan and wrote a book upon his observations, *Occult Japan*. It is a fascinating and apparently little-known work. Herein he describes many of the older traditions, ceremonies and beliefs. The "Ordeal by Boiling Water" was then in vogue, and is graphically depicted. This is followed by the "fire-walking ceremony," very similar to that observed in other countries. (This I have treated at some length later on.) The ceremony of climbing a ladder of swords with bare feet is next described; it bears, of course, a suspicious resemblance to many of our "side show" performances,—many of which I have explained in a little book entitled *Side-Show and Animal Tricks*. "Bringing down fire from Heaven" was a spectacular feat, in which a fire was kindled apparently by supernormal means—Mr. Lowell thought by means of a concealed magnifying glass, as the priest refused to attempt the miracle except on clear, sunshiny days. Finally, we are told much concerning incarnations and possessions—the latter very similar to those observed in China. By Incarnation is meant the personal embodiment of a God.

One or two extracts will be of interest, describing an incarnation of the kind; it will be observed that many of the symptoms are strikingly similar to those noted in our own mediums. Students of Hodgson's and Hyslop's Reports on Mrs. Piper will be particularly struck, doubtless, by these analogies. Thus we read:

"We now come to the subjective side of the trance, the first point being the getting into it; the cause, that is, as distinguished from the occasion. Entrance is effected, in fact, in the simplest possible manner. It consists of shutting the eyes and thinking of nothing. From the moment the *nakaza* takes the *gohei-wand* into his hands, at which time he closes his eyes, he makes his mind as much of a blank as he can.

"The ability to think of nothing—not the simple matter even to the innately empty-headed it might be imagined—has been increased by the previous etherealizing process of the austerities. . . . Some *nakaza,* in order the easier to enter the trance, rest one end of the *gohei-wand* upon the ground, and, leaning forward, throw their weight upon the other, pressing against the forehead at the base of the nose between the eyes. The act is thought to be helpful to a speedy possession. It is an interesting fact that this *zone hypnotique* should have been discovered by the Japanese long before the thing was scientifically known in Europe. . . .

"Of the trance itself most, if not all, of the possessed remember afterwards nothing. One man indeed said that it was like dreaming, only more vague—the dream of a dream, which certainly is very vague indeed. Even here I think he mistook the feelings fringing the trance state for the trance state itself. For certainly the average *nakaza* is quite emphatic on the point, and this particular man was not a specially able specimen.

"All agree in the sense of oppression which is their last bit of consciousness before going-off and their first on coming to. . . . Possession begins, they say, at the *gohei.* The hands that hold it are the first part of the man to be possessed. In the incipient cases they are all that are visibly affected. As the control deepens, the cataleptic condition creeps on like paralysis, till it involves all the body not actually in use by the god. Possession ends much as it begins. The subject's arms and hands are the last part of him to lose their induced catalepsy. After the man is well waked, and to all intents and purposes himself again, it is difficult to take the wand away from him. Only after being rubbed and kneaded will the fingers let go their hold.*

"In the trance itself the anæsthesia is usually marked. I have repeatedly stuck pins into the entranced at favorably sensitive spots without the god's being aware of the pricks. In some cases, however, where I had no reason to suspect fraud, the pin was felt. So that apparently want of feeling is not invariably produced in the state; but it is certainly a usual concomitant of it.

"The pulse is quickened to a varying extent.... During the height of the possession the subject's body is in a constant subdued quiver; evidence of the same nervous thrill that produces the initial spasm. Not till the comatose condition comes on does this cease. And it is capable of being revived to greater or less fury by reincantation, at any moment....

"The development of the voice is always an acquired art; dumb possession preceding the ability to converse in the trance. It takes the god no inconsiderable time to learn to talk. When he does do so the tone is peculiar. It is not the man's natural voice, but a stilted sort of voice, one which a god might be supposed to use in addressing mere mortals. It would be theatrical were it not sincere. It is the man's unconscious conception of how a god should talk, and commends itself artistically to the imagination."

Mr. Lowell, of course, writes as a complete skeptic, but his observations are shrewd, accurate and illuminating. He has preserved for us a valuable account of traditional Japanese psychism, permitting us to draw

* These points are of particular interest because of their connection with the phenomena of "dowsing."

analogies between these facts and the more closely studied psychic phenomena in our own countries. If more of this had been done in the past, we should be richer in knowledge today.

From Japan we now turn to Siberia, and shall consider, briefly, the magic and sorcery of the Shamans, or necromancers, concerning whom a few scattered reports have come to us.

### Siberian Shamanism

Throughout Mongolia and Siberia a variety of Sorcery exists which is generally known as Shamanism. It consists partly in a form of primitive religion and partly in a series of magical rites performed by a caste of priests who maintain that they are enabled to commune with the world of spirits. Absurd and degraded as some of these ceremonies are, they are nevertheless of considerable interest because of the light they throw upon the mechanism of the primitive mind, and also by reason of their connection with certain forms of spiritism. The Shaman is really a necromancer and sorcerer, the literal meaning of the word in Manchu being "one who is excited," evidently because of the epileptoid fits into which the Shaman falls while prophesying. Jochelson says that "people who are about to become Shamans have fits of wild paroxysms, alternating with a condition of complete exhaustion. They will lie motionless for two or three days without partaking of food or drink. Finally they retire to the wilderness, where they spend their time enduring hunger and cold in order to prepare themselves for their calling."

Mr. Lewis Spence, writing upon this subject in the *Occult Review* (November, 1923), says:

"When the Shaman accepts the call he also accepts the guardianship of one or more spirits by whose means he enters into communication with the whole spirit world. In this he resembles our own spiritualists, who are usually under the guidance of at least one, and sometimes as many as four or five, 'controls.' But the Shaman receives his call through the agency of some animal or plant or other natural object, which he encounters at the critical period when he is meditating on the life shamanic. This is, of course, precisely what the Red Indian does when he goes out to seek his totem, and it seems to me as if this analogy might throw a very considerable light upon the nature and origin of Totemism, regarding which there is at present great dubiety in scientific circles. Totemism, we know, has a root connection with spiritism, and is also connected with ancestor worship. The spirit often appears and addresses the would-be Shaman, precisely as does the totem among the American tribes. . . ."

Part of the training of the Shaman (which is extremely long and arduous) consists in learning to play the drum with the right rhythm and power, which is said to be a difficult procedure. Long fasts are essential. The initiation of the Shaman is in nine steps or stages, and, according to the grade of the sorcerer, are his powers revered. There are great, middling and little Shamans; there are also black and white Shamans, the former dealing with evil spirits and the latter with beneficent ones only. The Shaman usually begins operations by putting out the lights in the house in which the manifestations are to take place. He then commences to beat his drum softly, accompanying it by imitations of the howling of the wolf and other animals. These sounds then appear to come from various parts of the room (probably ventriloquism) and the drum playing suddenly ceases. When the lamps are re-lighted, the Shaman is found in a deep trance, in which condition he utters his prophecies and predictions. Various observers have reported that the Shaman frequently speaks in a tongue unknown to him, when in the trance state. Jochelson, for example, tells of a Tungus Shaman whose spirits were of Koryak origin, and who declared that, although they spoke to him in that tongue, he was ignorant of the meaning of what they said. "At first," writes Jochelson, "I thought he was deceiving me, but I had several opportunities of convincing myself that he really did not understand any Koryak."

Sieroszewski (O. R., p. 290) gives a vivid account of a séance given by a well-known Shaman. The preparations were made at dusk, the floor of the hut was carefully swept, and those who were to witness the ceremony ranged themselves along the walls, the men on the right and the women on the left. The Shaman, who was secured to the onlookers on either side by strong cords, "lest the spirits should carry him away," unwound his plaited hair, muttering the while. His eyes were steadily fixed upon the fire, which was allowed to die out.

The room was now almost entirely dark. The Shaman put on his wizard's cloak. Then he was given a pipe of narcotic tobacco, at which he puffed for a long time, inhaling the smoke. A white mare's skin was placed in the middle of the room and the Shaman asked for water. This he drank, and, going to the center of the room, he knelt, bowing solemnly to all four points of the compass, and sprinkling the ground about him with some of the water which he had retained in his mouth. A handful of white horsehair was then thrown on the fire, putting it quite out. The audience scarcely breathed, and only the unintelligible mutterings of the Shaman could be heard. Then the silence was broken by a loud yawn, "like the clang of iron," followed by the piercing cry of a falcon. The drum was once more beaten gently and with a sound resembling the humming of gnats on a summer's day. The music swelled until it reached the highest pitch, the small bells on the tympanum jingled, a cascade of strange sound fell on the ear. Silence came once more, to be broken shortly by the chanting of the Shaman invoking the spirits, the Mighty Bull of the Earth, the Horse of the Steppes. Wild shouts and meaningless words followed. Communication was now established with the spirits. The *amagyat* came down. The Shaman rose and began to leap and dance in wild excitement, first on the white horse skin, then in the middle of the room. Wood was quickly piled on the fire and the Shaman was seen dancing in wild gyrations, those who held him with the cords having the greatest difficulty in adapting their movements to his. More and more maniacal he grew. "His fury ebbs and rises like a wave. Sometimes it leaves him for a while, and then, holding his drum high above his head, he solemnly and calmly chants a prayer and invokes the spirits until the cause of the sick person's illness is revealed by them."

It is interesting to note that the Shaman does not take on the personality of a deceased *human being,* during the trance state—in this sense differing from the spiritistic type of manifestation. Some, who have witnessed these performances, are inclined to attribute the resultant phenomena to sub-human intelligences, of the type operating in so-called poltergeist cases. The degree of validity in this hypothesis depends, of course, upon the degree of certitude attained that poltergeist phenomena are ever instigated by such extraneous entities, in the historic cases known to us.

From the icy steppes of Siberia we fly on the wings of imagination, to the sun-baked tropics, and find ourselves in Malay!

### *Malay Magic and Spiritualism*

A leading authority upon this subject is undoubtedly Mr. Walter Skeat, who has written an extensive book on *Malay Magic,* and contributed an illuminating article upon the subject to the S.P.R. *Proceedings,* (Vol. XVII, pp. 290-304). (See also "Folk-Lore," June, 1902; *Journal* S.P.R., Vol. X, p. 259, etc.) Mr. Skeat says:

"The first class of spiritualistic ceremonies ... consists of a simple form of automatism, as represented by the movement of inert objects....

"A second class of automatisms includes a large number of ways of divining by means of the apparently intelligent movements of inanimate objects in *contact* with the magician.

"A third class, which requires to be distinguished to some extent from automatic phenomena, consists mainly of ceremonies by which certain demons, animals or even inert objects are made to act upon persons at a distance. This kind of ceremony corresponds to what is usually known as a 'sending.'

"The fourth and last class of ceremonies includes such rites as are intended to induce possession, either for divinatory purposes or for that of exorcism. . . ."

It will be seen from the above that classes one and two consist of phenomena allied to table-tipping, the divining rod, etc., and possibly telekinesis. The third is a variety of witchcraft, while the fourth includes possession-phenomena and also the curing of those who have been possessed by evil spirits—the supposed cause of most diseases.

We need not dwell at length upon these various classes of alleged phenomena, since they differ but little from those found among primitive peoples everywhere. We shall come to a discussion of native magic and witchcraft later on. The following remarks upon possession are, however of unusual interest, inasmuch as they illustrate the seeming analogies between these savage phenomena and those observed in the presence of our own mediums. Mr. Skeat says (pp. 302-3):

"Of the ceremonies of the fourth class, viz., Possession and Devil dancing, I have seen, perhaps, altogether about half a dozen performances, though I need scarcely remark that it is a most difficult task for a European to obtain permission to attend such ceremonies at all, and it can only be done by possessing a strong friend at court.

"At these performances, the magician and a large

number of his friends and relations being assembled in the sick man's house, the magician seats himself on the ground facing an attendant who chants an invocation, accompanying himself upon the Malay three-stringed viol. After much burning of benzoin and scattering of sacrificial rice, the spirit descends, entering the magician's body through the fontanel. The magician is at once seized with convulsive twitchings, which seem to spread all over his body, and these are accompanied by a rapid rotary motion of the head which he makes rotate from right to left at a tremendous pace, shaking at the same time his shoulders and thighs, and getting more and more violent until the whole body is quaking like a jelly, thus producing an almost painfully vivid imitation of an epileptic fit. Soon, however, he falls down in a state of what is doubtless real exhaustion, and after an interval rises again and commences to dance. The entire process is repeated several times; and a quiet interval then follows, during which the magician, sitting on the ground, replies in a high, speaky, unnatural voice to any question that may be put to him, not merely as regards the welfare of his patient, but even as regards private and personal matters, which are of interest only to the patient's friends and relatives. In the course of this catechism the magician expounds the cause and nature of the sick man's illness, as well as the remedies which should be adopted for his recovery...."

It will be seen, from this, that clairvoyant diagnosis is very old, and has been practiced by medicine men from the earliest times, in all countries. To what extent such diagnoses are accurate has never been definitely ascertained, so far as I am aware; it would necessitate a large statistical inquiry to settle that point. It will be observed however, that such diagnoses are interblended with general information, apparently supernormal in character, dealing with the subject's own life; also, that the method of giving the message is identical with that noted in other countries. The magician, or medium, is entranced and the voice is different from his own, suggestive of another personality. It would be unprofitable for us to pursue this line of inquiry further, however, at the present time; for, if we have such difficulty in deciding upon the authenticity of the communicators and communications received through our own mediums, who have been subjected to such prolonged analysis, it is hardly to be expected that we should be enabled to arrive at any definite conclusions as to the character of the messages received through savage mediums, concerning whom such scant reports have been obtained! We must accordingly be content to leave the matter here for the time being.

### In Tibet—The Astral Body

Aside from the Shamanism, magic and witchcraft common in Tibet, one factor of particular interest is to be noted in connection with this country and its mystical beliefs: that is the detailed teaching concerning the astral body which has been in existence for hundreds of years, and which today constitutes an integral part of their religious teachings. Just as the ancient Egyptians believed in the KA, its wanderings and trials being traced in detail in the *Book of the Dead,* and other writings, so, in the *Tibetan Book of the Dead,* we find stated in great detail the belief in the astral body, and precisely how it leaves the physical body, at death. This valuable book has lately been translated by Dr. W. Y. Evans-Wentz, and published by the Oxford University Press (1927). This work—the *Bardo Thodol* —was probably first committed to writing in the eighth century A.D., and embodied teachings much older. The manuscript from which the present translation has been made is judged by experts to be between 150 and 200 years old. As the reader may have surmised, it deals with the same general topic as the ancient Egyptian work; but, from our modern point-of-view, is far more rational, and many of its teachings correspond, in a remarkable way, with those of Occult and Psychical Science. A brief summary of those portions of the book which deal more or less directly with our theme will doubtless prove of interest.

When a man is about to die, a *Lama* is called in, whose duty it is to attend to the dying man and usher him properly into the next world. The arteries on the sides of the neck are pressed. This is done to keep the dying person conscious, with the consciousness rightly directed. For the nature of the death-consciousness determines the future state of the "soul-complex," existence being the continuous transformation of one conscious state to another. The pressing of the arteries regulates the path to be taken by the out-going vital current (*Prana*). The proper path is that which passes through the Foramen of Monro. "If the expiration is about to cease, turn the dying one over on the right side, which posture is called 'The Lying Posture of a Lion.' The throbbing of the arteries on the right and left sides of the throat is to be pressed. If the person dying is disposed to sleep, or if the sleeping state advances, that should be arrested, and the arteries pressed gently but firmly. Thereby the vital energy will not be able to return from the median nerve and will be sure to pass out through the Brahmanic aperture. Now the real setting face-to-face is to be applied. At this moment, the first glimpsing of the *Bardo,* of the Clear Light of Reality . . . is experienced by all sentient beings."

All the time the patient is dying, the *Lama* urges him to keep his mind tranquil and poised, so that he may see and enter into the Clear Light of Reality, and may not be troubled with hallucinations or thought forms, which have no objective existence, save in his own mind. The *Lama* superintends the whole process of the withdrawal of the astral body from the physical at death. "It is commonly held that the process (of separation) takes from three and one-half to four days, unless assisted by a priest called *hpho-bo* [pron. pho-o], or extractor-of-the-consciousness-principle; and that, even if the priest be successful in the extracting, the deceased ordinarily does not wake up to the fact of being separated from the human body until the said period of time has elapsed."

If the mind of the dying person has not been properly concentrated upon the Clear Light, he is liable to see scores of devils and demons of all sorts! But it is emphasized over and over again in the book that these demons have no actual, objective existence; they are merely hallucinations, or thought-forms, having no actuality, save in the mind of the seer. They are all purely symbolical. The mind is capable of manufacturing these, or creating them, just as we do every night in our dreams. He must cleave his way through these into the Clear Light of the Void. The sooner he can do this, the sooner is "liberation" attained.

Readers of the *Projection of the Astral Body,* by Sylvan J. Muldoon and myself, will see how closely all this tallies with the latest discoveries and findings of psychic science, based upon actual experimentation in this field. The teachings are likewise in conformity with those of modern Spiritualism, and the communications received through Mrs. Piper and other well-known mediums. In our book will also be found a reproduction of an old Chinese print, depicting the projection of the astral body, during trance, and the "cord" or "cable," connecting the two bodies. It is, I think, of no little significance and interest that statements made by Tibetan priests, a thousand and more years ago, should have been quite independently verified by a young man living in a small Western town in the United States! It seems incredible indeed that all this should be mere coincidence, and leads us to a belief in the actuality of the astral body, which, of course, has been believed in by primitive peoples in all times, and constitutes, as we have seen, an integral part of their magical doctrines and ceremonies.

. . . . . . .

We may now turn our attention to two particular aspects of savage magical practices which have no precise parallel in our own countries: I refer (1) to the Fire Walk Ceremonies, and (2) to Rain Making and Rain Makers. In the former, the priest or celebrant seemingly walks through fire or over red-hot stones unscathed; in the latter the witch-doctor professes to control the elements, and "make rain" or cause its cessation, at will. We may briefly consider these in turn, summarizing very rapidly the accounts which have been published concerning them.

Let us first consider

### The Fire Walk

It is perhaps not generally known that the Fire Walk Ceremony yet exists in Southern India, Fiji, Japan, Tahiti, Trinidad, The Straits Settlements, Mauritius, and elsewhere—the ceremony, that is, of walking unscathed and uninjured, through or over red-hot stones or through flames. Tylor, in his *Primitive Culture,* has touched upon the subject in several places (Vol. I, p. 85; Vol. II, pp. 281, 429, etc.), but evidently did not consider it of sufficient interest to treat it exhaustively, or to inquire what actual foundation there might be for these stories. As a matter-of-fact, numerous firsthand and recent accounts *are* available, supplied by eye-witnesses and may be verified by any one sufficiently interested to visit the localities in question, and see for himself. Mr. S. P. Langley, of the Smithsonian Institution, witnessed the Ceremony in Tahiti in 1901, and published an account thereof (rather non-committal) in the *Smithsonian Institution Reports* (1348, pp. 539-44), and also in *Nature,* August 22, 1901. Mr. Andrew Lang published a lengthy paper on the subject in the *Proceedings* S.P.R., Vol. XV, pp. 2-15, and to this paper I am indebted for several of the extracts which follow. Subsequent lengthy correspondence on the subject took place in the Society's *Journal* (Vols. IX and X). Mr. Harry Price contributed a "Note" upon the subject in the *Journal* A.S.P.R., September, 1928, p. 530. A splendid first-hand case may be found in the

*Journal of the Polynesian Society,* March, 1899, and a further account in the *Transactions of the New Zealand Institute,* Vol. XXXI, 1898. Mr. Percival Lowell's accounts, in his *Occult Japan,* have been referred to elsewhere in this paper. Colonel Andrew Haggard also witnessed the fire-walk ceremony in Japan, publishing his account of it in *The Field,* May 20, 1899, p. 724. With regard to the fire-walk ceremony in India, I may refer the reader to the accounts given by Mr. Stokes, in *The Indian Antiquary* (II. p. 190); Dr. Oppert, in his *Original Inhabitants of India,* (p. 480), and Mr. Crookes, in *Introduction to Popular Religion and Folk-lore in Northern India* (p. 10). In Tonga, the fire walk was witnessed and described by Miss Teuira Henry (*Journal of the Polynesian Society,* Vol. II, pp. 105-8). As to Fiji, one of the best accounts is that given by Mr. Basil Thomson, son of the late Archbishop of York, in his book *South Sea Yarns* (p. 195 *et seq.*). *Photographs* of the fire-walk ceremony in operation were published by Mr. S. P. Langley, in his Report, before referred to, and also in the *Folk Lore Journal,* September, 1895. A lengthy article on this subject was contributed by Dr. Th. Pascal to the *Annales des Sciences Psychiques,* July-August, 1899, entitled "Les Dompteurs du Feu." Many similar references could be given, but the above will suffice to show the universality of the ceremony, and the fact that first-hand reports have often been published concerning it by trustworthy and competent witnesses.

And what do these accounts say? A few extracts will serve to show the type of performance witnessed, and its general characteristics. Dr. H. M. Hocken, F.L.S., for example, in his account of the Fiji fire ceremony says:

"In this remarkable ceremony a number of almost nude Fijians walk quickly and unharmed across and among white-hot stones which form the pavement of a huge native oven—termed *Lovo*—in which, shortly afterwards, are cooked the succulent sugary roots and pith of the *Cordyline Terminalis*, one of the cabbage trees, known to the Maoris as *Ti*, and to the Fijians as *Masawe*. . . .

"So far we had seen nothing of the main actors. . . . Now they came on, seven or eight in number, amidst the vociferous yells of those around. The margin reached, they steadily descended the oven-slope in single file, and walked, as I think leisurely, but, as others of our party think, quickly, across and around the stones, leaving the oven at the point of entrance. The leader who was longest in the oven, was a second or two under half a minute therein. Almost immediately heaps of the succulent leaves of the hibiscus, which had been gathered for the purpose, were thrown into the oven, which was thus immediately filled with clouds of hissing steam. . . .

"Whilst walking through the fire, Dr. Colquhoun thought the countenances of the fire walkers betrayed some anxiety. I saw none of this; nor was it apparent to me at either examination. The stones, which were basaltic, must have been white hot, but due to the brilliance of the day this was not visible. . . ."

Mr. Thomson states that:

"The pit was filled with a white-hot mass, shooting out little tongues of white flame.... The bottom of the pit was covered with an even layer of hot stones ... the tongues of flame played continually among them.... The walkers planted their feet squarely and firmly on each stone...."

Similarly, Mr. Hastwell states that: "The stones were heated to a red and white heat.... The natives walked leisurely across five times; there was not even the smell of fire on their garments." *

Three questions at once arise in the mind, in connection with these performances. (1) Were the stones across which the natives walked really hot? (2) Were the soles of the feet treated or prepared in any way to render them partially immune to fire? (3) Were the participants in an ecstatic or abnormal mental state at the time? A brief discussion of each of these points may be in order.

(1) There can be no question that the under layers of stones, in all these cases, were practically white-hot, and the upper layers quite hot also. The accumulated testimony is unanimous as to this. The question is: Were the uppermost stones as hot as they appeared to be? There is confliction of evidence on this point. Professor Langley took some of these stones with him and analyzed them in his laboratory, coming to the con-

* Other accounts of a like nature are given by Mr. Henry K. Beauchamp, F.R.H.S., Fellow of the University of Madras, *Journal S.P.R.*, Vol. IX, pp. 312-21; Mr. George Ely Hall, Vol. X, pp. 132-34; Mrs. G. S. Schwabe, Vol. X, pp. 154-5; Mr. John Piddington, X, pp. 250-53; Mr. J. A. Sharrock, X, p. 298, etc. Inasmuch as these and other accounts are very similar, it would be useless to quote them at greater length. The latest report is that by Mr. Harry Price: "An Account of Two Experimental Fire Walks," in which every scientific precaution was taken.

clusion that the stones employed were of extremely low conductivity, and that it was even possible to hold one end of a small stone in the hand without discomfort, while the other end was repeatedly heated in the flame of a blow-pipe. The lower surface of the layer might be red-hot, provided stones of this type were used. At the same time, there is evidence to show that the general and radiated heat issuing from the furnace must have been very considerable. Dr. Hocken tested this out, by means of a thermometer, and states:

"Our thermometer was suspended by a simple device over the center of the stones, and about 5 ft. or 6 ft. above them; but it had to be withdrawn almost immediately, as the solder began to melt and drop, and the instrument to be destroyed. It, however, registered 282° Fahr., and it is certain that, had not this accident occurred, the range of 400° would have been exceeded, and the thermometer burst."

The general degree of heat over the improvised furnace, therefore, must have been very great—much too hot for comfort! Mr. Thomson states that a handkerchief was dropped on the surface of one of the stones, and that it was immediately charred. Dr. Oppert likewise states that "the heat is unbearable in the neighborhood of the ditch." Further, natives are occasionally badly burnt, either through some accident, or because they have not suitably prepared themselves before attempting the fire walk. The evidence is in some ways conflicting, but may perhaps be summed-up by saying that, while the surfaces of the uppermost stones are not generally red-hot, in these ceremonies, nevertheless the heat must be very great, and the whole performance extraordinary and often difficult to account for by purely normal means.

It must also be emphasized that native fire-walking ceremonies do not invariably follow this routine. In many cases, *no stones were employed;* the celebrants walked through beds of glowing charcoal or live embers—far more extraordinary performances! Such a test was recently underaken, in England, by Kuda Bux, under excellent conditions of scientific control. This test was arranged by Mr. Harry Price, the details being given in his *Bulletin,* "Two Experimental Fire Walks," published by the University of London Council for Psychical Investigation (1936). The feet of the fire walker were carefully examined both before and after the walk, the temperature of the oven tested, etc., by well-known physicists and medical men. No normal explanation was forthcoming. A summary of this recent case is given in Price's *Confessions,* pp. 355-80, together with photographs.

(2) As to the possible preparation of feet, many skeptical Europeans have examined the feet of the participants, both before and after the ceremony, and have asserted that no special preparation was attempted. It has been suggested, and even asserted, that the soles of the feet were previously rubbed with a solution of alum, or the juice of the aloe, just before the ceremony. This, however, is denied by other investigators. Further, in certain cases, Europeans have walked across, without injury. Certainly, the feet of the natives are probably much tougher than those of white men, but Dr. Hocken (who examined them) asserts that they were *not* leathery, while the feet of

one of the Europeans who walked across were particularly tender. In some instances, it is true, little pools of wet mud were prepared, in which the natives stepped immediately before and after crossing the hot stones; but if these were sufficiently hot they would certainly scorch the soles of the feet, even if moist or subjected to chemical preparation—which some observers are emphatic in saying they were *not*.

(3) As to our third question—the mental condition of the priest or performer at the time—this is a purely subsidiary one, for, as Mr. Lang points out, "it is conceivable, barely, that in certain abnormal states of mind, men might be insensible to the action of fire. But no such state of mind would prevent fire from doing its normal work on the body." In other words, an exalted mental condition might make an individual *insensible* to pain (as appears to have been the case with numerous martyrs, burnt at the stake) but this would not prevent the tissues of the body from being burnt and destroyed. Why the natives' feet are not actually injured during these fire-walking ceremonies is the problem!

These phenomena are of course analogous to those witnessed in the presence of the medium D. D. Home, whose celebrated "fire tests" are well known. In these cases there can be no reasonable doubt that the *coals* (not stones) handled were actually red-hot. The Earl of Crawford, for instance, writes:*

"I have frequently seen Home, when in a trance, go to the fire and take out large red-hot coals, and carry them about in his hands, put them inside his shirt, etc. Eight times I have myself held a red-hot coal in my

* *Report of the Dialectical Society,* pp. 208-9.

hands without injury, when it scorched my face on raising my hands. Once, I wished to see if they really would burn, and said so, and I touched the coal with the middle finger of my right hand, and I got a blister as large as a sixpence; I instantly asked him to give me the coal, and I held the part that burnt me in the middle of my hand, for three or four minutes, without the least inconvenience...."

Sir William Crookes, again (*Proceedings* S.P.R., Vol. VI, p. 103) states that:

"Mr. Home again went to the fire, and, after stirring the hot coals about with his hand, took out a red-hot piece nearly as big as an orange, and putting it in his right hand, covered it over with his left hand, so as to almost completely enclose it, and then blew into the small furnace thus extemporized until the lump was nearly white hot, and then drew my attention to the lambent flame which was flickering over the coal and licking round his fingers; he fell on his knees, looked up in a reverent manner, held up the coal in front, and said, 'Is not God good? Are not his laws wonderful?'"

It might be suggested, of course, that Home made use of some non-conducting substance, such as asbestos, while handling the coals, but how are we to account for those instances when *the sitter* took the red-hot coals in *his own* hands, holding them there without injury? The same fatal criticism might be leveled at the suggestion that the hands of the medium were in some way chemically prepared. I have given a number of these formulæ in my *Physical Phenomena of Spiritualism*, pp. 402-5, (and in *Side Show and Animal Tricks*), but Sir William Crookes, who tried a number of them out, asserted that many of them do not actually work, and that, in any case, the hands of the sitters were certainly unprepared. We are thus left with an unexplained problem on our hands. These fire tests of Home certainly give us pause, and prevent us from coming to any too-hasty conclusion with regard to the fire-walking ceremonies, such as those we have described. If the one set of phenomena are genuine, the other may be also. We can only hold our judgment in suspense. There may be an extraordinary, supernormal element in these fire-walk ceremonies, but only a prolonged, first-hand investigation can settle this matter one way or the other.

[NOTE: It may perhaps be of interest to the reader to know that a tentative explanation of these fire tests was put forward many years ago by students of the Occult: this was that the body is protected, in all such cases, by a semi-fluidic emanation or aura, which thus acts as a sort of protective coating or sheath, preventing injury to the surface of the body. I merely give the theory, as stated, adding that this same explanation has been independently advanced in many different quarters, and that some such theory seems to be held by the natives undertaking the fire walk.]

### Rain Making and Rain Makers

We now come to our consideration of rain making by native magicians—a universally believed-in magical phenomenon among primitive peoples. The reader may perhaps be inclined to become impatient that I should even stop to consider anything so manifestly preposterous, judged by our Western standards. Considering the question merely from the psychological point-of-view, however, it has great interest, and, at the very lowest estimate, throws a valuable side-light upon the workings of the primitive mind. Further, in psychical research, we should accustom ourselves to consider accounts of reputed phenomena of *every* character impartially, no matter how impossible they may appear to us *a priori*. These accounts, on any theory, have a definite historic interest, and should be considered accordingly.

A careful distinction must be made between the savage rain maker, who endeavors to influence the elements by means of his magic, and the modern, scientific attempts to produce the same results by physical and electrical methods. There is a wide-spread belief, for instance, that rain can be produced by explosions, and that, because of this "rain almost invariably follows a battle." Much money has been spent in experiments along this line, but it may be said that this idea is no longer credited, and the belief is now given up by meteorologists. The same may be said of the numerous chemical and electrical methods which have been tried. Neither will great fires, nor the liberation of great clouds of smoke or dust produce rain. In fact, the consensus of expert opinion today is that there is no known method by which rain can be produced artificially and at will. All experiments along this line have ended in disappointment and failure. (See, in this connection: "Weather Making, Ancient and Modern," by Mark W. Harrington, *Smithsonian Institution Report*, 1004, pp. 249-70; *Meteorology*, by Charles F. Talman, of the American Meteorological Society, pp.332-45; *Weather Science,* by R. G. K. Lempfert, etc.)

It is rather surprising, therefore, to say the least, to learn that there are, in Africa, America and elsewhere, certain witch-doctors, medicine-men, etc., who claim actually to control the elements and to make rain! They do not rely upon any of the above methods, but depend for their results upon magical ceremonies alone! The natural reaction of common sense is, of course, that such claims are preposterous, and we cannot *seriously* believe that these men interfere with the processes of nature and cause the downfall of rain. Nevertheless, the belief in this power among primitive peoples has been almost universal, and there are many facts connected with it which are at least striking and curious. The belief of the average man, for instance, is that, whenever there is a drought, a witch-doctor is called in, and he performs the customary ceremony. Sometimes it rains shortly afterwards, and sometimes it does not; it is all a matter of luck or chance; those occasions in which he was successful are remembered, while those when he was not are forgotten or overlooked. This is far from being the case. It is a serious matter indeed for the professional rain maker to fail, when called upon by his tribe. The first failure may be perhaps overlooked—though even then the magician "loses face" to a greater or lesser extent. The second failure, however, almost invariably means death to the rain maker. I have looked up the records of many tribes, and I find that this is the all-but-universal rule. Yet many of these medicine-men are very old, and have been making rain for many years! They seem rarely to have failed. These facts are, as I have said, at least curious and interesting, and should at any rate justify our tolerant examination of the evidence. A few extracts will illustrate the methods employed. Sir J. G. Frazer, in that great storehouse of myth and folk-lore, *The Golden Bough,* says:

"Of the things which the public magician sets himself to do for the good of the tribe, one of the chief is to control the weather and especially to insure an adequate fall of rain. In savage communities the rain maker is a very important personage; and often a special class of magicians exist for regulating the heavenly water supply."

Frazer devotes some ninety pages of his work to a rapid survey of the methods of controlling the weather that have found credence among the various races of mankind. These range all the way from the most complicated ceremonies to the summary expedient of throwing a passing stranger into a river to bring rain!

In America, many Indian tribes have attempted to produce rainy or dry weather, according to requirements. Among these may be mentioned the Mandan, the Muskingum, the Moqui, the Natchez, Zuni, Choctaws, and others. For this purpose pipes were smoked, tobacco was burned, prayers and incantations were offered, arrows were discharged towards the clouds, charms were used, and various other methods were employed.

Catlin, in his *Life Among the Indians* (p. 78), says that he found that the Mandan had rain makers and rain-stoppers, who were respected medicine men "from the astonishing facts of their having made it rain in an extraordinary drought, and for having stopped it raining when the rain was continuing to an inconvenient length."

Heckewelder, in his *Account of the Indians of Pennsylvania* (p. 229) says:

"There are jugglers, generally old men and women, who get their living by pretending to bring down the rain when wanted. . . . An old man was applied to by the women to bring down rain, and, after various ceremonies, declared that they should have rain enough. The sky had been clear for nearly five weeks, and was equally clear when the Indian made this declaration; but about 4 o'clock in the afternoon the horizon became overcast, and, without any thunder or wind, it began to rain, and continued to do so until the ground became thoroughly soaked."

Heckewelder adds that "experience had doubtless taught the juggler to observe that certain signs in the sky and in the water were the forerunners of rain."

Among the Blackfeet Indians, according to W. P. Clark, in his *Indian Sign Language* (p. 72):

"The Medicine Man has a separate lodge which faces the East. He fasts and dances to the sun, blowing his whistle. . . . The dance continues for four days, and should this medicine man drink it is sure to cause rain, and if it does not rain no other evidence of his weakness is wanted or taken. He is deposed as high priest at once." *

* See also, in this connection, E. A. Smith, *Myths of the Iroquois;* Father Charlevoix, *Voyage to North America*, Vol. II., p. 203; J. Owen Dorsey, "Third Report of the Bureau of Ethnology," p. 227; John Frost, *The Indians of North America*, p. 109; Schoolcraft, *History,* etc., Vol. III., p. 208; Capt. J. G. Bourke, *The Snake Dance of the Moqui*, p. 120; Stevenson, "Second Ann. Rep. Bureau of Ethnology," p. 371; Acosta, *History of the Indies*, Hakluyt Society Edition, Vol. II., pp. 312, 313, etc.

Turning now to Africa, we find the following graphic account of a native rain maker in active operation in Charles Beadle's book *Witch Doctors* (pp. 55-60):

"As a pallid moon rose, as if fearfully, above the deep ultramarine of the banana fronds, was a magic potion brewed from certain herbs in enchanted water, with which the King, Zalo Zako, his son, and the King's wives were laved. Amid a tempest of screams and drums rose Kawa Kendi purified, to be driven by the wizards back to the hill of his father, leaving the assembled chiefs squatting humbly and in dread of the spirits abroad in the night. . . .

"The Keeper of the Fires came forward upon his hands and thrust the other sacred gourd in front of the King, a deep one containing water, and a wand made from a sacred tree which had upon the end a crook. To the groaning of the magicians, the King took from the one gourd two stones of quartz and granite, the male and the female, and spat upon each one, thus placing part of his royal body upon them. . . . Save for the distant wailing, there was the silence of those waiting for a miracle. In the sky, at the back of the idol, was the paling of dawn. . . . Suddenly, as if exasperated by the non-obedience of the elements, Kawa Kendi sprang to his feet, with the magic wand in his right hand, turned and stared apparently into the face of the idol. For a full two minutes he stood as if carven, while the doctors and the chiefs moaned dismally. Around him like a pall still hovered the smoke of the magic fire. . . . Then, shooting out his right hand, Kawa Kendi made gestures as if hooking something invisible, and began to scream furiously. . . . In a slight puff of wind, the smoke, lace-edged with the dawn-light, swayed, seeming to twine about the figure of the King as he stood with the wand outheld, as if firmly hooked in the guts of the recalcitrant elements. . . . Against the rose of the dawn appeared a dark line which increased as the magicians and chiefs moaned and groaned in sympathy with the furious efforts of the rain maker, who threatened and pulled with the magic crook, so that everybody could see that he was indeed dragging the reluctant clouds from over the end of the earth. As the dark mass swelled the more he wrestled and screamed abuse at the dilatory spirit of the rain.

"And behold, within half an hour, the great black spirits sailed across the scarlet sunshine and wept exceeding bitterly; while from the village went up a great shout of praise to the triumphant King, still prancing and cursing to such good effect up on the hill. . . ."

The above account, of course, is intended to be merely descriptive of the general character of a rain-making ceremony—without intending to be in any way evidential of the phenomenon itself. As such, however, it has (it seems to me) no little interest, enabling us to obtain a sort of bird's eye picture of the ceremony in active operation. Actual *instances* of alleged rain making have rarely been investigated or recorded—which is greatly to be regretted, in view of the universality of the belief. At all events, a brief mention of rain making and rain makers must necessarily be included in the present account, which aims to present a fairly comprehensive summary of savage psychism and magic.

.     .     .     .     .     .     .

We come, now, to a study of magical rites and ceremonies, properly speaking. It must not be thought that
the belief in Magic is limited entirely to savages: on
the contrary, many learned men in all ages have believed in and practiced it; and in our own day it finds
representatives such as Eliphas Levi, Papus and
Aleister Crowley. Even the belief in witchcraft is still
very much alive—as Theda Kenyon showed in her book
*Witches Still Live*. Limiting ourselves, for the present,
to primitive peoples, however, we may first of all consider the Secret Organizations wherein such magical
practices flourish.

### Secret Occult Societies

In all ages and countries students of the Occult have
more or less banded themselves together in secret organizations. In former times, this was doubtless due
largely to fear of punishment, torture and death, in-
flicted by the ecclesiastical and civil authorities, for
their unorthodox "prying into the secrets of Nature,"
or "the Mysteries of God." The "secrets" imparted
were evidently considered precious and dangerous by
those imparting them! While many of these were
doubtless natural phenomena—now included as a matter-of-course in our text-books on physics, chemistry
and biology—there is evidence that some of these
secrets related to psychic phenomena, and that what
we might call séances were regularly held in these
meetings. Such Societies still exist, in all parts of the
world, and it is only natural that they should be found,
also, among primitive peoples.

Captain F. W. Butt-Thompson has recently published an exhaustive work upon the subject: *West*

*African Secret Societies,* in which he has furnished us with much valuable information concerning them, and here we find (as we might have suspected) that initiation into mediumship constitutes one of their most important rites. Many cases of psychic phenomena are given, which compare with those investigated by our modern scientists. These include augury, crystal-gazing, geomancy, sortilage, clairvoyance, clairaudience, psychometry and even direct voice. Trance is common and telepathy taken almost as a matter-of-course. It is interesting to note that "if any one dares to practice as a 'doctor' unless properly initiated, he is executed—unless in territory governed by Europeans. . . . That is their way of disposing of frauds and keeping mediumship pure. . . ." Many interesting cases are given in this book, as well as in the same author's *Black Magic.*

But why, today, the need for such secrecy? Perhaps the answer to this question is that given by Mr. John W. Vandercook who, in an article on "The Case for Magic Science in West Africa," * says:

"Since the white aggression began its swarming slaughter over the lands beloved by the Blacks, they have felt with ever-increasing force that their one last hope for survival is to keep their wisdom hidden. They realize—and state frankly—that if magic, too, passed into destroying hands there would be nothing left at all."

And he continues:

"There is perhaps nothing genuinely magical, i.e., inexplicable in either cure of disease or hypnotism. But

* *Harper's Magazine,* February, 1928.

telepathy—still for the want of a better word—as practiced in West Africa, attains reaches of sheer marvel that defy explaining, surely till we have learned far more than we at present understand. The most straight-forward and common telepathy in the jungles ...survives, namely, the uncanny prewarning of a visitor's approach relayed invisibly from one witch-doctor to another.... Many natives can deliberately convey by mental projection the most elaborate and minute details of an event of importance, or of a person for whose arrival preparations are to be made.... The magicians admit the gift, say it can be taught to any intelligent pupil—but never of course to a white man...."

Of the secret Orders which exist, none perhaps is more fascinating than the *Dervishes*. This order still flourishes in Northern Africa, Arabia, Turkey and along the southern strip of Asia adjoining India. There are said to be twelve original Orders: the Rufaee, the Sadee, the Suhraverdee, the Shibanee, the Mevlevee, the Kadiree, the Nakshibondee, the Vaisee, the Jelvettee, the Khalvettee, the Bedawee, and the Dussookee. Of these, the Mevlevee, or dancing Dervishes, and the Rufaees, or so-called howling Dervishes, are the best known in the Occident. The Dervishes would doubtless characterize themselves as a religious body; as a matter of fact, they are also ascetics, Fakirs, fanatics, priests, followers of Yoga, students of the Occult Sciences, and a dozen other things combined. A lengthy study of their customs and beliefs was made by Mr. John P. Brown, late Secretary of the U. S. Delegation at Constantinople, and he published his findings in a work entitled *The Dervishes: or, Oriental Spiritualism*—to which I would refer the interested reader for further particulars.*

The interesting thing about these Dervishes, from our present point-of-view, is that they are apparently enabled to inflict severe pain and injury upon themselves, without suffering in consequence—stab themselves with knives and daggers, eat live spiders and scorpions, and permit themselves to be bitten by poisonous snakes, without any ill effects! Such, at least, are the tales of numerous eye-witnesses. All these things take place when the performer is in an exalted or ecstatic state of mind. Several accounts of this nature were collected and published by Mr. Campbell Homes, in his *Facts of Psychic Science and Philosophy* (pp. 482-86), and also in my own book *The Story of Psychic Science*. What credence can be attached to these accounts is a matter for debate. That these men have an extraordinary control over the general functions of the body there can be no doubt; further, it is highly probable that they possess much secret knowledge concerning antidotes for poisons, as well as of poisons themselves. The point is: to what extent may such explanations be carried before admitting anything definitely supernormal? For my own part, I must be content, for the present, with having no opinion—leaving my judgment in suspense.

The Dervishes are great users of *Hasheesh*, a drug which is known to produce visions and hallucinations of all sorts. It is certainly possible that Hasheesh and similar drugs may, in addition to their normal physio-

* See also an article on the "Dervishes" in the *Occult Review*, June, 1912.

logical and psychological effects, enable the subject to become genuinely clairvoyant, as the natives themselves believe. Some recent experiments with Peyotl seem to indicate this quite strongly.* This, however, is a subject about which a whole article could be written, and we have not time to consider it now. Suffice it to say that many savage sorcerers combine drug-taking with their other magical ceremonies—just as the medieval witches rubbed their bodies with "witches' unguent," and the Pythoness of Delphi inhaled the vapor issuing from a cleft in the rock, before uttering her famous Oracular discourses.

## Voodooism

We now come to a particular branch or aspect of magical practices, which has, of late years, received considerable attention from students and travelers, and concerning which a good deal has been said in the public press and elsewhere. I refer to the Voodoo rites and ceremonies, which have from time to time caused the authorities no little anxiety. While blood sacrifices undoubtedly play an important part in any Voodoo ceremony, it is now generally admitted that *human* sacrifice is exceedingly rare; being limited, in all probability, almost exclusively to certain savage tribes in Central Africa. The Spell cast by a Voodoo doctor is known as a "hoodoo"—a word which has found its way into the English language almost without our being aware of the fact! A brief summary of Voodoo witch-magic will doubtless suffice for our present purposes.

* See *Journal*, A.S.P.R., November, 1925, pp. 661-3, and November, 1926, p. 666.

Voodooism may roughly be defined as a form of witchcraft, in which the voodoo doctor seeks to influence, or cast a spell upon, another person by means of black magic. Certainly, voodooism is more than this; it is a vitally active religion also, in which ceremonials play a prominent part, and altars, incense, songs, etc., are included. It is a religion in much the same sense that witchcraft originally was. However, voodooism is invariably associated in the public mind with its practical aspects, and it is in this sense, and not as a religion, that we are to discuss it. The word is of doubtful origin, but as Mr. Theodore Besterman points out (in his article on "Voodooism," in the *Occult Review*, July, 1927) it is probably derived from the Ewe (West African) word *vodu,* god. It originated in Africa and was carried to Haiti by the slaves, and also into the Southern States of America. Haiti is now considered the headquarters of voodooism, where it still flourishes extensively, despite the efforts of the authorities to stamp it out.

The voodoo doctors are often known in Africa as Wonder Workers, Black Magic Men, Necromancers, The Devil's Own, and by similar titles, and are greatly feared by the natives. There can be no question whatever that, after a voodoo doctor has cast a spell upon a man, that man often sickens and dies; there are hundreds of well-authenticated cases to prove this. The only question is: What causes this sickness and death? Believers in voodoo, of course, say that it is the spell which the witch doctor has cast, but powerful autosuggestion may be credited with a large share of the result, while it is practically certain that many of their victims are merely poisoned. That these natives possess an extensive knowledge of subtle poisons is certain, one of them, I understand, being made from the intestines of a certain caterpillar, native to Africa. To what extent telepathy, hypnotism and genuine supernormal powers may be associated with voodooism is of course a problem. Mr. W. B. Seabrook, after living with the voodoo people for several months, and after having been allowed to witness certain of their ceremonies, came to the deliberate conclusion that genuine Magic was at work—as we shall see presently. For the moment, however, let us take a sample case of voodooism from Africa, by way of illustration. I quote from an article in the *Occult Review* (September, 1914), on "Voodooism in West Africa," by Irene E. Toye Warner, Member of the British Astronomical Association—being narrated to her by an eye-witness.

"One day," (the account runs) "whilst at a place called Axim, on the Gold Coast, Prince Karatsupo came to me and asked if I had ever seen the voodoos at work, to which I replied that I had not. 'Then,' said he, 'a marvelous opportunity presents itself for you to see them, and with my introduction I do not think there will be any difficulty in allowing you to witness their work. Mind you, a lot of their business is what you would call hellish, beastly and repugnant, but that they accomplish results there is no doubt on this earth!'

"Accordingly that afternoon I was conducted to the hut of a woman, who might have seen forty-five summers, and what seemed to me two daughters, aged eighteen and twenty-three respectively. The woman eyed me very suspiciously at first, put two or three questions to me, and then said 'He'll do!' for evidently I was considered worthy to be allowed to observe their ceremonies intact. . . .

"Through the Prince, they explained to me that they were being paid a large sum of money by a native exporter to remove a certain white man, who was fast supplanting him in the palm oil business on the Gold Coast. . . .

"Accordingly, at about 3 o'clock, the hellish work commenced. Herbs were burnt by way of incense, and to any one standing by, they would quickly have known that the devil had got his own, for the stench was unbearable! Then certain chants and incantations took place, and, to look at the faces of those three women, the elder one especially, you could easily conceive that hell and hate were typified therein. A poor innocent cockerel was then seized: I think three feathers were pulled out over his heart, and his neck wrung off in very quick time. What incantations took place I am unable to say, but I am sure they were diabolical.

"Then the younger girl tore open the skin over the heart and plunged the feathers into the blood, soaking them thoroughly. After which she proceeded to the residence of the white man, and, being in touch with his servant, a Kroo-boy, got into his hut and safely planted the feathers, with their cursed weight of villainy and murder, in a crevice near the bed.

"To all intents and purposes this man was well and healthy at the time to which we refer. This at least was the unanimous opinion of the public. . . . In the middle of the night the doomed man was reported to have yelled with excruciating pain, which continued at intervals until morning, when he seemed to have revived. During the day he had the pains at intervals and consulted a medical man who was located at Axim, on one of the Gold Company's concessions.... On the third day at the same hour the man died."

Several similar instances are given in the article referred to, and might be amplified from other sources.

A striking and graphic account of a voodoo ceremony is given in W. B. Seabrook's *The Magic Island* before referred to. After describing the preliminary ceremonies—the chants, invocations, the sacrifice of cocks, doves, a white turkey, etc.—Mr. Seabrook continues:

"The ceremony of substitution, when it came, was pure effective magic of a potency which I have never seen equaled in Dervish monastery or anywhere.... The girl was now on her hands and knees in the attitude of a quadruped, directly facing the goat, so that their heads and eyes were on a level, less than ten inches apart, and thus they stared fixedly into each other's eyes, while the *papaloi's* hands weaved slowly, ceaselessly above their foreheads, the forehead of the girl and the forehead of the horned beast, each wound with red ribbons, each already marked with the blood of the white dove. By shifting slightly I could see the big, wide, pale-blue, staring eyes of the goat, and the big, black eyes of the girl, and I could have almost sworn that the black eyes were gradually, mysteriously becoming those of a dumb beast, while the human soul was beginning to peer out through the blue. But dismiss that, and still I tell you that pure magic was here at work, that something very real and fearful was occurring...."

"While the *papaloi* still wove his spells, his hands moving ceaselessly like an old woman carding wool in a dream, the priestess held a twig green with tender leaves between the young girl and the animal. She held it on a level with their mouths, and neither saw it, for they were staring fixedly into each other's eyes as entranced mediums stare into crystal globes, and with their necks thrust forward so that their foreheads almost touched. Neither could therefore see the leafy branch, but as the old *mamaloi's* hand trembled, the leaves flicked lightly as if stirred by a little breeze against the hairy muzzle of the goat, against the chin and soft lips of the girl. And after moments of breathless watching, it was the girl's lips which pursed out and began to nibble at the leaves. Human beings, normally, when eating, open their mouths and take the food directly in between their teeth. Except for sipping liquids they do not use their lips. But the girl's lips now nibbling at the leaves were like those of a ruminating animal.... It sounds a slight thing, perhaps, in the describing, but it was weird, unnatural, unhuman....

"As she nibbled thus, the *papaloi* said in a hushed but wholly matter-of-fact whisper, like a man who had finished a hard, solemn task and was glad to rest, '*Ca y est*' (There it is).

"The *papaloi* was now holding a machete, ground sharp and shining. Maman Celie, priestess, kneeling, held a *gamelle,* a wooden bowl. It was oblong. There was just space enough to thrust it narrowly between the mystically identified pair. Its rim touched the goat's hairy chest and the girl's body, both their heads being thrust forward above it. Neither seemed conscious of anything that was occurring, nor did the goat flinch when the *papaloi* laid his hand upon its horns. Nor did the goat utter any sound as the knife was drawn quickly, deeply across its throat. But at this instant, as the blood gushed like a fountain into the wooden bowl, the girl, with a shrill, piercing, then strangled bleat of agony, leaped, shuddered, and fell senseless before the altar."

It must be understood, of course, that the above account represents merely a part of Mr. Seabrook's initiation into the Voodoo Cult, and is not intended to depict the usual Voodoo magical rite, in which some individual is bewitched, or has a spell cast upon him, by the native practitioner. It gives us, however, a vivid picture of a savage magical ceremony, and, inasmuch as Mr. Seabrook is, I believe, one of the few white men who have ever been initiated into the Voodoo Cult, it constitutes a document of first-rate historic and psychological importance.

As to the actual *results* obtained by Voodoo doctors, these have been, of course, very imperfectly studied by intelligent observers; partly, no doubt, because of the secrecy of the natives, and partly because of the intolerant skepticism with which white men have invariably regarded such practices. That strange results *are* obtained by Voodoo doctors there can be no doubt: these results are probably due, in large part, to fear, anticipation, and the baneful effects of auto-suggestion, working upon superstitious and credulous minds. It has been pretty conclusively established, also, that poison is extensively used, as a means of doing away with the intended victim. It is largely because of this fact that such drastic measures have recently been adopted to suppress Voodooism in Africa, wherever the native population has come under European sway.

### Magic and Witchcraft
### (General Discussion)

"You will hardly find a white man who has lived long alone in West Africa who does not think there may be something in Fetish," writes Miss Mary H. Kingsley, in her article on "The Forms of Apparitions in West Africa," (*Proceedings* S.P.R., Vol. XIV, pp. 331-42). According to Tylor, Fetishism consists essentially in "The doctrine of spirits embodied in, or attached to, or conveying influence through, certain material objects,"—hence the employment of charms, talismans, etc., and the basis for much of the belief in witchcraft. "In many cases," says the *Encyclopædia Britannica,* "the fetish-spirit is believed to leave the 'god house,' and pass for the time being into the body of the priest, who manifests the phenomena of possession." The trance-like sleep—whether induced or spontaneous—plays an essential rôle in many forms of Magic, and has been known to the natives of many countries for centuries. It is in this trance state that many of their prophetic utterances are given.

It is only natural that abnormal states of body and mind should have been associated with supernatural powers by primitive peoples; that certain forms of insanity should be revered, and that epilepsy should have been regarded as a god-given gift. The abnormal and the supernormal are closely allied. The connections between genius and degeneration have formed the theme for more than one learned monograph! Lombroso, who of course had a special nose for such things, expatiated at considerable length upon these connections. In his book *After Death—What?* (Chapter: "Mediums and Magicians in Savage Tribes") he says:

"Among the Zulus, the Bechuanas, and the Walla-Wallas the profession of medicine is hereditary, therefore the fathers choose certain sons, to whom they give counsel.... The same is true with the Siberian shamans.... Among the Kafirs, before electing a diviner, it is necessary to test his skill in the discovery of malefactors, finding lost articles, and recognizing a disease and its cause.... With the Aleout, as among the yogis and fakirs of India and the shamans of Siberia, their supreme aspiration is to attain the rapt, trance-like state of ecstasy. They exhibit symptoms which may be classed with epilepsy. They possess strange lucidity of mind and hyperæsthesia, and believe in the persecution of demons who come to torment them.... During their prophetic fury they abandon themselves to strange convulsive fury, contortions, to unearthly howlings, foaming at the mouth, with face and eyes so congested that for the time they lose their sight.... Another method is to incite convulsions by rapid motions of the head and by intoxicating substances.... Thus the pathological, epileptoid origin of the medium is attested by the universal consensus of all ancient and barbarous peoples.... In the case of the Bilculas the initiation into medicine is accomplished with fastings and prayers; among the red Pollis, with fastings, dreams, and withdrawal into the forest and into solitude; among the black aborigines of Australia, by solitary search for the spirit of a dead doctor.... It is the custom of the Indians of Gamina to have their candidate for the 'doctor's degree' eat leaves of a special kind and live alone in the forest until the spirit appears...."

At the same time, Lombroso was among the first to call attention to the fact that these abnormal conditions open the doors, so to say, very often, to the influx of genuine supernormal phenomena, for he says:

"The special conditions of the trance ... give to the medium at a stated moment extraordinary faculties, which she certainly did not have before the trance and which ordinary persons do not have. Above all, the action of the unconscious is intensified. Those centers which seem dormant in the ordinary life come into activity and predominate. Matters forgotten years ago are recalled. The thought of persons present is divined and assimilated. . . . When she (i.e., Eusapia) is about to enter the trance state, she lessens the frequency of the respiratory movements, just as do the fakirs, passing from 18 inspirations to 15 and 12 a minute; while, on the other hand, the heart-beats increase from 70 to 90, and even to 120. The hands are seized with jerkings and tremors. The joints of the feet and the hands take on movements of flexure and extension, and every little while become rigid. The passing from this stage to that of active somnambulism is marked by yawns, sobs, perspiration on the forehead, passing of insensible perspiration through the skin of the hands, and strange physiognomical expressions. Now she seems a prey to a kind of anger, expressed by imperious commands and sarcastic and critical phrases, and now to a state of voluptuous-erotic ecstasy.

"In the state of trance she first becomes pale, turning her eyes upward and her sight inward and nodding her head to right and left; then she passes into a state of ecstasy, exhibiting many of the gestures which are frequent in hysterical fits, such as yawnings, spasmodic laughter, frequent chewing, together with clairvoyance. She comprehends the thought of those present when they do not express it aloud. . . . Toward the end of the trance, when the more important phenomena occur, she falls into true convulsions and cries out like a woman who is lying-in, or else falls into a profound sleep, while from the aperture in the parietal bone of her head there exhales a warm fluid, or vapor, sensible to the touch. . . . Politi, when out of the trance, does not exhibit any anomaly: in the trance this medium has convulsions, anæsthesias, terrific zoömorphic hallucinations, delirious ideas of persecution. . . ."

The point to be emphasized, in the above quotation, is that abnormal mental and bodily states and conditions may frequently be associated with supernormal powers, but that the latter are in no way *explained* by the former. That is a point which is frequently confused or overlooked by our modern psychiatrists—as I have endeavored to show at considerable length elsewhere.*

When we encounter these same abnormal conditions in savage mediums, magicians and witch-doctors, therefore, we are not entitled to dismiss them as mere epileptics or madmen—as is usually done—but must study the phenomena produced through their instru-

---

* *Modern Psychical Phenomena,* pp. 14-35: Ch. "Abnormal vs. Supernormal Psychology."

mentality, to see whether or not supernormal knowledge may at times become manifest through them also. This, it will be observed, is a new method of regarding the facts, and throws an entirely new light upon these manifestations. We must study them impartially, as we must (or should!) study our own mediums.

With these thoughts in mind, then, let us turn our attention to a few accounts of magic and witchcraft, as practiced by native magicians in Africa, India, Afghanistan, Australia, the Fiji Islands and elsewhere. A rapid summary of this will be sufficient.

According to the Rev. J. A. Chalmers, there are six classes of witch-doctors among the Kafirs, and careful distinction must be made between these men and the wizards or sorcerers, such as those found on the West Coast of Africa, for instance. The latter work harm and evil, and cause death, while the witch-doctor is trusted by the natives, and regarded as their friend. He is the one who cures them of sickness and smells out the guilty one when, for instance, a theft or a murder has been committed. This ceremony of smelling out the guilty man is very curious and interesting. It consists essentially in having all the men of the village brought together, while the witch-doctor walks amongst them, often with a small rod in his hands, resembling a divining rod. He is almost invariably enabled to select the guilty man, who thereupon confesses. He rarely fails in his selection.*

---

* See "Black Magic in South Africa," by I. E. Toye Warner, *The Occult Review,* October, 1914; "Psychic Faculties of the Kafirs," by I. T. Warner-Staples, F.R.A.S., *ibid.,* February, 1929; "Some African Occult Doings," by Oje Kule Kun, May-June, 1907; etc. In modern Egypt, we also find the distinction between High and Low Magic, or Divine and Satanic. (O. R., April, 1916.)

Writing on "Algerian Magic," Mr. Vere D. Shortt says:

"Algerian professors of magic are divided into three classes. The Dervish, who is solely a religious magician, and claims to hold his powers direct from Allah; the white magician, who is very often little more than a *hakim,* or doctor, with a considerable knowledge of the properties of herbs, and whose stock-in-trade consists of this knowledge and a few inconsiderable tricks designed to impress the ignorant; and the black magician, who claims to hold his power solely from his own personal mastery over the evil forces of nature.... Powers of some kind, which are at present unknown to the Western world, these men certainly have.... In all magic, white as well as black, it is an understood thing that *thought* is *force,* and under certain circumstances is capable of creating an entity or entities. According to Eastern belief, a practitioner of magic can by following prescribed rules, and by concentrating his thought in a certain way, actually either liberate from another sphere, or even actually *create* an entity which, under strictly regulated rules and within certain limits, will do his bidding. This entity may be either good or bad, its malevolence or otherwise depends entirely upon its creator, but if used for malignant purposes, and if set to do a task beyond its powers, or especially if used against any one in the possession of a stronger spirit, it will infallibly return and destroy its master, afterwards becoming free, and one of the host of *afrites,* or evil spirits, which according to Eastern belief, are everywhere...." (O. R., July, 1914.)

Much the same extraordinary powers are credited to the Marabouts of North Africa and Morocco, concerning whom Mr. L. Grant says:

"Their wonderful and mysterious power of occult telegraphic communication with each other is a fact, and in the case of a general uprising might be a source of serious import...." (*Ibid.*, June, 1921.)

In Africa as elsewhere, however, careful distinction must be made between the higher and lower forms of magic and witchcraft, for the lowest forms are degraded and crude indeed. Mr. Frank H. Melland has drawn a lurid picture of this type of magic for us in his book *In Witchbound Africa.* The magicians are said to traffic in elementals and transform themselves into animals (*lycanthropy*). Helen M. Boulnois, F.R.A.I., has narrated the tale of a "leopard man" in her article on "Sorcery in France and Africa," (O. R., March-April, 1926). Curious and incredible as it may appear, some accounts of animal transformations of the kind have recently been forthcoming from otherwise credible witnesses. In the *Cornhill Magazine,* for October, 1918, appeared an article entitled "The Hyenas of Pirra," by Richard Bagot. A summary and comment on this article by John Mostyn Clarke appeared in the *Journal* S.P.R., July, 1919. Mr. Clarke writes:

"The subject of this article is the supposed power of some individuals of a race in No. Nigeria to change into animal form,—a somewhat startling proposition though not unknown to legend. Mr. Bagot's article describes some experiences reported by Lieut. F. personally, and an experience of the late Capt. Shott, D.S.O. With variation of detail both narratives deal with the killing of natives when in the form of supposed hyenas. There is so much in the details which excludes commonplace explanations, and the officers to whom the experiences happened seemed so deeply impressed with what they learned, on further inquiry, that one is led to wonder whether here is not some new psycho-physiological phenomenon. . . .

"Of the accounts themselves the main facts are as follows. Raiding hyenas were wounded by gun-traps, and tracked in each case to a point where the hyena-traces ceased and were succeeded by human footprints, which made for the native town. At each shooting a man mysteriously dies in the town, all access being refused to the body. In Lieut. F——'s experiences the death wail was raised in the town almost immediately after the shot; but Capt. Shott does not mention this. In Capt. Shott's experience the beast was an 'enormous brute,' readily trackable, which after being hard-hit made off through the guinea-corn. It was promptly tracked, and a spot was come upon where 'they found the jaw of the beast lying near a large pool of blood.' Soon after the tracks reached a path leading to the native town. The natives next day came to Capt. Shott —and this is the curious part of the affair—and told him, without any regrets, that he had shot the *Nefada* —a lesser head-man—who was then lying dead with his jaw shot away. The natives gave their reasons as having seen and spoken to the *Nefada,* as he was, by his own admission, going into the bush. They heard the gun and saw him return with his head all muffled up and walking like a very sick man. On going next morning to see what was the matter ... they found him as stated. ..."

In response to further inquiries, Mr. Bagot, who was himself a member of the S.P.R., replied:

"In the article in question I merely reproduced *verbatim* the reports and letters sent to the said official ... by British officers well known to him, and said that the authenticity and good faith of the writers can be vouched for entirely. I have evidence of precisely similar occurrences that have come under the notice of Italian officials in Eritrea and Somaliland; and in all cases it would seem that a gravel patch thrown up by the small black ants is necessary to the process of metamorphosis. I drew the attention of Sir James G. Frazer (author of *The Golden Bough*) to this coincidence, and asked him if he had come across in his researches anything which might explain the connection between gravel thrown up by ants and the power of projection into animal forms; but he informed me that, so far as he could recollect, he had not done so. Italian officials and big game hunters assure me that it is considered most dangerous (by natives in Somaliland, Abyssinia, etc.) to sleep on ground thrown up by ants; the belief being that any one who does so is liable to be 'possessed' or obsessed by some wild animal, and that this obsession once having taken place, the victim is never afterwards able entirely to free himself from it, and is compelled periodically to assume the form and habits of some beast or reptile. ..."

Here we have a modern case of reputed lycanthropy! It is perhaps hardly necessary to assure the reader that I cannot believe, any more than he does, that a man can transform himself into a leopard, a wolf or a hyena; but the puzzling question once more arises—Why do such stories come to be told? The evidence, in the above cases, evidently proved impressive to the narrators, and the facts are certainly most curious. It is hardly necessary, again, to remind the reader that this belief—that a human being can, under certain conditions, transform himself into an animal—is widespread and extremely old. The wer-wolf (the *loup-garou* of the French) is a standard tradition. How it came into being is a question of extreme importance and interest. It is well known that there are subjects of lycanthropia, an imitative madness, in which the unfortunate individual *believes* himself thus transformed into a wolf or other animal. M. Morel, in his *Etudes Cliniques* (Vol. II, p. 58) gives such a case, coming under his own observation:

" 'See this mouth,' he cried, touching his lips with his fingers, 'it is the mouth of a wolf, and see the long hairs which cover my body and my paws. Let me bound away into the woods so that you may shoot me there!' When his family endeavored to caress him, he cried out that they were embracing a wolf. He asked for raw meat, the only food he could touch, but on tearing it apart he found it not to his liking, as it had not been freshly killed. Thus he went through the tortures of the damned until released by death."

In many cases, the subject merely wears the skin of the animal, prowling about at night and terrifying the inhabitants, for it is believed that merely wearing the animal's skin imparts to the wearer some of the attributes and characteristics of the animal. Such transformations were of course common in witchcraft cases, as well as instances of repercussion, or the injury received by the witch, after the animal's body had been injured, which the witch occupied for the time being. Much could be said concerning this question of lycanthropy—still implicitly believed in by the African Blacks—but we have perhaps already devoted too much space to it, for the purposes of the present review, and I shall have to content myself by giving, in conclusion, a few of the more important references, where the interested reader may find the subject fully discussed: Frazer, J. G., *The Golden Bough,* Vol. I, pp. 155-56; Hamel, Frank, *Human Animals;* O'Donnell, Eliott, *Werwolves,* and *Animal Ghosts;* Fiske, J., *Myths and Myth Makers;* Levi, Eliphas, *Mysteries of Magic,* pp. 237-8; D'Assier, Adolphe, *Posthumous Humanity;* Salverte, E., *The Philosophy of Magic,* Vol. I, p. 289; *Human Leopards,* by K. J. Beatty; *The Ethiopian,* by Major T. C. Grant; etc.

.    .    .    .    .    .    .

Let us now return to our study of magic and witchcraft among primitive peoples, from a more general point-of-view. Mr. Theodore Besterman, in an article on "Evocation of the Dead and Kindred Phenomena among the Natives of Madagascar," (*Proceedings* S.P.R., Vol. XXXVIII, pp. 209-21), gives an account of the general ceremonies, in which the spirit of some dead ancestor is evoked and talks through the mouth of an entranced medium, concluding that "one cannot help feeling that the immensely long and troublesome preliminaries a medium has to go through, before being recognized as a channel through which supposed spirits of the ancestors are willing to manifest, put deliberate fraud out of court as a general explanation of the phenomena of mediumship among the easy-going Malagasy...."

I may perhaps conclude this rapid summary of magic in Africa by the following quotations from an article by Mr. John W. Vandercook, which appeared in *Harper's Magazine,* February, 1928. It is entitled "The Case for Magic Science in West Africa," and in it Mr. Vandercook says:

"Magic among the Negro tribesmen of West Africa seems to include a variety of practices. Under this heading, first of all, comes their science of healing. Closely allied to therapy, and branching off into innumerable other departments, is hypnotism. Then comes telepathy, which the witch-men seem to have lifted to a status of a literal, teachable technic. And lastly there is that wholly mysterious craft which deals with man's transmutation into animal shapes, and man's friendly fellowship with trees, night and wind...." *

Turning now to New Zealand, we find very similar beliefs and practices among the Maoris. "Although a

---

* Before leaving this subject of magic and witchcraft in Africa, I should like to call the reader's attention to Mr. Harry Price's "Notes" on this subject, which have appeared from time to time in issues of the A.S.P.R. *Journal.* I merely give the dates and pages for ready reference: January, 1926, pp. 55-58; October, 1928, p. 598; July, 1929, p. 401; August, 1929, p. 456; October, 1929, p. 567; November, 1929, p. 629, etc.

chief might lose his temporal power," says Mr. Horace Leaf, in an article on "Tapu Among the Maoris," (*Occult Review*, May, 1924), "he never could lose his spiritual powers by means of which he often held the exalted rank of *upoko-ariki* (high priest). In common with ordinary chiefs and priests, an *upoko-ariki* was believed to possess the mysterious power of 'mana.' . . . Mana may be regarded as a mediumistic quality, as it was derived from *ayua* (ancestral spirits), and through their agency increased, diminished, or even made to cease. . . . It is well known that all forms of psychic phenomena familiar to spiritualists and psychical researchers have long been practiced by the Maoris. . . ."

In Australia, black magicians were said to have been very plentiful until the arrival of the white man, when they rapidly decreased in numbers. (See *The Native Tribes of South-East Australia,* by A. W. Howitt, D. Sc.) "The chief articles used in the making of charms appear to have been mainly as follows: human fat, kangaroo fat, quartz crystal, human fibula bone, sinews, black and white round pebbles, wood of the oak-tree, human hair, eagle-hawk's feathers, etc. These articles, or any other substances used as charms, are known as *Joias,* and the 'throwing of a *Joia'* is the projection of a magical substance invisibly, on the victim by a magician. . . . If the chief material used by the Egyptians, and other races, in their black magic, was *wax,* the primary substance of the Australian sorcerer was certainly fat. . . ."

In an article entitled "Black Magic in Australia," I. E. Toye-Warner, F.R.A.S., says (*Occult Review,* September, 1916) :

"As a rule a boy is selected for training because of the psychic power seen in him by a magician, i.e., he may be clairvoyant and have described the spirits of ancestors; or have dreamed, whilst sleeping at a grave-side that the deceased had visited him. Clairvoyance either before or after initiation seems to have been the rule; levitation during such ceremonies was also firmly believed to take place. Much occult knowledge was revealed to the initiate in dreams, and it is a remarkable fact that psychic power left a man if he took to drink or became ill.... Whatever is fanciful about the method by which a man becomes a magician, one thing is certain, and that is, he completely believes in the reality of his own power....

"The belief that evil may be wrought by magical means seems to have some foundation in actual fact, if we take into consideration the power of the human will when properly concentrated and directed. I believe that much actual evil and sickness has been produced by the black magician when his will has been sufficiently powerful. The faith in evil magic is too widespread and long continued to be absolutely without some substratum of truth. The power of hypnotic suggestion throws a flood of light upon the methods and practices of the Black Art. The latter's successes and failures can be accounted for by the supposition that all are not sensitive in the same degree to the psychic force of the magician.

"Another point to notice is the fact that the magician, when casting a spell, usually becomes partly hypnotized himself, so that he can come into *rapport* with the victim.

"Except in cases where real poison is used, my

opinion, after careful study of the various methods, is that evil magic works harm by the psychic power directed by the concentrated *will* of the operator on to the sub-consciousness of the victim. If my theory be correct, then the most certain cure for such cases will be found in counter-hypnotic suggestion, and indeed we find traces of this also in the fact that a more powerful sorcerer can 'break the spell.' "

We find precisely the same form of magic and witch-craft in Dutch Guiana, (see "White Magic and Black," by John W. Vandercook, *Harper's Magazine,* October, 1925), with some interesting additions, while similar practices are to be found in numbers of the small islands of the Pacific and Indian oceans (see "Black and White Magic," by Rosita Forbes, *Fortnightly Magazine,* January, 1928; etc.).

In India, as might be expected, magical practices are very common, and implicitly believed in by the natives. (See *Omens and Superstitions of Southern India,* by Edgar Thurston, C.I.E., and "Black Magic in India," by Ethel Rosenthal, *Occult Review,* November, 1927. An interesting account of certain hill sorcerers may be found in *Borderland,* Vol. I, pp. 477-79.) Regarding psychic phenomena in India generally, Mr. S. Eardley-Wilmot, Inspector-General of Forests to the Government of India, says:

"Can it be possible that these people . . . possess in some little measure the powers attained by their more pious ancestry? How otherwise can we explain the fact that they can converse with each other at distances far beyond the reach of the human voice; that they can to some extent foretell the future, whilst the possession of these faculties is sufficiently common to create no surprise amongst their fellows? . . . For my own part I would not willingly incur the ill-will of one who claims supernatural powers; I treat him with respect and consideration, and am glad to see him go in peace. . . .

"It is best to acquiesce outwardly in his theories, for only by so doing do you learn much that would be otherwise hidden from you; only by so doing can you hope to succeed in gradually gaining the confidence of your companion, though the penalty may be that your own skepticism is shaken." (O. R., October, 1908.)

Regarding the belief in, and occurrence of, psychic phenomena generally among North American Indians, the following excerpts from an article by Miss Alice C. Fletcher, of the Peabody Museum, will be of interest. They are quoted from her article entitled "The Supernatural Among the Omaha Tribe of Indians," published in the *Proceedings* of the (Old) American S.P.R., pp. 135-50. A point of particular interest, perhaps, is that the typical ghost of the Omahas is audible rather than visible—thus differing from the ghost of more civilized white races, where the contrary seems to be the case. Miss Fletcher says:

"The Omahas believe that after death the spirit travels four days seeking for the path that leads to the home of the dead. . . .

"Heaven is thought to be a place like this world. Each one enters heaven as he left this world; the adult is still an adult, the child a child. Friends welcome each other and relatives are united. . . . There is said to be a succession of heavens, each one better than the preceding. How many heavens there are no one could state to me. Each succeeding heaven is reached as was the first, the person dying in the heaven where he may be, and entering the next above him.

"The knowledge of the hereafter seems to have been received by visions coming to persons in a swoon. Those having such visions declare they remain several days where the dead live, but are finally forced to return from loneliness; for, although they see their friends and watch them at their occupations, these will not speak to the newcomer, and ignore his presence. . . . There are men in the tribe who spend much of their time in seeking by fasts and other rites to have visions, and a few persons become adepts in obtaining them. Their dreams are supposed to have a peculiar hold upon the supernatural and there are those among them who profess to have constant dealings with the spirits of animals and men. . . . The sick, when about to die, see their deceased relatives, who bid the dying ones to hasten and join them. . . . Among this tribe ghosts are more frequently heard than seen. The presence of a ghost is made known by a whistling sound. . . . It may be stated as a rule, among this tribe of Indians, that the potency of a supernatural appearance depends upon the physical presence of something that belonged to the apparition in its natural existence. This, and the fact that the folk-lore of the people has much to do with the peculiarities of the phantasms that appear among them, may explain why the manifestations of the supernatural fail to transcend the experience and vocations of daily life. . . ."

The above remarks are of peculiar interest in view of the fact that the beliefs expressed (based upon seeming experiences) are so closely paralleled by the tenets of modern spiritualism, and by sporadic psychic phenomena, as noted, throughout the world.

## Conclusion

We have now completed our brief summary of metapsychic phenomena among primitive peoples. I cannot claim, of course, that it is in any way exhaustive. I possess neither the data nor the erudition of a Frazer or a Tylor, and in any case the subject is doubtless well nigh inexhaustible! But I have endeavored to give a fairly comprehensive summary of those practices and beliefs, among primitive peoples, which bear more or less directly upon our own psychical investigations—backed-up, whenever possible, by the citation of cases which appear to be well authenticated. Studies by academic anthropologists in the past have all been made on the assumption, seemingly, that *of course* none of these phenomena could possibly be genuine—that they represented, merely, the mythical beliefs of savage minds. That was largely because these men had no actual knowledge of genuine supernormal phenomena, and no belief in them. (Mr. Andrew Lang was a worthy exception.) This attitude is greatly to be regretted, since it doubtless influenced their conclusions, to a great extent, and deprived us of much valuable information which we might otherwise have acquired. My object, in the present book, has been to show that genuine phenomena of the type well known to us have also been noted among primitive peoples, in all times and in all countries, and that these phenomena bear a striking resemblance to our own. If genuine psychic phenomena exist, and are frequently reported in civilized communities, it is surely only natural to suppose that they may exist in savage countries also, and our investigation of the subject—cursory as it may have been—has, I think, shown us that this is in fact the case.

Amid the mass of myths, traditions and superstitions of primitive peoples, therefore, we find a *residuum* of genuine, supernormal facts, comparable in every way to our own, and strikingly similar in their reported details. Cases of telepathy, clairvoyance, prediction, apparitions, haunted houses, poltergeists, physical manifestations, mediumistic phenomena—we find them all, just as we find them in our midst. If the one set of phenomena be true, the other may be also! Just because they occur among savage peoples is no excuse for disbelieving them *a priori*. They should be impartially investigated, just as we investigate our own. These phenomena seem to be quite independent of culture, locality and general environmental conditions, save to the extent that they are colored, in minor details, by such influences, as we have seen. The actual magical practices and ceremonies are doubtless limited to the members of various secret Cults and Organizations; but the spontaneous phenomena are noted everywhere, and the possession of some sort of psychic power seems to be far more common among primitive races than among the more highly civilized. This is, perhaps, only what we should expect. Professor Charles Richet, in his book *The Sixth Sense,* has endeavored to show that psychic faculty is far more general and universal than has been commonly supposed; and, if this be true of practical, skeptical Europeans and Americans, it is doubtless still more true of the so-called uncivilized races. At all events, I have endeavored to show that psychic phenomena of the type known to us may be found among these peoples also; and I can only hope that this preliminary survey will serve to draw the attention of other students to these questions, to the end that a more detailed and exhaustive study may be made of them at some time in the future.*

* Since the above was written, several valuable additions have been made, notably M. Caesar de Vesme's two volumes, *Primitive Man* and *Peoples of Antiquity,* and Mr. Max Freedom Long's *Recovering the Ancient Magic*—all of extreme value to the student of psychic phenomena.

# INDEX

# Index

Lightning Source UK Ltd.
Milton Keynes UK
UKHW012124150223
417099UK00011B/238